Pindar's Mythmaking: The Fourth Pythian Ode

Pindar's Mythmaking

The Fourth Pythian Ode

CHARLES SEGAL

Princeton University Press, Princeton, New Jersey

Copyright © 1986 by Princeton University Press

Published by Princeton University Press, 41 William Street,
Princeton, New Jersey 08540

In the United Kingdom: Princeton University Press, Guildford, Surrey

All Rights Reserved

Library of Congress Cataloging in Publication Data will be found
on the last printed page of this book

ISBN 0-691-05473-8

Publication of this book has been aided by a grant from
The Andrew W. Mellon Foundation

This book has been composed in Linotron Trump

Clothbound editions of Princeton University Press books are printed
on acid-free paper, and binding materials are chosen for strength
and durability

Printed in the United States of America by Princeton University
Press, Princeton, New Jersey

For Froma Zeitlin

σοφίαι μὲν αἰπειναί

Contents

Preface	ix
Abbreviations	xii

PART I. MEDEA'S CRAFT AND APOLLO'S WISDOM

Introduction	3
1. Heroic Guile: The Craft of the Hero and the Art of the Poet	15
2. The Language of Gods and Men	30
I. MANNERS OF SPEECH	30
II. ORACLES, OMENS, AND GIFTS FROM THE GODS	42
3. Trials of the Hero: Sexuality, Generational Passage, and the Seeds of Creation	52
I. EROS	52
II. THE SEEDS OF CREATION	68
4. Mythic Patterns I. Wandering and Foundation	72
I. NARRATIVE STRUCTURE: SEA, LAND, AND TIME	72
II. FIXITY, MOVEMENT, AND POETRY	85
5. Mythic Patterns II. The Voyage Beyond and Primordial Beginnings	89
I. *NOSTOS*: TRITON AND HADES	89
II. BIRTH AND CREATION	94
6. The Wisdom of Oedipus	106

CONTENTS

PART II. CULTURAL MODELS: LANGUAGE, WRITING, AND SEXUAL CONFLICT

7. Poetry and/or Ideology	123
I. IS POETRY A SALABLE COMMODITY? THE POSITIVE AND NEGATIVE HERMENEUTIC	123
II. ANALOGY, DISCREPANCY, AMBIGUITY	130
III. CONTINUITY, DISCONTINUITY, DECONSTRUCTION	134
IV. AMBIGUITIES OF THE PROPHET: MEDEA AND APOLLO	136
V. AMBIGUITIES OF THE KING: BATTUS AND OEDIPUS	145
VI. COMMUNICATION WITH GODS: LOSS AND RECOVERY	150
8. Pindar's Post-Oral Poetics: Between Inspiration and Textuality	153
I. *PNEUMA* AND *GRAMMATA*	153
II. MEDEA, JASON, AND PINDAR (WOMAN, HERO, AND POET)	161
9. Sexual Conflict and Ideology	165
I. CONQUEST OF THE FEMALE	165
II. MASCULINE *MĒTIS: PYTHIAN 9*	168
III. THE MYTH OF PATRIARCHY	171
10. Conclusion. *Chronos*: Time and Structure	180
Select Bibliography	195
Index of Works and Passages	201
Index of Names and Subjects	205

Preface

OF MAJOR ancient poets, Pindar seems perhaps the most intractable to recent critical methodologies. That is partly because his work is so deeply rooted in the historical circumstances and social and political contexts of its time. I believe it possible, however, to look at the poetics of Pindar in the fresh perspectives opened by the study of Greek myth and literature over the past twenty years without thereby losing sight of the distinctive qualities of this poetry or dissolving its historical specificity. Though focussing in detail on a single ode, this study, I hope, will have applications to all of Pindar and to other archaic and early classical poets as well. I have tried to write not only for the professional Pindarist but also for the generalist—student, scholar, or lover of Greek poetry—interested in seeing how early classical poetry uses myth to organize reality and to express its implicit views of art.

In viewing Pindar largely in terms of mythical patterns, narrative structures, and ideological constructions, I have necessarily paid less attention than many Pindarists would like to the formulaic and conventional aspects of the victory ode. The great danger of the formulaic approach, indispensable as it is, is to leave aside Pindar's most striking quality as poet and storyteller: imagination. The fully developed Pindaric ode needs to be read at least three times: once from the point of view of the victorious athlete, involved in human time; once from the point of view of the mythical hero who, like the blessed souls in *Olympian 2*, have won some measure of eternity or at least a "life free of tears" and "without suffering"; and once from the point of view of the gods, far from age and

PREFACE

death. The Bundyist reading, concentrating on encomiastic strategies, neglects the second two perspectives.

A Fellowship from the John Simon Guggenheim Memorial Foundation and a sabbatical leave from Brown University 1981-82 made possible the leisure in which to reread and rethink Pindar. To both institutions I owe deep thanks. During the time of this work's gestation I enjoyed once again the lively atmosphere of the Centre de Recherches Comparées sur les Sociétés Anciennes in Paris, and I am grateful to Jean-Pierre Vernant, Marcel Detienne, Nicole Loraux, Alain and Annie Schnapp, Pierre Vidal-Naquet, and many others for friendship, hospitality, and stimulating discussion. The opportunity to lecture on Pindar at the Ecole Normale Supérieure, J.F., in April 1982 helped me to clarify the direction of my work; and I wish to thank Mmes. Sérre, Follet, Leclerq-Neveu, Saïd, and Trédet for their interest and collegiality. I am also most grateful to M. Petitmengin, Director of the Library at the Ecole Normale Supérieure, for generously allowing me to make use of the excellent facilities of the Ecole.

Several friends and colleagues were kind enough to read and comment on the manuscript, and I thank Deborah Boedeker-Raaflaub, Vincent Farenga, and Peter Rose for helpful suggestions. I owe a long-standing debt of gratitude to John H. Finley of Harvard University for having introduced me to Pindar some thirty years ago and for his warm encouragement over the years. The thanks that I here express to my colleagues and students in the Departments of Classics and Comparative Literature at Brown University for much kindness and support in a difficult time are meant as far more than a formality. So too my thanks, once again, to Joanna Hitchcock, Assistant Director of Princeton University Press, to my editor Elizabeth Powers, and to the staff of the Press for interest, helpfulness, and attentive care to all aspects of this work's pro-

PREFACE

duction. I also thank the two readers of the Press for helpful comments. Naturally whatever errors and faults remain are solely my responsibility.

My dedication expresses a long-felt gratitude to a scholar whose penetrating work on the mythopoeic imagination of the ancient Greeks has been an unfailing inspiration to me and to all those working in the field of archaic and classical literature. I take this occasion too to convey my deep thanks to her for generous friendship and help over many years and particularly during a time of sorrow and loss.

Providence, Rhode Island
July 26, 1985

Abbreviations

AJP	*American Journal of Philology*
BICS	*Bulletin of the Institute of Classical Studies, University of London*
Bo., Bowra	*Pindari Carmina* (Oxford 1947) (Oxford Classical Texts).
CJ	*Classical Journal*
CQ	*Classical Quarterly*
CW	*Classical World*
Dr.	Drachmann, A. B., ed., *Scholia Vetera in Pindari Carmina* (Leipzig 1903-27) 3 vols.
DK, Diels-Kranz	Diels, Hermann, and Walter Kranz, eds., *Die Fragmente der Vorsokratiker*, ed. 6 (Berlin 1952) 3 vols.
GRBS	*Greek, Roman and Byzantine Studies*
HSCP	*Harvard Studies in Classical Philology*
ICS	*Illinois Classical Studies*
JHS	*Journal of Hellenic Studies*
M-W	Merkelbach, R., and M. L. West, *Fragmenta Hesiodea* (Oxford 1967)
N, Nauck	Nauck, Augustus, ed., *Tragicorum Graecorum Fragmenta*, ed. 2 (Leipzig 1889), with Supplement, ed. B. Snell (Hildesheim 1964)
P	Pearson, A. C., ed., *The Fragments of Sophocles* (Cambridge 1917) 3 vols.
Page, PMG	Page, D. L., ed., *Poetae Melici Graeci* (Oxford 1962)
QUCC	*Quaderni Urbinati di Cultura Classica*
RhM	*Rheinisches Museum für Philologie*
Sn., Snell	Snell, Bruno, and Herwig Maehler, *Pindari Carmina cum Fragmentis* (Leipzig 1971, 1975) 2 vols.
TAPA	*Transactions of the American Philological Association*

ABBREVIATIONS

W., West	West, Martin L., ed., *Iambi et Elegi Graeci* (Oxford 1971-72), 2 vols.
YCS	*Yale Classical Studies*

The text of Pindar is generally cited from the Oxford Text of Bowra, with deviations as noted. *Isth.* = *Isthmian Odes; Nem.* = *Nemean Odes; Ol.* = *Olympian Odes; Pae.* = *Paeans; Pyth.* = *Pythian Odes*. Other abbreviations follow the standard usage for classical citations. Unless otherwise noted, translations are by the author.

I

Medea's Craft and Apollo's Wisdom

He hears the earliest poems of the world
In which man is the hero. He hears the words,
Before the speaker's youngest breath is taken!
Wallace Stevens, "Montrachet-le-Jardin"

Introduction

ARE Pindar's poems able to transcend the limited occasion of their origin and the narrow class ethos of their intended audience? This question, secretly or openly, torments all those who have studied the Epinicia and fallen in love with their splendid language. My answer, which is in the affirmative, lies not so much in studying verbal patterns (sound, rhythm, diction) as in examining the myth-making and myth-using operations of the ode.

This approach requires a thematic rather than a line-by-line or strophe-by-strophe analysis. I attempt to combine a study of the internal coherence, symmetries and contrasts, and language of the ode with a consideration of subsurface narrative patterns drawn from the myths in the background and influenced by the cultural assumptions of Pindar's time and class. Hence the discussion falls into two parts. The first explores the means by which Pindar weaves his network of analogies between the various myths and parts of myths. Part II views the mythical patterns underlying the narrative in a more theoretical perspective. A concern with Pindar's poetics, explicit or implicit, informs both parts; and there are inevitable crossings over. Some of the results, I hope—particularly the material on the hero, time, the myth of origins, and male-female conflict—may apply beyond this ode and beyond Pindar.

In one respect my approach will appear unfashionable, at least to some Pindarists, for this is a relatively non-Bundyist study. This is not because I do not admire Bundy's work or fail to recognize its revolutionary impact on Pindaric scholarship, but because my concern is the narrative design and the verbal textures rather than the encomiastic

INTRODUCTION

structure of praise, with the attendant *topoi* that Bundy has so well elucidated. It is in the study of the myths that Bundy's methodology is least helpful.[1] And in *Pythian* 4, as in the majority of the longer odes, the myths are truly the heart of the poem. Pindar's myths and images give the Epinicia their splendor of spirit; and it is this eagle-like soaring that has inspired readers and poets from Horace and Longinus to Hölderlin and Valéry.

The Fourth *Pythian* is the longest of Pindar's Epinician Odes and the longest independent choral work extant from classical antiquity. It is unique in the grandeur and richness of its themes, its bold organization of different time frames, and its picturesque detail and elliptical synopsis. By skillfully mixing fulness and brevity, Pindar surrounds the events of the tale with an aura of numinous mystery. By selecting intense moments and rendering their quality of the marvelous through strong metaphors, he impels the hearer or reader to share the imaginative recreation of the mythic past in its elusive beauty and remoteness.

The newly discovered fragments of Stesichorus show us what archaic choral lyric could achieve in extended narration through the pathos of direct discourse and the elaboration of decorative detail in colorful settings.[2] *Pythian* 4

[1] See, for instance, the review article of Ettore Cingano, "Problemi di critica pindarica," *QUCC* 31 [n.s. 2] (1979) 169-82; Bernadini, *Mito e attualità*, 78. For the limitations of a Bundyist approach to *Pythian* 4, see also Gigante, 27f. For evaluations of Bundy's contributions and limitations, see David C. Young, "Pindaric Criticism," in Calder and Stern, 86-88; Paola Bernadini, *QUCC* 2 (1966) 171f.; Rose, "First Nemean," 149f.; H. M. Lee, "The 'Historical' Bundy and Encomiastic Relevance in Pindar," *CW* 72 (1978-79) 65-70; Mary Lefkowitz, "Pindar's *Nemean* XI," *JHS* 99 (1979) 49ff.; E. Christian Kopff, "American Pindaric Criticism after Bundy," in Ernst Günther Schmidt, ed., *Aischylos und Pindar* (Berlin 1981), 49-53; Crotty, *Song and Action*, viii-ix.

[2] For the new Stesichorus, see D. Page, *Suppl. Lyricis Graecis* (Oxford

INTRODUCTION

combines the limpidity, expansiveness, and richness of detail that we can see in Stesichorus' poems on Geryon and on Thebes, in Simonides' Danae fragment, and in Bacchylides' longer odes with Pindar's own peculiar ability to convey the epic wonder of heroic deeds in bold images and powerfully condensed narrative. Even so, earlier choral poetry has nothing comparable to Pindar's great ode. Wilamowitz's characterization of the poem some sixty years ago is still apt: "Dies längste Gedicht ist wahrlich ein seltsames Gebilde, chimaerahaft, wenn man näher zusieht, unrubrizierbar für jeden Systematiker der Poetik."³

A work as ambitious as *Pythian* 4 tends to emerge only late in an artist's career and at the end of long tradition. When Pindar came to compose *Pythian* 4 in 462 B.C., he had been producing epinicia for over thirty years. Now he brilliantly manages the art of amplification and of silence; he knows the *kairos* of when to expand and when to hasten to his end (247). And he is fully aware of his own supremacy in the art: "To many others," he boasts, "I am a guide in the skill of poetry" (248).⁴ Modern critics agree.

1974), especially frags. S11ff., and the Lille Stesichorus, *P. Lille*, 73 and 76. For a recent summary and bibliography, see my remarks in *Cambridge History of Classical Literature* I, ed. P. E. Easterling and B.M.W. Knox (Cambridge 1985) 188ff. with the bibliography. Burton 153 remarks of *Pyth.* 4, "Perhaps nowhere more than in reading this poem may we regret the loss of Stesichorus' narrative poems; possession of these might have established how far Pindar's technique in storytelling was original to himself, and how much, if anything, he owed to the poet whom Quintilian described as supporting on the lyre the weight of epic poetry." What the new fragments do show us is that the effect of creating pathos by extended use of direct discourse (which, of course, Stesichorus shares with Homeric epic) was already well developed in earlier lyric. Thus Jason's long speeches in *Pyth.* 4 are well within the traditions of archaic lyrical narration. Compare the speeches of Geryon and his mother Callirhoe in Stesichorus, frags. S11 and S13, or "Jocasta's" speech in the Lille fragment.

³ Wilamowitz, *Pindaros*, 392.
⁴ On line 248, see Burton, 153 and 166; Méautis, 247; Maehler, 95;

INTRODUCTION

To quote Farnell, "The mellow golden diction of the ode shows Pindar at his height as a master-artist of speech."[5]

Medea's prophecy at the beginning springs upon us with an abruptness appropriate to her shadowy western kingdom and the mysterious sea-realm of her tale. Niece of Circe and the granddaughter of Helios, she at once brings into the story the atmosphere of a fabulous world close to the gods.[6] The narrative on either side of her prophecy refers to the Argonauts as half-divine sailors (12) and godlike heroes (58). The first direct speech in the ode comes from her, and it contains her ennobling address, "children of high-spirited mortals and gods" (παῖδες ὑπερθύμων τε φωτῶν καὶ θεῶν, 13). The heroes' varied divine parentage is in fact catalogued at length some hundred and fifty lines later.

Medea is, appropriately, the focal point of the fabulous elements in the ode. Around her play the love-magic of Aphrodite, "mistress of sharpest missiles" (214ff.), the drugs that protect Jason from the fire-breathing bulls (233ff.), and the ominous power of her father, Aeetes. He is given his potent epithet, "wondrous son of Helios," at the moment when he reveals the location of the "brilliant hide" of the Golden Fleece, but he presumably conceals the existence of the dragon that guards it. This creature "surpassed in thickness and length a fifty-oared ship which the blows of iron have completed" (241-46). With this marvelous detail Pindar breaks off his narrative.[7] He

---

Gianotti, 98f. The fact that such statements are also a conventional feature of the ode, the poet's praise of his superlative craft, does not lessen Pindar's self-consciousness of his achievement. Cf. Ol. 1.111ff. or Ol. 2.83ff.

[5] Farnell, 1.115.

[6] For Medea, see Theogony 956-62. For the atmosphere of wonder, see Pyth. 4.242, Aeliou thaumastos huios, and also 163, thaumastos oneiros. See also below, p. 40.

[7] To underline the fabulous (and sinister) quality of the penteconter to

INTRODUCTION

has told the myth at great length; "completed," τέλεσαν, is an appropriate note on which to close. Ship-building also leads into the break-off motif of the journey: "I have far to go on my path" (247); the poem, as it were, returns to land. Now three rapid lines of his summarizing style suffice for the remaining essentials of Jason's tale (249-51) and effect a transition back to the founding of Cyrene with which he had begun some two hundred and forty verses earlier.

In this work Pindar's power of incisive characterization is at its height. The mythical personages reveal themselves at once through their manner of speech and a briefly caught essential gesture or quality: Medea's prophecy has its appropriate vatic mystery (cf. 10f.). Jason is forthright, restrained, and polite. He has the modesty and reverence of the ideal young adult, and he displays an instinctive leadership in the heroic magnificence and ritual expansiveness of entertaining his kinsfolk (129-33). His father Aeson's spontaneous emotion (120-23) contrasts both with Pelias' cautious self-control (96-100, 156-67) and with Aeetes' distant majesty (230). Events are pregnant with their divine meaning as oracles are fulfilled in the day or night appointed by destiny (*moiridion amar*, 255f.). But they also resonate with the feelings that they stir in the participants: the awed silence of the young heroes at the great enterprise awaiting them (57f.); Aeson's tears of fatherly joy; Aeetes' astonishment and chagrin; and the Argonauts' joyful triumph and enthusiastic affection when their leader, no older than themselves, accom-

---

which the dragon is likened, Pindar is probably echoing the description of the Cyclops' olive stake in *Odyssey* 9.319-24. This too is described in nautical terms; it is compared to the mast of a black twenty-oared ship: "Such was its length, such its thickness to look upon" (τόσσον ἔην μῆκος, τόσσον πάχος εἰσοράασθαι, 9.324). Cf. Pindar's πάχει μάκει τε, 245. This combination occurs only here in both Pindar and Homer.

INTRODUCTION

plishes the deed that the barbarian king has put to him (238-41). Performing a hopeless task against overwhelming odds: this is the undaunted confidence of youthful energy at its best. The companions, like a winning football team, ecstatically mob their captain, and we want to join in the congratulatory embraces.

Like all of Pindar's great odes, *Pythian* 4 is a meditation on the relation between the cosmic and the moral order, on kingship and divinity, on the power of eros and the power of song, on the restless energy of superb young heroes and the sage wisdom of just monarchs, on the heroic spirit that would achieve great deeds in an open and exciting world, and on the corrupting and narrowing effect of greed and treachery. Poetics, politics, sexuality, the vocation of a divinely given destiny are all interwoven.[8] By allowing himself the unprecedented breadth of thirteen triads, Pindar brings together in a tour de force epic adventure, foundation legends, love, magic, family conflict, and cosmogonic myths.[9]

I have not argued specifically for the unity of the ode—once a favorite pastime of Pindarists—but it is obvious from my study that I consider the ode a unified whole. This unity derives not from any single element in isolation—an image or a fundamental idea—but from a more complex clustering of interrelated themes, narrative patterns, imagery, verbal echoes, parallelism and contrasts in the form and in the subject matter. The themes of travel, founding cities, kingship, and the fulfilment of a divinely appointed destiny in time are central and interrelated concerns. The model of heroic action underlying these ele-

[8] For this kind of coherence and interrelation of the various aspects of the world order, see my remarks on *Pyth.* 1 in *Cambridge History of Classical Literature* 1.228-30.

[9] On the triadic organization of the ode (3 + 7 + 3), see Mullen, *Choreia* 95f.

INTRODUCTION

ments is also defined by contrast to trickery, greed, and lack of the moral restraints of shame or respect (*aidōs*).

Pindar begins with the *kōmos*, the formal celebration of the victory for the ruler of a land "good in horses" (*euhippou Kuranas*, 2). The "glory in the horse-racing" at the end of the third strophic system rounds off the first section of the ode in what could be in effect a complete epinician in itself.[10] After this point, Pindar never again mentions the occasion of the poem: King Arcesilaus' Pythian victory in the chariot-race of 462 B.C. Having performed his formal obligations to the genre in the first section, as it were, he allows the myth to expand to unprecedented length.

In its lack of athletic detail *Pythian* 4 bears some resemblance to *Pythian* 3, also addressed to a tyrant and more like a poetic epistle than a victory-ode. The Fourth *Pythian*, unlike the Third, however, has the requisite formal features of the full-fledged Epinician, as described by Schadewaldt, Bundy, and Thummer.[11] In *Pythian* 5, which celebrates the same victory as the Fourth, Pindar had given a spectacular account of the Delphic victory for the sportsmen (*Pyth.* 5.26-34, 49-53); thus in *Pythian* 4 he had the liberty to expand his mythical material and to deepen the moral seriousness and grandeur of tone beyond what was often possible in the "standard" epinician. Like Hieron, commissioning the First *Pythian* to glorify his new foundation, Aetnaea, Arcesilaus had probably requested a work of proportions appropriate to the magnificence of an occasion of state.

We may speculate whether Pindar also enjoys another kind of freedom, that of a poet who makes increasing use of writing in his mode of composition and perhaps even thinks of literate as well as oral / aural reception for his

[10] *Kudos . . . hippodromias*, 66f. See Lattimore, 19; Burton, 150.
[11] Schadewaldt, passim; Bundy, passim; Thummer, 1.19-158.

INTRODUCTION

work. We know too little about the details of either composition or performance to do more than speculate; but there are a few references to reading and writing in the Epinicia that suggest that Pindar at least had the idea of a written text.[12] Pindar seems to think of himself primarily as an oral poet, a public voice bestowing praise and blame in communal gatherings and preserving for the future what is memorable, noble, exemplary, and therefore useful.[13] The complexity of Pindar's style and organization, which both qualitatively and quantitatively mark an enormous step beyond earlier choral narrative (so far as we can judge from the fragments of Alcman, Stesichorus, and Simonides), may also reflect a poet in transition between the oral tradition, with its formulaic elements,[14] and an increasingly literate society.

Among the indications of this transitional status of Pindar between oral and literate composer, I would suggest, is his greater self-consciousness about the craft, artistry, and potential deceptiveness of his poetry. Such concerns are of course expressed as early as Hesiod and Solon,[15] but in Pin-

[12] E.g., *Ol.* 10.1-3; cf. the suggested emendation to a form of ἀναγιγνώσκειν, "read," in *Ol.* 13.3 by A. Wasserstein, *CQ*, n.s. 32 (1982) 278-80.

[13] Cf. *Pyth.* 2.67f. and *Ol.* 10.1-15, with my remarks on the latter in *Poétique*, 50.141f., with further bibliography. For the relation of poet-audience in oral poetry, see Havelock, *Preface to Plato*, especially 26ff. and 145ff., and *The Literate Revolution*, 174ff.

[14] The formulaic aspect of Pindaric composition has been most fully developed in recent years by C. O. Pavese, *La lirica corale greca* (Rome 1979). For a balanced view of convention and originality in Pindar, see Paola Bernadini, "Linguaggio e programma poetico in Pindaro," *QUCC* 4 (1967) 80-97. For formulaic elements in Stesichorus, see now G. Vagnone, "Aspetti formulari in Stesicoro," *QUCC* 41 (1982) 35-42, stressing Stesichorus' intermediate place between the recreative art of the rhapsodic tradition and the style of a literate poet. By comparison with Pindar, however, the rhapsodic tradition of oral epic is by far the dominant strand for Stesichorus.

[15] Hesiod, *Theogony* 27f.; Solon, frag. 29 W. See Pucci, *Hesiod and the*

INTRODUCTION

dar they are more pervasive and more insistent. There is a greater awareness of the careful premeditation and "plotting" that go into the make-up of his work. Such an attitude is perhaps more comprehensible for one who thinks of himself as a writer, the producer of a written text that will be performed by others, rather than as an oral poet who composes and improvises (with whatever amount of premeditation) directly before his audience. The use of writing, I would suggest, was a further catalyst for the growing professionalism of the poet over the course of the sixth century.[16]

Pindar's odes certainly do not look like improvised works; yet he still maintains the direct personal relationship with his audience characteristic of the oral poet, and he still affirms the role of spokesman for communal, collective values.[17] What particularly concerns us here is the other side of this role, the self-awareness of the craft and elaboration behind these productions. Here, perhaps, we have an indication of a new mentality of poetic creation, and one that belongs to the age of tragedy as well as the age of epic, for the tragic poets, too, stand in this intermediate position. They are oral poets who create works to be per-

---

Language of Poetry, 9ff.; For recent discussion, see Verdenius, "Gorgias' Theory of Deception" 123f.; W. Rösler, "Die Entdeckung der Fiktionalität in der Antike," *Poetica* 12 (1980) 296ff.; Walsh, *The Varieties of Enchantment,* 26ff.

[16] One should, of course, not discount other influences, like the tyrants' wish to have poets in residence at their courts. For a recent examination of the whole question of poetic professionalism, see Bruno Gentili, "Lirica greca arcaica e tardo arcaica," 77ff., and "Poeta e musico in Grecia," in Mario Vegetti, ed., *Oralità Scrittura Spettacolo* (Torino 1983), 53-76, especially 58ff. and (on Pindar) 62-66, with the bibliography, 75f.

[17] For poet and audience in the archaic period, see Bruno Gentili, "Aspetti del rapporto poeta, committente, uditorio nella lirica corale greca," *Studi Urbinati* 39 (1965) 70-88; Paola Bernadini, *Mito e attualità,* 39-74, especially 40ff.

INTRODUCTION

formed before a live audience, but they are also the producers of a written text.[18]

These subjects take us far beyond the scope of this study. They directly touch the concerns of *Pythian* 4, however, in the ode's emphasis (again, hardly unique in the Epinicia) on the notions of clever skill, craft, guile, and drugs (*sophia, mētis, dolos, pharmaka*).[19] Here, as elsewhere (notably in *Nemeans* 7 and 8 and *Isthmian* 4), Pindar draws analogies between these elements in his mythical actions and his own poetics. In *Pythian* 4 he is particularly concerned with the ambiguities of his hero, which in turn reflect on the ambiguities of the poetic craft that creates and describes him. At one level the ode masks the ambiguous qualities of guile and magic that lie behind its hero's success and the poet's own techniques of artful persuasion and adornment. At another level the ode not only reveals but also celebrates the process of crafting myths, inventing details, elaborating a persuasive and seductive surface that enables the poet to believe his story and makes us want to believe it too.

Given the occasion, the victory of the King of Cyrene at a panhellenic festival in the Greek homeland, Pindar is careful to bestow eloquent praise on stable monarchy and on the inherited possession of a land through generations of ancestors (*Pyth.* 4.256-62). But political affairs in Cyrene had been turbulent and precarious throughout the previous century, and the 460s were no safer for kings and tyrants.[20] At the end of the sixth century Arcesilaus III al-

[18] See my remarks in *Poétique* 50, passim; also my "Greek Tragedy: Truth, Writing, and the Representation of the Self," 42ff. For further discussion, see chap. 8 below.

[19] See Giannini (1977-80) passim and (1979) 49ff.

[20] For the history of Cyrene in the archaic period, see Hdt. 4.159-67, 200-5; schol. to *Pyth.* 4 and 5; Chamoux, 128-210; Méautis, 202-5, 217, 220; Giannini (1979) 43ff.; Helmut Berve, *Die Tyrannis bei den Griechen* (Munich 1967), 1.124-27.

ready had to contend with serious internal dissension—the efforts of the popular faction, led by one Demonax, to revise the constitution, limit regal power, and extend the privileges of full citizenship. Externally, the kingdom, though protected by the vast desert to the east, had to pay tribute to the Persians after the Egyptian conquest of Cambyses. Expelled once in an outbreak of *stasis*, Arcesilaus III managed to return, but did not long survive. Persian intervention, obtained through his mother, the formidable Pheretime, brutally avenged his death and put down the rebels (Herodotus 4.162-67, 200-204).

Battus IV, Arcesilaus' grandson and successor, held together the restored monarchy for some forty years (ca. 510-470). He enriched his kingdom with the lucrative export of silphium, but he still had formally to recognize Persian sovereignty.[21] His successor, Pindar's Arcesilaus (Arcesilaus IV), seems to have ruled until about 440. His reign, like those of his predecessors, was marred by internal dissension; and one of his first undertakings was to suppress a group of discontented citizens. Among those exiled was the Damophilus for whose restoration Pindar pleads in the ode.[22] Around 440 B.C. a democratic faction overthrew the monarchy and brought about Arcesilaus' violent death, extinguishing the Battiad dynasty.[23]

Arcesilaus' reign was still new at the time of his Pythian victory of 462; and, like Hieron in 470, he seems to have taken advantage of the originally religious occasion for political propaganda. Of this function in *Pythian* 4 there is an indication in Pindar's vivid account of Battus' visit to

[21] See Chamoux, 163ff.

[22] On Damophilus' exile, see schol. inscr. a (2.92.18ff. Dr.); also Bowra, *Pindar*, 137, 141; Giannini (1979) 61f.

[23] Few details of Arcesilaus IV's reign are known, and the dating of his death rests on archeological evidence: see Chamoux, 202ff.; also Bowra, *Pindar*, 141f.

INTRODUCTION

Delphi and the oracle that announces the succession of Battiad kings (59-66). Herodotus reports a disagreement between Thera and Cyrene on the correct version of the founding legend (4.154). Pindar obviously follows the Cyrenean story, with its strong Delphic legitimization of the ruling dynasty. But, whatever his personal feelings and personal politics, he also shows us, inevitably, how myths of patriarchal succession and domination can be enlisted to support this kind of power.[24]

[24] See below, chap. 7.

1. Heroic Guile: The Craft of the Hero and the Art of the Poet

PINDAR frequently associates craft (*mētis*), clever skill (*sophia*), *erōs*, drugs (*pharmaka*), and seductive persuasion (*peithō*) with the shifting, ambiguous side of the bard's daedalic craft.[1] He is concerned to distinguish his poetry of praise and truth from the deceptive potential inherent in the poet's power to adorn men and things through his artful language. He often projects these poetic concerns upon the heroes of his myths. Like the poet himself, Jason, the principal hero of *Pythian* 4, must find his way between the helpful and the evil properties of guile, drugs, persuasion, and love. His success depends on neutralizing the dangers inherent in them; he has to use the gifts of Aphrodite and Medea without succumbing to their magic.

Both hero and poet follow a mythical pattern of which the most celebrated literary example is the tale of Odysseus, and particularly Odysseus confronting Circe and turning her witchcraft from harm to help. One of Jason's strengths throughout the ode is his ability to use or receive the "drugs" of language, love, and magic in a positive way (136f., 184f., 214ff., 233).[2] When Pelias sends him on his

[1] On the ambiguities of *mētis* and related terms, see Vernant and Detienne (1974, 1978); for applications to *Pyth.* 4, see Giannini (1977-80) passim and (1979) 43ff. and 62, who stresses the role of *themis* as a counterbalance to *mētis*. See also Farenga, 13f., 19f.; Gianotti, chap. 3. On *sophia*, see Bowra, *Pindar*, 4-6; Gundert, 61ff.; Gianotti, 85ff., especially 95-106; Maehler, 94ff.; Giuliana Lanata, *Poetica Preplatonica* (Florence 1963), 83f., ad *Ol.* 2.86. See also below, notes 19 and 20.

[2] On parallels between the ode and the Circe episode of the *Odyssey*, see Duchemin, *Pythiques*, 104; also Farenga, 14. Note too the verbal parallel between Jason's encounter with the dragon in 241-46 and Odysseus'

CHAPTER 1

mission of "taking away the wrath (*mēnis*) of those below" (158f.), he draws (perhaps unknowingly) on this power of healing mildness.

Like Odysseus, Jason has the ambiguity of a hero who uses *mētis* rather than *bia*, craft rather than open force.[3] Like Odysseus, he is a hero of the sea and its shifting movement rather than a hero of the land and face-to-face martial combat.[4] He explicitly rejects an Achilles-like hand-to-hand passage at arms when he sets up the terms of his trial against Pelias: "It does not behoove us with bronze-piercing swords or with javelins to divide the great honor of our ancestors" (147f.; cf. *Iliad* 1.188ff.).

As in the *Odyssey*, sea, sex, and feminine wiles all go together. Jason's ability to make use of the wiles offered by Aphrodite and Medea is another aspect of his Odyssean

---

defeat of the Cyclops in *Od.* 9.319-24, discussed above, Introduction, note 7. For the importance of healing in the ode, see Robbins (1975) 211ff. There are also some parallels between Euphamus' meeting with Triton and Menelaus' with Proteus in *Odyssey* 4, on which see below, chap. 5, sec. i. The tales of the Argonauts and Odysseus became intertwined and influenced one another at an early date, whether or not one accepts the still popular theory that a pre-Homeric *Argonautica* was the direct source of the wanderings in the *Odyssey*: see Karl Meuli, *Odyssee und Argonautika* (Berlin 1921) and Albin Lesky, "Homeros," Pauly-Wissowa, *Real-Encyclopädie der classischen Altertumswissenschaft*, Supplementband 11 (1968), 795-97. In any case the crossing over between Odysseus (or Odyssean characteristics) and Jason in *Pythian* 4 doubtless lay to hand in the poetic and mythical material (perhaps mostly oral) long before Pindar.

[3] For Odysseus, see in general W. B. Stanford, "The Untypical Hero," in *The Ulysses Theme*, ed. 2 (Oxford and New York 1964), chap. 5. Note Odysseus' definition of his *kleos* in terms of *dolos* in *Od.* 9.19f., and see my "*Kleos* and its Ironies in the *Odyssey*," *L'Antiquité Classique* 52 (1983) 22-47.

[4] This aspect of Jason is developed by Apollonius of Rhodes: cf. Gilbert Lawall, "Apollonius' *Argonautica*: Jason as Anti-Hero, *YCS* 19 (1966) 121-69; Charles R. Beye, "Jason as Love-Hero in Apollonios' *Argonautica*," *GRBS* 10 (1969) 41-55. In a similar way the crafty side of Odysseus' guile is developed into anti-heroic features by Sophocles and Euripides.

HEROIC GUILE

heroism. The ode presents two kinds of drugs, the ambiguous *pharmaka* of Aphrodite and Medea on the one hand (cf. 213ff. and 233), the Olympian medicines of Apollo and the martial *pharmakon* of glory associated with Hera on the other (187). It is part of Pindar's strategy of healing that underlies this ode to identify the two forms of art and to incorporate the erotic wiles into the Apolline wisdom.[5] Apollo's priestess is far from the sexual Medea, associated with seduction and magic: she is the "bee-woman" (60), a figure connected with chastity and purity.[6] The god's Olympian healing and his priestess's upright speech (cf. 60) serve as foils to the magical drugs and devious wiles that the young hero must encounter on his journey and, like the poet, learn to use for his own ends.

To Pelias' propensity for tricky profit (*kerdos dolion*, 139), Jason opposes not merely the righteous behavior of *themis*, but also another kind of trickery. Pelias' crafty mind (*pukinos thumos*, 73), places him on the side of the ambiguous arts of *mētis* (73).[7] Yet Jason too has Medea's crafty guile (*pukinan mētin*, 58) on his side. To counter Pelias' trickery, he has a skillfulness (*sophia*) of his own,

[5] For the myth of the Olympian appropriation of feminine *mētis* underlying this strategy, see below, chap. 9. Hera's helpful *pharmakon* and Pelias' practice of guile indicate that Pindar does not frame the problematical quality of "craft" in terms of a simple dichotomy by gender.

[6] On the bee and honey in Pindar's imagery of poetry, see Duchemin, 251f.; Maehler, 91 with notes 2 and 3; Stern, "The Myth of Pindar's Olympian 6," 339f. with note 27; Boedeker, 91f. Cf. Plato, *Ion* 534a. Farnell, ad 60, notes that *melissa* of the Delphian priestess occurs only here, but cf. the rather mysterious bee-women of *H. Merc.* 558-63, on which see Fontenrose, *Python*, 427f., and more recently Susan Scheinberg, "The Bee Maidens of the *Homeric Hymn to Hermes*," *HSCP* 83 (1979), 1-28, especially 16ff. and 23ff.; also Laurence Kahn, *Hermès passe* (Paris 1978), 178; Pucci, *Hesiod*, 19-21 and 27f. On bees and purity, see Marcel Detienne, "D'Orphée au miel," *QUCC* 12 (1971) 7-23, especially 12ff.

[7] In *Ol.* 13.52 *pukinos* is used of the guileful Sisyphus. For this contrast between Pelias and Jason, see Giannini (1977-80) 137 and (1979) 59f.; Darcus (1977) 98f.

17

CHAPTER 1

the "good drug" and "wise words" of his gentle speech (136-38). Pindar emphasizes this "good" *sophia* by contrasting it at once with Pelias' guile, *dolos*, against which the hero utters a stern warning:

ἐντὶ μὲν θνατῶν φρένες ὠκύτεραι
κέρδος αἰνῆσαι πρὸ δίκας δόλιον τρα-
χεῖαν ἑρπόντων πρὸς ἐπίβδαν ὅμως. (139f.)

There are minds of mortals too quick to praise tricky gain before justice, though they come nonetheless to the harsh day of reckoning.[8]

Jason's association with the "good" drug of mild speech also gives a positive and helpful cast to the enchantments and persuasive seduction of Aphrodite (*epaoidai, peithō*) with which she makes him skilled or clever (*sophon*, 217-19). Yet this love-magic of Aphrodite also has the morally dubious power of "taking away shame" from Medea (218) so that she helps him with her "drugs." Pelias would use a thievish spirit (*kleptōn thumōi*, 96); yet Jason will "steal away" Medea on the *Argo* (*klepsen*, 250). Jason slaughters the dragon not by force, but through crafty arts (*technai*).[9]

The neutralization of guile operates also at the verbal level in the etymological associations of names, of which

---

[8] On the *dolos* of Pelias here, see Darcus (1977) 98f. With these greedy *phrenes* of 139 cf. also the forgetful *phrenes* of Pelias' *leukai phrenes* in 109, on which see Darcus (1977) 109-12. Burton, 157f., thinks that the *leukai phrenes* indicate "unhealthy" organs of thought and feeling that lead Pelias to his plotting. However interpreted, the phrase contrasts Pelias' mentality with the forthright *phrenes* of direct-dealing Iliadic heroes. Note too Pelias' insult about lies in 99, a charge more appropriate to him than to Jason.

[9] The "shifting light" on the dragon's scales (*poikilonōtos*, 249) reminds us perhaps of the ambiguous and shifting quality that pervades this heroic world, including the "shifting" movements of the whirling iynx that makes Jason's victory possible (*poikila iunx*, 214). For the pejorative connotations of *poikilos* cf. *Ol.* 1.29. Pindar, however, can use the word in a positive sense to describe the intricate craft of his art: e.g., *Ol.* 6.86f., *Nem.* 8.15; cf. Maehler, 90.

Pindar is fond.[10] The skill of Jason / *Iasōn*, the "healer," is able to turn to good the craft and wiles of Medea / *mētis* / *mēdea*.[11] Healing Jason, who "drips mild converse," like a medicine, on his "soft voice" (136-38), counters the potential poisons of the female enchantress with good drugs that stem ultimately from the "most timely healer," Paean Apollo (ἰατὴρ ἐπικαιρότατος, 270). In this healing function too, he proves his education from Chiron (102), famous for his healing arts (*Pyth.* 3.1ff.). Thus he can serve as a mythical model for King Arcesilaus, enjoined to "tend the festering wound by applying a soft hand" (μαλακὰν χέρα, 271).[12]

Jason cites Chiron's teaching in attempting to restore the rights and honors of his own parents (*tokeis*, 110) and later solemnly invokes the Moirai as guardians of *aidōs*, "respect," between kinsmen:

Μοῖραι δ' ἀφίσταντ', εἴ τις ἔχθρα πέλει
ὁμογόνοις αἰδῶ καλύψαι. (145f.)

The Moirai stand apart if any enmity comes among kinsmen to cover up the respect that should exist between them.[13]

Yet later he himself would rob Medea of respect or shame toward her closest kin, her parents (*tokeōn aidō*, 218). The result is their "mingling sweet marriage shared together

---

[10] See J. H. Quincey, "Etymologica," *RhM* 106 (1963) 142-48, especially 144f..

[11] On Iason / healer, see Finley, 85; Thummer, 1.43f.; Robbins, 211ff.; Giannini (1979) 56. On Medea / *mētis* / *mēdea*, see Giannini (1977-80) 142 and (1979) 57-59. The word *mēdea* also has sexual connotations, e.g., Hesiod, *Theog.* 180. Note too the epithet *thrasumēdēs* that Jason applies to his Aeolid ancestor, Salmoneus, in 143, whom Hesiod (frag. 10 M-W), quoted by the scholion ad loc., couples with Sisyphus αἰολομήτης and describes as ἄδικος. See below, chap. 5, note 12.

[12] Cf. Jason's "soft voice," *malthakos*, in 138 and his "honeyed words," *meilichioi logoi*, to his kinsfolk in 128.

[13] In the interpretation of this controversial passage, I follow, essentially, Farnell, ad loc. For other aspects of the Moirai, see below, chap. 10.

CHAPTER 1

with one another" (223f.): καταίνησάν τε κοινὸν γάμον / γλυκὺν ἐν ἀλλάλοισι μεῖξαι. But this union seems to begin with one of its essential qualities lacking.¹⁴ In another Cyrenean ode, *Pythian 9*, Aphrodite "casts *aidōs* on the sweet bed" of Apollo and the Nymph Cyrene, "fashioning a marriage mingled in sharing for the god and the daughter of Hypseus of the broad force" (12f.): ξυνὸν ἁρμόζοισα θεῷ τε γάμον μειχθέντα κούρᾳ θ᾽ / Ὑψέος εὐρυβία. In robbing Medea of her "shame towards her parents" (218), he behaves as a seducer rather than as a husband; but he does not, presumably, lose his own firmly implanted *aidōs* (cf. 145 and 173). Again, his success seems to involve unheroic modes of action (seduction and "stealing," 250); but Pindar has kept the contradictions in the background.

Medea both uses and suffers the power of drugs (*pharmaka*). Her gift of *pharmaka* to protect Jason from the fire of Aeetes' bulls (221, 233) results from Aphrodite's "first" invention of the iynx (213-16), the love-charm whose supplicatory enchantments (*epaoidai*) she (Aphrodite) taught to clever (*sophos*) Jason in order that he might take away from Medea her shame towards her parents (217-19). Jason, soon to be helped by Medea's *pharmaka* against real fire, uses Aphrodite's erotic magic to set Medea "afire in her heart" (*en phrasin kaiomenan*, 219). Aphrodite gives him a cleverness, *sophia*, to overcome the *sophia* of Medea (217b, 219).

At the end of the myth Pindar resumes the theme of Jason's arts (*technai*, 249) and his exercise of guileful theft against the initial source of *mētis*, Medea herself. The par-

¹⁴ On the importance of *aidōs* in the union of Cyrene and Apollo in *Pyth.* 9, see Woodbury (1972) 567-69 and (1982) 246-69. See also Illig, 36-47. Pindar's abbreviated version of Medea's story in *Ol.* 13.53f. has a milder statement of her unconventional behavior: "establishing marriage for herself before her father," τὰν πατρὸς ἀντία Μήδειαν θεμέναν γάμον αὐτᾷ. Note too the importance of *aidōs* elsewhere in *Pyth.* 4, especially 29, 146, 173.

HEROIC GUILE

allel clauses coordinate the stealing of Medea with the killing of the dragon. The dense phrasing of the next line also links the serpent slaying with the killing of Pelias:

κτεῖνε μὲν γλαυκῶπα τέχναις ποικιλόνωτον ὄφιν,
ὦ Ἀρκεσίλα, κλέψεν τε Μήδειαν σὺν αὐ-
τᾷ, τὰν Πελίαο φονόν ... (249f.)

With devices he killed the grey-eyed dragon of the scaly back, O Arcesilaus, and he stole away Medea with herself (willing), the killer of Pelias.

The stylistic device of jamming together these three events puts the heroic deed of the "godlike" Argonauts under the ambiguous sign of craft, art, deception, and thievery (*mētis, technē, dolos, kleptein*).[15]

Mētis has been operative in Jason's life from the very beginning. His account of his origins contains the familiar folktale motif of the birth of the hero: ruse, disguise, or concealment protects the newborn from an evil father-figure, in this case his uncle, Pelias.[16] Amid "fear," "concealment," and the cover of "night" the infant Jason escaped from the *hybris* and *bia* of the bad uncle (*deisantes, krubda, nukti,* 112-15). Years later, when the full-grown Jason arrives at Iolcus, Pelias responds with "thievery" and "fear": "Concealing fear in his heart, he addressed him" (κλέπτων δὲ θυμῷ δεῖμα προσήνεπε, 97f.). Pindar so orders his narrative that the deception practiced at Jason's birth follows directly upon Pelias' reception of the grown

---

[15] Note the striking zeugma of 250, coordinating Medea, Jason's prize and new bride, with the killer (or killing) of Pelias. The verbal expression highlights the different results of using *mētis* on the two men. The reference to Pelias' death is to Medea's trick of the caldron by which she deceives Pelias' daughters into killing their father. The story was frequently depicted in vase-painting of the archaic period and was the subject of Euripides' first entrance into the dramatic competitions in 455, only a few years after *Pyth.* 4.

[16] Compare the stories of the birth of Zeus, Cyrus, Cypselus, etc.

CHAPTER 1

Jason in Iolcus, with another turn of the Bad Uncle's characteristic weapons of trickery back upon their originator.

Unlike Pelias, however, Jason can also use openness and gentleness. "Tell me clearly," he says to the citizens of Iolcus in looking for the house of his father (117b); and he declares his identity openly in the next line. It is characteristic of Jason's forthrightness that even before he knows for certain whom he is addressing he replies to Pelias' question about his identity with the honest, unflattering truth about his behavior (*athemin Pelian*, 109).

This presence of the various forms of *mētis* on Jason's side can be seen as part of the poetic justice over which *dikē* presides, a dynamic reversal which hoists Pelias with his own petard. Yet it also reaches more deeply into a fabric of ambiguity that Pindar recognizes within his own art.

The model for the rightful use of craft and drugs is the doctor's healing medicine, implied in the mildness which Jason "drips" upon his words in his temperate rejoinder to Pelias (136f.). Just after the myth of the founding of Cyrene, Pindar's transition to his own advice to Arcesilaus takes the form of a summary of Apollo's gifts to the ruling dynasty (259-63), including "upright counselling craft" (*orthoboulon mētin*, 262). A few lines later he invokes Apollo Paian as the source of Arcesilaus' own capacity as a healer (270) and draws on the old Solonian metaphor of good rule as a healing medicine for the wounds or sores of the city.[17] This *mētis* too is not only balanced by *themis*,[18] but is transformed into its positive, Apolline aspect.

Within *Pythian* 4, as elsewhere, Pindar calls his own poetry "skill" (*sophia*, 249, 295);[19] and Aphrodite gives such

[17] Solon 4.17ff. West. On this passage, see most recently Giannini (1977-80) 140 and (1979) 56. Burton, 168, notes the importance given to *orthoboulon mētin* by the enjambement and its place first in the verse.
[18] See Giannini (1977-80) 143.
[19] As Gianotti, 86ff. points out, *sophia* can imply not just technical skill but also a larger wisdom, including moral wisdom. So too Walsh, 47 and 50f., who suggests that the poet's *sophia* is also the knowledge of

HEROIC GUILE

a skill, with its full complement of ambiguity, to Jason when she "teaches him the supplicatory enchantments" of her love-magic (217f.; cf. 250). Among his Cyrenean fellow countrymen, who are endowed with the *sophia* that can appreciate the gifts of the poet (295), the hopefully restored Damophilus, schooled by Pindar, is to "lift the elaborately crafted lyre" (*daidalea phorminx*, 296); and that adjective belongs to the same semantic field as *mētis*. In *Olympian* 1 Pindar uses a form of *daidallein* to describe the dangers that inhere in the craft of poetry, its capacity to adorn deceptive tales with cunningly wrought and pretty, shifting lies (*Ol.* 1.29f.).[20]

Pindar's *sophia*, like Jason's, is to be a healing communication between Damophilus and Arcesilaus (cf. 136-38 and 270f.; also 293). Damophilus' "daedalic lyre" in 296 appears in a context of healing a sickness and of Apollo's divinity (293f.). Pindar thus implies that this poetic skill and *sophia*, so closely identified with his own (299), exemplify the "good" craft, like the *mētis* that defeats Pelias and wins Medea. The evil uses of *mētis*, however, are projected upon Pelias. Just as Medea speaks both the inspired utterance of an "immortal mouth" (10f.) and "dense craft" (57), so Jason uses both Apolline healing skill (136f.) and thievish trickery (e.g., 250).[21]

Apollo's oracle told that Pelias would die by an Aeolid's strength of "hands or by plottings not to be turned away" (χείρεσσιν ἢ βουλαῖς ἀκάμπτοις, 72). Force and guile are juxtaposed as alternative modes of action. The phrasing of 72, in keeping with oracular pronouncements, leaves the

---

what is worthy of being memorialized by the technical skill, that is, "his knowledge of god's abiding presence in human history" (50f.).

[20] On the ambiguities of such *mythoi* in Pindar, see Detienne, *L'invention de la mythologie*, 99; also Komornicka (1972) 245 and 251f. On the ambiguities of *daidalos* in general, see F. Frontisi-Ducroux, *Dédale* (Paris 1975), especially 68ff. and 79ff.

[21] For the theme of healing and medicine, see also 136-38, 217, 270f., 293; see in general Robbins, 211-13.

CHAPTER 1

outcome ambiguous. In the sequel Pelias' doom does not in fact come by heroic force. The Aeolid in question (cf. 142f.), who has the heroic epithet *agauos* in 72, wins out by Odyssean "plottings": he "steals away" a woman who will be the killer of Pelias (250).[22]

The "unbendable plots" that cause Pelias' death (72) belong to the same semantic field of *mētis* as the "unloosable circle" of Aphrodite's iynx (*alutos kuklos*, 215). Both passages draw on the imagery of the "nets" and "entrapments" of *mētis* characteristic of the language of love rather than war.[23] The phrase of 72 reminds us too of the ambiguities of *mētis*, as a form of heroic action. Instead of the straightforward movement of traditional heroism, *akamptoi boulai* suggest the devious entanglements of what Vernant and Detienne call "the circle and the bond," the infinitely encircling and enfolding nets that immobilize in a never-ending, untraversable, disorienting space.[24]

Jason's second confrontation with Pelias also combines Odyssean and Iliadic heroic modes. He "drips mild converse upon his soft voice," but he also "lays a foundation of clever words" (136-38).[25] His speech appears as a Medea-like ministration of drugs; but the architectural image also connects him with stability, civic life, and the firm,

---

[22] The "stealing" of Medea, however, is qualified by the phrase σὺν αὐτᾷ in 250, if in fact this means "of her own accord," "of her own free will" ("avec son aveu, même avec son concours," Duchemin, *Pythiques*, ad loc.), the most plausible interpretation if the text is sound.

[23] See Bruno Gentili, "Sul testo del fr. 287.2 P di Ibico," *QUCC* 2 (1966) 125-27; also Giannini (1977-80) p. 142 with note 40.

[24] Vernant and Detienne, *Cunning Intelligence*, 279-326. Tartarus, for example, "is not just a prison from which there is no escape; it is itself a space which binds; the expanse of it is indissociable from inextricable bonds" (294). The nets that Hephaestus devises for Ares and Aphrodite in *Od.* 8.272ff. and 296ff. are the most famous example.

[25] For the pharmacological associations of "dripping" such "mild" speech, cf. *Ol.* 13.68 and 85. On the form of *mētis* in this passage, see Vernant and Detienne, *Cunning Intelligence*, 18ff.

HEROIC GUILE

visible achievements that belong to successful males.[26] This "foundation of skillful words" that Jason's healing speech lays down (krēpid' sophōn epeōn, 138) uses an architectural image that Pindar often employs for his own art (e.g., krēpid' aoidân, "foundation of songs," Pyth. 7.3; frag. 184 Bo. = 194 Sn.). The metaphor also prepares for the heroic act of reverent foundation on the voyage later and for the political responsibility and stability that distinguish a good ruler. The act of "founding" (ktizein) characterizes heroes and heroized kings.[27] The Argonauts' first deed at sea is to "set up a holy temenos to Poseidon of the sea" (ἔνθ' ἁγνὸν Ποσειδάωνος ἔσσαντ' ἐνναλίου τέμενος, 204), with its altar's "newly built surface" (νεόκτιστον λίθων βωμοῖο θέναρ, 206).

After the Argonaut myth, Pindar exhorts Arcesilaus to exercise the clemency that belongs to good kingship, "for to shake a city is easy, even for men of nought, but to settle it again in its place is difficult" (ἐπὶ χώρας αὖτις ἕσσαι δυσπαλές, 273). We may recall too the image of the upright column that supports the lordly hall in the "wisdom of Oedipus" (267). The imagery of "uprightness," orthos, also characterizes Delphic prophecy in 60 and the wise counsel of the Cyrenean rulers in 262 (orthoboulon mētin). There is perhaps a further connection between the uprightness of Jason's deeds and speech and the divine purposes of the oracles in the untranslatable echo between

[26] Cf. Ol. 6.1-4, Pyth. 6.5-15, Pyth. 7.1-4. This architectural imagery, from a different point of view, also embodies the kind of technological mētis involved in carpentry, building, making straight lines, or directing a journey (as of a ship) on a straight course: see Vernant and Detienne, Cunning Intelligence, 237f.

[27] So Battus here, Pyth. 4.6-8. In Pythian 5 too Battus is said to have "founded the gods' groves" at Cyrene (κτίσεν δ' ἄλσεα μείζονα θεῶν, Pyth. 5.89). Cf. also Heracles as "founder" of the Olympian games in Ol. 10.24ff. (ἐκτίσσατο, 25). On the heroization of "founders," see Rohde, Psyche, 127f.

CHAPTER 1

the *monokrēpis* ("single-sandled," "with single base") in the oracular warning to Pelias in 75 and Jason's own *krēpis* ("base," "foundation") of wise words in 138. The danger that Pelias expects to come in the tangible form of physical violence takes the gentler, but no less effective form, of a metaphorical "base" of words.

Jason's readiness to profit from *mētis* and its ambiguous brood implies an ability to use *mētis* to counter *mētis* that is also relevant to Pindar's poetics. Generally Pindar is emphatic about choosing the straight over the crooked path.[28] But on occasion he may accept—reluctantly, of course—the "tricky way of life" inherent in the changefulness of the human condition (*dolios aiōn*, *Isth.* 8.15f.). All *mētis* requires special care on the user's part. The skills of the poet's verbal craft are ever prone to lead on to crooked paths (cf. *Nem.* 8.25-35) and encourage the dishonest "profit" to which such "skill is bound" (*Pyth.* 3.54). But, Pindar advises, "Even for the clever craftsman the guileless skill proves better" (*sophia adolos*, *Ol.* 7.53). Hence he needs the help of the gods, especially Zeus and Apollo, to keep his words and deeds on the "simple roads of life" (*Nem.* 8.36). The poet's words too have the power of medicinal healing (*Nem.* 4.1ff.) and need to be employed in righteous ways (cf. *Pyth.* 3. 52-58 and 63-67).

The controversial passage in *Pythian* 2.76-89, which seems to contradict Pindar's praise of the upright speech of his poetry of truth, can perhaps be understood in terms of using *mētis* against *mētis* in the myth of *Pythian* 4. When Pindar states his willingness to attack an enemy with the slyness of a wolf, "sometimes treading in crooked paths"

[28] Cf. *Pyth.* 11.38f., *Nem.* 1.25, *Nem.* 8. 32-36. In *Ol.* 7 Pindar suggests parallels between the upright *logos* (21) of his poetry, the "guileless art" of the Rhodian craftsmen (*sophia adolos*, 53), and the "straight road" (*euthuporei*, 91) traversed by the "skillful" athlete, Diagoras, as he follows the admonitions that come from the "upright thoughts" (*orthai phrenes*, 91) of his fathers. See in general Gundert, 42; Komornicka (1972) 244f.

HEROIC GUILE

(85), the words need not be explained away as the utterance of an imaginary interlocutor, as some interpreters have suggested,[29] but may instead reflect the necessity of using *mētis* in dire circumstances (cf. *allote*, "sometimes," *Pyth.* 2.85), as Jason does when confronting Aeetes' power. Even on such occasions, however, there are dangers (cf. *Pyth.* 2.91f.), and Pindar carefully qualifies his use of *mētis* by the moral presence of the god. In *Pythian* 2 Rhadamanthys refuses "to take joy in deceptions" (74), and the poet must not "struggle against the god" (88). In *Pythian* 4, as we have seen, the uprightness of Delphic prophecy (at least as Pindar views it in this ode)[30] balances the ambiguities of *mētis* in Medea's prophecy and Jason's success through seduction and female magic.

Like other late archaic poets, Pindar is acutely aware of the affinities between poetic speech and erotic seduction.[31] "The master of truth is also a master of deception. To possess truth is also to be capable of deception."[32] Jason's success in utilizing Medea's *mētis* in the service of Apollo's justice-fulfilling oracle corresponds to Pindar's success in utilizing the seductive *peithō* and potentially deceitful *mētis* and *sophia* of his art to inculcate the austere ideals of Dorian heroism, valor tempered by Delphic

---

[29] See Gildersleeve, ad loc.; Farnell, 2.131f. See contra C. M. Bowra, *Problems in Greek Poetry* (Oxford 1953), 87-89; Finley, 96f.; Burton, 127-29, with a review of earlier scholarship. The parallels with *Isth.* 4.52 and with the Heracles poem (frag. 169 Sn.) also support the possibility that Pindar could be supporting "tricky" behavior when justified by the ends. See also Martin Ostwald, "Pindar, *Nomos*, and Heracles," *HSCP* 69 (1975) 109-38, especially 129-31 = Calder-Stern, 228-31; most recently Bernadini, *Mito e attualità*, 72-74, citing frag. 235 Bo. = 43 Sn. For other views, see Schadewaldt, p. 326, note 1; Thummer, 1.89f.; Lefkowitz, 29.

[30] Delphic oracles, of course, can be notoriously ambiguous (cf. Herodotus passim or the prologue of Sophocles' *Electra*), but Pindar suppresses that side.

[31] See Detienne, *Maîtres de vérité*, 65ff.

[32] Ibid. 77. See also Maehler, 70ff. and 90ff.; Verdenius, "Gorgias," 117ff.

CHAPTER 1

wisdom, knowledge, and moral probity (cf. *Pyth.* 5.63-69, 9.44-51).

In *Pythian* 9 Apollo comes to grips with *erōs* and through Chiron's *mētis* (38) is initiated into the seductions and deceptions of Aphrodite's realm (κρυπταὶ κλαῖδες ἐντὶ σοφᾶς Πειθοῦς ἱερᾶν φιλοτάτων, "Secret are wise Persuasion's keys to holy loves," 39).[33] But the wise teacher Chiron presides over this moment. Immediately afterwards he extols Apollo's knowledge of all things (44-49), including his freedom from deception and misleading speech (*pseudos, parphasis*, 42f.). The high hymnic style of the passage (relieved, however, by a touch of playful irony) is meant as an effective antidote to the dangerous erotic tone of the young god's meeting with the nymph Cyrene (36-38). Pindar's treatment of Apollo's love-affair with Coronis in *Pythian* 3 similarly contrasts Apolline upright wisdom with the secrecy, thievishness, and lies in the realm of eros (cf. *Pyth.* 3.14, 29f.).

These three Pythian Odes—3, 4, and 9—display both the Aphroditic and Apolline side of Pindar's art. The Apolline wisdom eventually dominates, but only after appropriating (if uneasily) the Aphroditic. The balance between feminine wiliness and masculine straightforward heroism on the level of myth corresponds to the delicate balance between crafty technique and honest contents, artistry and morality, on the level of poetics. Thus *Peithō*, Aphrodite's erotic seduction in *Pyth.* 9.39, here accompanies not the love-goddess's iynx in 213ff., as one might expect,[34] but Hera's inducement of valor that burns into the Argonauts

[33] On Chiron's craftiness here, see Méautis, 210, who identifies it with the playful irony of one who knows the truth and feigns ignorance. See also R. P. Winnington-Ingram, "Pindar's Ninth Pythian Ode," *BICS* 16 (1969) 10f.; Woodbury (1972) 570ff. For further discussion of the relation between *Pyth.* 9 and *Pyth.* 4, see chap. 9, sec. II, below.

[34] See M. Detienne, *Les jardins d'Adonis*, 160-72.

a "sweet, all-persuading desire" for the ship and the quest (τὸν δὲ παμπειθῆ γλυκὺν ἡμιθέοισιν πόθον ἔνδαιεν Ἥρα, 184; παμπειθής only here in the extant Pindar).

When Jason makes his first appearance in Iolcus, Apollo and Aphrodite are named: "Surely this is not Apollo," one of the townsmen conjectures, "nor the bronze-charioted consort of Aphrodite" (87f.).[35] A further guess soon after mentions Tityos and the Aloades, Otus and Ephialtes, and brings with it a warning about "touching the loves in one's power" (92).[36] This ominous erotic element is left in abeyance for well over a hundred lines, but the Aphroditic dimension of this Apolline hero appears at his first entrance upon the scene.[37] By placing the erotic overreachers alongside the restrained Apollo and the married Ares, Pindar also suggests the ambiguities and moral dangers inherent in this erotic power, even when it helps a good man.[38]

[35] Note also Apollo's presence as a sponsor of inspired poetry in 176f.: "From Apollo came the lyre-player, father of songs, well-praised Orpheus."

[36] Tityos is punished in Hades for having tried to rape Leto, according to Homer (Od. 11.580f.). The Aloades tried to rape Artemis and aspired to love for Hera: see the schol. ad loc. (156a Dr.). Their attack on Olympus is well known (Od. 11.313-17; Pindar, frag. 148a Bo. = 162 Sn.). Homer also mentions their exceptional beauty (Od. 11.310) and their youthful bloom (319f.). Apollodorus (1.7.4) relates their sexual violence against Hera and Artemis. See in general Fontenrose, *Orion*, p. 114, with note 11 on p. 135. Burton, 154, finds their appearance here "strange." Crotty, 117, suggests that the comparisons connect Jason to "gods and to heroes capable of threatening the gods." Perhaps they also reflect the themes of cosmogonic myth and the establishment of the Olympian order implicit in 289-91; see below, chap. 5, sec. i.

[37] There is another erotic suggestion in the panther skin of 81: see below, chap. 3, sec. I.

[38] Crotty, 117, recognizes the dangers here but interprets them rather differently, as part of the "special powers of the person returned from the wilderness." Since Apollo is the one who kills the Aloades in the Homeric version (Od. 11.317), the alternatives—disorderly eros and Olympian order—are even sharper in the passage.

2. The Language of Gods and Men

I. MANNERS OF SPEECH

THE previous chapter has suggested that the heroism of Jason in the ode is cast not in the simplex mold of Achillean forthright action but rather is shot through with the ambiguities of a more devious model, the craft or guile of Odysseus. This divided heroism is, in turn, related to Pindar's self-consciousness of his poetry. This is a poetics of *alētheia* and *mētis*, of both truth and craft. Like his hero who "drips mildness upon his words" (136-38), the poet practices an ambiguous pharmacology.[1] His craft contains the double possibility inherent in all artifice of language: its poison of duplicity and its healing drug of truth. The poet needs his crafty art and guile to create his "truth"; but the very nature of his medium also casts a shadow of artificiality and deviousness upon that truth, and vice versa.

In calling attention, here and elsewhere, to this quasi-magical power of poetic language and the indissoluble polarity of its two faces, the curative and the poisonous, Pindar also takes the first steps toward a poetics of textuality: a self-consciousness about the processes by which language fabricates meanings and persuades, seduces, or entices the reader / listener to accept them. Instead of disguising the play of differences between word and object, signifier and signified, that makes representation possible, such a poetry allows us to glimpse the dynamic power—metaphorically, the magic, seduction, or medicine—through which it takes hold of our minds. At the same

[1] I have in mind, of course, Derrida's analysis of the drug / poison of writing in the myth of Plato's *Phaedrus*: "La pharmacie de Platon," in *La Dissemination* (Paris 1972), especially 108-13.

time this poetry reveals the potential instability or reversibility of the elements by which it exercises this power over us: hence the ambiguity of the drugs or craft that serve as the metaphorical or symbolic correlates of poetry. Pindar, it must be emphasized, is only at the early stages of such an awareness. What makes his work particularly interesting, as we shall see in more detail later, is the interaction between this nascent poetics of textuality and his underlying poetics of "presence," a belief in the full power of poetry to reveal eternal truth through access to divine authority.

The choice between the good and bad sides of craft, *mētis*, and between a hero of guile and a hero of force, determines not only the nature of poetry, but also the ways in which men communicate with one another and with the gods. Thus the concern in *Pythian* 4 to neutralize *mētis* takes the pervasive form of a contrast between honest and deceptive speech. As in Herodotus too (4.155), the story of Battus gives speech and silence an important role, and the circumstances of speaking and listening are strongly marked at critical points (57-63, 127-29, 135-38). Kindly or gentle words recur as a leitmotiv, and they particularly characterize Jason (128, 137) and his followers (240). The mythical model for righteous speech extends to the present, for Damophilus, as Pindar assures Arcesilaus, allows no place to an evil tongue ("deprives the evil tongue of a clear voice," ὀρφανίζει κακὰν γλῶσσαν φαεννᾶς ὀπός, 284).

The speech and actions of the ancient heroes have an urgency and spontaneity that mark their honesty, directness, and frank openness. The disguised Triton "at once" seizes the clod (εὐθὺς ἁρπάξας, 34) and "seeks eagerly" to give it (μάστευσε, 35). The recipient, Euphamus, "does not disobey" but "rushes forward" (θορών) to press hand to hand and accept the gift (35). Jason, entering the agora of Iolcus, comes with sudden speed (τάχα δ' εὐθύς, 83).

CHAPTER 2

When his presence is known, his kinsfolk come quickly (ταχέως, 126). From their house, after serious talk (132), Jason at once rises up from the feasting for his important conference with Pelias (αἶψα δ' ἀπὸ κλισιᾶν ὦρτο σὺν κείνοισι, 133f.), and they surge or speed inside to confront the usurper (ἐσσύμενοι δ' εἴσω κατέσταν, 135). Pelias claims the rapidity of response as authority for the oracle that sends Jason on his dangerous mission: "Quickly (ὡς τάχος) it urges me to fashion a voyage with a ship" (164). In the fabled realm of Colchis, Aeetes, baleful king though he is, is a man of honor, and after the trial at once (αὐτίκα) tells Jason the location of the Golden Fleece (241). Pindar himself follows the heroic manner when he breaks off abruptly and takes the path of brevity (οἶμον ἴσαμι βραχύν, "I know a short path [of song]," 248).

The meeting between the Argonaut Euphamus and the disguised Triton early in the poem and in the earliest chronological stratum of the narrative sets the tone for courteous exchange among peers. These words of friendship (*philia epea*, 29) establish a model of heroic discourse. Their meeting fulfils the requisite norms of hospitality that men of generosity and good will (*euergetai*) should show to strangers (*xenois. . . . elthontessin*, 30). The god displays polite understanding of the Argonauts' haste and excuses his abrupt arrival and departure (γίνωσκε δ' ἐπειγομένους, 34). Throughout the ode haste seems to characterize the energy of heroes; they do nothing slowly.

The motifs of guest-friendship, the proffered banquet, and the courtesy of address carry over to Jason's behavior at Iolcus (127ff.) and to Pindar's recommendation of Damophilus. The latter is reinforced by the citation of Homer's "greatest honor for a noble messenger" (*angelon eslon*, 278; cf. *angelias orthas*, 279; *epangellonti*, 30).[2] Pin-

[2] Cf. also frag. 61.18-20 Bo. = 70b.23-25 Sn. (a dithyramb for Thebes)

dar is just such a good messenger; he is one of a series of positive intermediaries through speech. He is the mouthpiece of the Muse (1-3), as the Pythia is of Apollo (5). Hence he is of assured probity as the mouthpiece of Damophilus in effecting reconciliation with Arcesilaus (276-99). Pindar in fact executes his commission as good messenger by giving a vivid account of the joy of being received by welcoming kinsfolk among whom full and frank speech is possible (120-34, especially 127f.; *panta logon*, 132). The scene diplomatically prefigures the happy return that Damophilus is to find among his relations in Cyrene (cf. 294-96).

This power of conciliatory speech has two other mythical exempla. Jason would persuade Pelias to release the kingdom before further evil. Release (*luson*, 155) is emphatically the first word of the epode. Zeus too released (*luse*) the imprisoned Titans (291). The poet's own song at the celebration "today" (1f.) partakes of the good speaking in the mythical banquets of the past (cf. 29-34, 127-30). It is also exemplified in the Cyrenean symposium that will celebrate the exile's return (294-96), an event in itself predicated on Damophilus' righteous speaking (283; note the repeated motif of the song's "increase" in 3 and 279).

The mode of speaking reveals the moral temper of the speaker. Jason introduces himself as a man decent in both deed and word (*ergon, epos*, 104f.). The epic fulness of direct discourse here and throughout the myth, nowhere else carried to such length in the Pindaric corpus, keeps these contrasts in the foreground.[3] Pelias' warning to Jason

---

and in general, Gundert, 54f.; Burton, 112f.; Segal, "Messages to the Underworld." Note too the motif of the herald in 170 and 200 (ὤρνυεν κάρυκας, κάρυξε δ' αὐτοῖς).

[3] See especially Sandgren, 18f. and Gigante, 34ff. Note the repeated formulas of speaking and listening in 11, 13, 58. Gigante observes the striking proportion of direct discourse in the ode.

CHAPTER 2

about "polluting (*katamiainais*) his race with hostile lies" (99f.) is at once refuted by the purity of Jason's origins (cf. *hagnos*, 103 and 204).[4] It is Pelias who needs warnings about guile and trickery (cf. 139f., 145f.), while Jason's gentle speech is a recurrent theme (101f., 127f., 136-38, 240).[5] Jason, then, can serve as the mythical paradigm for Damophilus (cf. 283) and exemplify the healing effect of words implied in his name (cf. 270f.).[6]

Uncowed by Pelias' overbearing attitude, Jason answers with bold courage (θαρσήσαις, 101); but he also uses subtle speech as a weapon against his crafty foe. Upon his arrival in Iolcus he implicitly lays claim to his authority in the city through his very mode of address. Although he is ostensibly answering Pelias, he is in fact addressing the citizens: "Taking courage, he replied thus with gentle words" (τὸν δὲ θαρσήσαις ἀγανοῖσι λόγοις / ὧδ' ἀμείφθη, 101f.). But he utters Pelias' name only in the third person, coupled with the uncomplimentary epithet, "lawless" (Πελίαν ἄθεμιν, 109). Only near the end of his speech does he reveal the real addressees: "Know ye the chief points of these words" (ἀλλὰ τούτων μὲν κεφάλαια λόγων / ἴστε,

[4] The tone of Pelias' in 99ff. has been much discussed; scholars have been cautious about assuming too brutal a spirit, but there is general agreement that the tone is, at the least, discourteous and not particularly friendly: in addition to the commentators ad loc., see Sandgren, 16f., Robbins, 208f., Carey, 149f., Burton, 155f., Lattimore, 23f., Méautis, 233-35. For Norwood, however, Pelias' ἔσομαι τοῖος in 156f. shows "a knightly manner" (p. 39) and "flawless courtesy" (p. 40). The contrast with Apollo's manner in *Pyth.* 9.33ff. is telling. Theseus in Bacchylides 17 is another example of the polite, calm, and self-assured young hero: cf. Carey, 146.

[5] See Giannini (1977-80) 140.

[6] For the etymological play see, inter alia, Robbins, 211ff. Despite the strong contrast of Jason and Pelias, we should beware of a simplistic one-to-one equation of Jason = Damophilus and Pelias = Arcesilaus, a view that would hardly do credit to Pindar's tact. See Lattimore, 23f., Carey, 165, Robbins, 207-9, and Sandgren, 18, for a review of previous scholarship. See also below, chap. 7, sec. II.

116, emphatically at the beginning of the strophe). The vocative κεδνοί πολῖται ("dear citizens") in the next sentence makes the address explicit (117b).[7] The epithet κεδνοί implies his special bond of inclusiveness and solidarity with them.

"Stranger" was Pelias' appellation for Jason (ὦ ξεῖνε, 97). The youth politely declines the term: "I do not come to this land as a place of strangers" (οὐ ξείναν ἱκάνω γαῖαν ἄλλων, 118).[8] He is, however, not merely a citizen returning "home" (οἴκαδε, 106) but a king's son seeking to restore the ancient honor of his house (106-8). Thus when he requests directions to "the house of his fathers of the white horses" (117, repeating the motif of "home" from 106), he has the right to address the Iolcans as "dear citizens." At this point he explains (γάρ, 119) that he is in fact "the child of Aeson, belonging to the place" (Αἴσονος παῖς ἐπιχώριος, 118). He thereby establishes the personal ties of ancient association and local habitation appropriate to κεδνοί. This term in Pindar nearly always denotes the bonds of family ties or an equivalent sentiment of familial affection.[9] In fact the two phrases that denote Jason's roots in the land, "house of (my) fathers" and "child of Aeson, belonging to the place," frame the address to the "dear citizens."

In his second speech, after Jason has been accepted and festively regaled by his clan, he begins with a direct and honorific address to Pelias: παῖ Ποσειδᾶνος Πετραίου

[7] The point about Pelias and the citizens is well made by Illig, 66f.

[8] The status of *xenos* is, of course, crucial to Jason's threat to Pelias' position in Thebes. In 78 the oracle warned Pelias to watch out for a man wearing a single sandal, "whether he is a stranger or townsman" (ξεῖνος αἴτ' ὦν ἀστός). The apparently adventitious addition to the sentence, as is the manner of oracles, proves to be the more significant detail.

[9] See Slater, *Lexicon*, s.v., who, however, unnecessarily isolates *Pyth.* 4.117 from the other occurrences and weakly translates, "*good* in respectful address."

CHAPTER 2

("son of Poseidon Petraios," 138). The difference between the two modes of address shows the temper of the young hero. Insulted, Jason coolly disdains to address Pelias at all (101-19), even though his own position at that moment of arrival is precarious. Strengthened by the support of his family, he generously opens his second address with an honorific patronymic (138).

The Pythia's spontaneous shout of prophecy to Battus at Delphi (60) and the flow of the poet's own ambrosial words from their Theban spring (299) are the most positive form of speaking in the ode: here mortal words are touched by divine authority or immortality. Pelias' premeditated reply to Jason (156) is at the opposite extreme from the Pythia's spontaneity. She shouts with joyful openness (60f.); he conceals in his heart the fear caused by an oracle (96; cf. 73). Jason's speech too, like the Pythia's, stirs an immediate emotional response, as his old father's eyes brim with tears (120-23).[10] At the banquet that follows, Jason again shows his warmth and frankness before kinsmen. Though he is in fact the guest rather than the host,[11] he is the one who "receives them with words of sweet kindness," provides the appropriate guest-gifts, and entertains them "with every festivity for five nights and days together in the holy bloom of lavish comfort" (129-31). Only on the sixth day does he "set forth the whole account in full seriousness from the beginning" (132f.):[12] ἀλλ' ἐν ἕκτᾳ πάντα λόγον θέμενος σπου-/δαῖον ἐξ ἀρχᾶς ἀνὴρ / συγγενέσιν παρεκοινᾶτ(ο).

The change from Jason's frankness to Pelias' dissimula-

[10] The contrast with Pelias is all the greater if Pelias' *leukai phrenes* in 109 refer to his cold, unfeeling, unemotional temperament: see above, chap. 1, note 8.

[11] See Duchemin, *Pythiques*, ad loc.

[12] On the scene, see Méautis 238.

tion accompanies the spatial shift from one house to another:

αἶψα δ' ἀπὸ κλισιᾶν
ὦρτο σὺν κείνοισι· καὶ ῥ' ἦλθον Πελία μέγαρον·
ἐσσύμενοι δ' εἴσω κατέσταν. (133-35)

At once with these [kinsmen] Jason rose up from the couches, and they came to the palace of Pelias. Moving with speed, they stood before him.[13]

Each house has its own mode of speech.

Ambiguously between the two modes of utterance, open and closed, spontaneous and controlled, stands the speaking of Medea. Like the Pythia, she speaks with divine inspiration (10f.); yet the "dense craft" of her words (58) has the ambiguity of everything in the sphere of *mētis*.[14] The architectural setting, with its sculptural adornments, places the Pythia's oracle in sacral, civilized space (4f., 53-55, 66f.; cf. 74, 163b). Medea's oracle, though localized at Thera (*epos Thēraion*, 9f.; cf. 14, 19, 42), is dominated by the watery wastes traversed by the *Argo* at a vaguely defined point in a long voyage (11ff., 57f.). Yet it too is enframed within the Delphic setting, as Pindar's craft is enclosed within its context of friendship (line 1) and defined by its moral aims of praising noble and lasting things.[15]

Silence as well as speech tests men's character as they respond to divinity entering their lives. The Argonauts are

[13] On the probable sense of *klisiai* in 133 (only here in Pindar), see Christ, ad loc., and LSJ, s.v. Slater's "camp" (*Lexicon*, s.v.) is less appropriate. The motif of "standing" also recurs emphatically at several places in the ode as a mark of energetic determination: cf. Pindar himself in 2 and Jason in 84.

[14] For the ambiguities of *mētis* in general, see above, chap. 1, notes 1 and 11. On Medea's prophecy, see below, chap. 7, sec. IV.

[15] Cf. the injunction to say "what is good about the gods," *amphi daimonōn kala*, Ol. 1.35.

CHAPTER 2

fixed in awesome, motionless silence when they hear Medea's prophecy (57f.). Pindar's break-off formula here in leading into the major myth (59), like his break-off formula near the end of the myth (247), suggests that he too knows how to keep silence where it is appropriate.[16]

Very different from the Argonauts' holy silence is the dumbstruck dismay of Pelias when he sees the fateful single sandal of Jason (τάφε δ' αὐτίκα παπταίναις ἀρίγνωτον πέδιλον, 95). This wonder is marked not by reverence and spontaneous feeling but by caution and calculation (96f.).[17] Pelias is quiet again in 156, just before he gives his answer to Jason's terms. The addition of the adverb "in silence" (or "after silence") here (ἀκᾷ ἀνταγόρευσεν, 156) indicates possible premeditation as he proposes to the young hero a long and dangerous journey.[18] Pindar is using a familiar folktale motif: Evil King sends off straightforward Young Hero on Impossible Quest; but the details of speech and silence add individual characterization.

Aeetes' speech at the end of the myth has far greater majesty than Pelias'. This doublet of the powerful Evil King who sets the impossible task is less prosaic than his Iolcan counterpart. Though possibly cruel, Aeetes is not presented as particularly crafty. A mythical grandeur and an aura of mysterious power, both of which are appropriate to his remote kingdom and his divine ancestry, envelop him. With the courtesy (and slightly mocking irony) of the powerful, he gives Jason his full regal title:

[16] Note also the deliberate silence about an evil story in *Nem.* 5.19.

[17] On Pelias' caution in this scene as part of his *mētis*, see Giannini (1979) 59f.

[18] See Farnell, ad 156-67. The phrase can also mean "answered softly," in which case Pelias cleverly takes his cue from Jason. Thus Mezger, ad 156, comments, "Der Heuchler ahmt Jasons Sanftheit nach." Duchemin, ad loc., sees in the adverb only the calmness of Pelias' reply, but she too admits that he is "ce roi plein de ruses." See also Puech, ad loc. (p. 77, note 2): "le vieux renard rusé et négocié."

LANGUAGE OF GODS AND MEN

τοῦτ' ἔργον βασιλεύς,
ὅστις ἄρχει ναός, ἐμοὶ τελέσαις
ἄφθιτον στρωμνὰν ἀγέσθω,
κῶας αἰγλᾶεν χρυσέῳ θυσάνῳ.   (229-31)

Let the king who rules over the ship accomplish for me this deed and then carry off the fleece imperishable, the skin radiant with golden tassel.

Pelias' tone in an analogous situation is very different: τοῦτον ἄεθλον ἑκὼν τέλεσον ("Do you willingly accomplish this trial," 165). His clipped phrase is bare of ornament. Though in the next line he swears (with equal bareness of language) to give up rule and kingship, he does not actually give Jason the title of "king," the point of conflict between them (cf. 106, 152f.).[19] His stark words have none of the resonance of Aeetes' "king who rules over the ship" in 229f.

Both rulers also describe the fleece in different ways. Pelias' language is unheroic and characteristically dry. He calls the fleece merely "the deep-woolled skin of a ram" (δέρμα κριοῦ βαθύμαλλον, 161). To Aeetes, however, it is a "coverlet imperishable, fleece radiant with tassels of gold" (ἄφθιτον στρωμνάν, κῶας αἰγλᾶεν χρυσέῳ θυσάνῳ, 230b f.).[20]

---

[19] The motif of kingship and the title of *basileus* is also a link between the stories of Jason and Battus: cf. 62; also *Pyth.* 5.15f. and 97f. Within *Pyth.* 4 Jason's request for the σκᾶπτον μόναρχον καὶ θρόνος ("sole-ruling scepter and throne") in his second, formal speech at 152 is echoed in Pelias' answer, with its obvious attempt to stall, in 165f., καί τοι μοναρχεῖν / καὶ βασιλευέμεν ὄμνυμι προήσειν ("I swear to give up sole rule and the kingship"). Pelias' ἑκών, "willingly," in 165 is perhaps taken up and counteracted by the divinely offered help of Boreas, another *basileus*, who "willingly, with joyful spirit," sends his Argonaut sons in 181. See also below, chap. 7, sec. v.

[20] On the emphatic placement of 231 at the opening of a new strophic system, see Burton, 165, and Mullen, 95. Aeetes later speaks of the fleece as a "skin" and even mentions the knife of Phrixos which layed it out

CHAPTER 2

Aeetes' response to Jason's success, correspondingly, has an openness and emotional force totally lacking in the crafty Pelias: he "cried out in grief, unspeakable though it was, astonished at the power" (ἴυξεν δ' ἀφωνήτῳ περ ἔμπας ἄχει / δύνασιν Αἰήτας ἀγασθείς, 237). The Delphic oracle had warned Pelias to keep a sharp lookout for "the man with a single sandal" (τὸν μονοκρήπιδα); yet at the critical moment this king's gaze is riveted less on the wearer than on what he wears: "At once he marvelled, discerning the easily known sandal on the right foot alone" (95). Aeetes, however, is gripped not by the physical object but by the marvelous sight of the young hero yoking the bulls and by the heroic quality of strength or power (*dunasis*).[21] Pelias' wonder centers anxiously on potentiality in the remote future, Aeetes' on the actuality of successful performance. Such open astonishment (ἀγασθείς, 238) is perhaps appropriate to one who is himself an object of wonder ("wondrous son of Helios," Ἀελίου θαυμαστὸς υἱός, 241).[22] The oxymoron-like collocation of shouting and speechlessness in 238 emphasizes the extraordinary quality of the moment. But where Pelias kept silence, Aeetes gives voice to his feelings, even though they defy speech (ἀφώνητον ἄχος). The speech of both kings, however, contrasts with the kindly speech of kinsmen or companions (cf. 127ff. and 240f.).

The verbal play on Aeetes' "shout" (*iuxen*, 238) and the *iunx* of Aphrodite's seductive power (214) brings together

---

(241f.) but adds the epithet "bright" (*lampron*). Cf. Euripides' "all-gold fleece," τὸ πάγχρυσον δέρας, *Medea* 5.

[21] Cf. Pelias' admission of Jason's force or ability in 158f., where, however, the mood is not of admiration but of an intentional manipulative persuasion, to lure him to undertake a perilous journey: δύνασαι δ' ἀφελεῖν μᾶνιν χθονίων ("You have the power to remove the wrath of those below the earth").

[22] Wilamowitz, 390, notes the striking quality of the epithet ("ein sehr seltenes Prädikat").

LANGUAGE OF GODS AND MEN

the two sides of Jason's victory, a male contest of force and the aid of feminine "drugs," Olympian help and Colchian witchcraft.[23] Behind Aeetes' cry of dismay at a deed of "force" (*dunasin*, 238) there stand the two instances of feminine guile, Aphrodite's love-magic (213-18) and the potent craft of Medea's advice (πῦρ δέ νιν οὐκ ἐόλει παμφαρμάκου ξείνας ἐφετμαῖς, "the fire did not press him, thanks to the behests of the stranger-woman, skilled in all drugs," 233). Behind his "speechless grief" at Jason's "power" stands the narrative model of Medea's prophecy to the Argonauts in 57f., namely awed, motionless silence in response to "craft":

ἔπταξαν δ' ἀκίνητοι σιωπᾷ
. . . πυκινὰν μῆτιν κλύοντες. (57f.)

(The heroes) crouched down unmoving in silence, hearing the dense craft.

ἴυξεν δ' ἀφωνήτῳ περ ἔμπας ἄχει
δύνασιν . . . ἀγασθείς. (237f.)

He shouted in grief, unspeakable though it was, wondering at the power.

In both cases masculine heroes of physical strength are beneficiaries of a mysterious feminine craft, be it the *mētis* of prophecy or the *pharmaka* of magical knowledge (the latter stressed by the repeated compounds of *pharmakon* in 221 and 233).

The awed silence produced by Medea's prophecy is carefully balanced by the Pythia's spontaneous shout in answer to Battus' inquiry about the "misspeaking voice" of

[23] As Duchemin, *Pythiques*, notes ad 237, this is the only occurrence of the verb *iungein*, "shout," in Pindar, and it stands in a bold combination with *aphōnētos*, "unspeaking." Note too the oral violence of the snake's *labrotatai genues*, "jaws most destructive," in 244.

CHAPTER 2

his stammer (56-63).[24] In like manner, Medea's drugs at the climax of the myth are made helpful by the Olympian Aphrodite's invention of the iynx; and the result is another spontaneous cry that redounds to the hero's glory, Aeetes' shout of grief (cf. 237f. and 61-63). Jason, like Odysseus, may ultimately owe his success to Zeus.

II. ORACLES, OMENS, AND GIFTS FROM THE GODS

Oracular utterance is a major subdivision of the theme of language. The first section of the ode (1-69) revolves about the oracles of Apollo to Battus and of Medea to the Argonauts (6-9, 10-58, 59-67). Just as the initial statement of Battus' oracle leads into Medea's prophecy (6-10), so in reverse order the end of Medea's prophecy leads back to Battus at Delphi in an ABBA pattern (Pythia-Medea; Medea-Pythia) (59-63).[25]

The vivid encounter between Euphamus and the disguised Triton recalls scenes like the meeting of Glaucus and Diomedes in *Iliad* 6.[26] The heroic tone embodies the spontaneity and energy that attend the right receiving of the gifts of the gods. These come unbidden and unexpected.[27] The gods choose the mortals worthy of their attention, and they choose their own moment and mode of utterance. Being singled out as the recipient of such a message expands a mortal life beyond its ordinary limits so

[24] In *Pyth.* 5.57-62, too, Apollo miraculously gives Battus the power to speak, and the voice frightens lions so that the god may not leave his prophecies about Cyrene unfulfilled.

[25] See Sandgren, 21, who also notes the step-like ("stufenweise") movement back to the past. Given the onomatopoeic importance of Battus' name and the etymological play on Jason's, we may wonder if the etymology of Eu-phamos is significant as well. On prophecy as a organizing principle of the ode, see also Ruck-Matheson, 28ff.

[26] On the Homeric coloring of *Pyth.* 4 generally, see Gigante, 37-41, and Sandgren, 14ff., both with further bibliography.

[27] For the gifts of the gods and the readiness to accept them cf. *Ol.* 1.75-87, 9.28, 14.5ff.; *Pyth.* 1.41f., 3.59f., 8.96f.; *Isth.* 5.22ff.

LANGUAGE OF GODS AND MEN

that it touches the realm of the ageless or imperishable—*athanaton, agēraon, aphthiton*. Such is the glory that accrues from a great and lasting deed: a victory in the games, the founding of a city, a heroic battle, a noble death in war.

Receiving a god's gift is a leitmotiv of the poem. Euphamus received the divine clod (*dexato*, 37) but lost it. At the start of the Argonaut myth the beginning of the sea-voyage received the heroes (70), as if this beginning (*archa*, a strong word in Pindar) were itself an active force and an extension of the gods' will.[28] The abortive receiving in the marshes of Lake Tritonis is then set right on Lemnos, where the fated day (*moiridion amar*) will receive not the imperishable seed of the divine clod (cf. 43 and 255) but the seed of Battiad prosperity (254-56).[29]

The motif of "receiving" is also associated with a momentous journey of descent to the place of exchange between human and divine.[30] Battus "descends" into the Pythia's chamber at Delphi (*katabanta*, 55), as Euphamus "descended" from the *Argo* to receive the divine clod (*katabas*, 22). Between the muster of the Argonauts in Homeric catalogue style and the launching of the expedition, the "bloom of the sailors came down into Iolcus" (188): ἐς δ' Ἰαολκὸν ἐπεὶ κατέβα ναυτᾶν ἄωτος. Here, as in the meeting between Euphamus and Triton, there are divine omens, the thunder of Zeus (23f. and 197-99). At such mo-

---

[28] For the power of the *archa* in Pindar, cf. *Ol*. 11.5; *Pyth*. 1.2 and 10.10; frag. 121 Bo. = 137 Sn.; frag. 194 Bo. = 205 Sn. On the striking phraseology of 70, see Bowra, 289. On *archē* in archaic thought, see Van Groningen, *In the Grip of the Past*, 17ff. and 89; Greengard, 119-24. Cf. *Pyth*. 4.132 here: Jason tells his story ἐξ ἀρχᾶς, "from the beginning." Cf. also *Pyth*. 1.2b; frag. 194 Bo. = 205 Sn.; *Ol*. 11.4f.

[29] For the text of 255, see below, chap. 3, note 37.

[30] *Katabainein* is also used elsewhere of the hero's or poet's contact with divine power, e.g., *Ol*. 6.58, *Pae*. 6.13; also *Ol*. 7.13; *Pyth*. 3.73; *Nem*. 1.38 and 3.42. Cf. the imitation in Theocr. 13.21, on which see K. J. Gutzwiller, *Studies in the Hellenistic Epyllion*, Beiträge zur Klassische Philologie 114 (Königstein 1981), 23.

CHAPTER 2

ments mortal life is opened to the divine perspective of the larger destiny, *moira* or *aisa* (cf. 145, 196, 255; 24, 107, 197; also πεπρωμένος in 61).

The task of right "receiving" originates in the gods' mysterious gifts to men, but it also serves as a model for man's relation with man. Hospitality (*xenia*), the art of receiving kinsmen and strangers, is a recurrent theme.[31] This too extends to the poet in Pindar's praise for the art of the good messenger, another kind of intermediary between men (277ff.).

As one would expect in a Pythian ode, the Delphic setting of prophecy is a prominent link between the stories of Battus and Pelias (cf. 4-6, 59-61, 74). Later Pelias tells of another consultation at Delphi (163f.), this time in response to a dream. The Argonaut myth ends, as it began, with an allusion to Apollo's gift of Libya (259), which in ring-composition recalls the initial prophecy (6), now for the third time:

χρῆσεν οἰκιστῆρα Βάττον
    καρποφόρου Λιβύας   (6f.)

He prophesied Battus as the founder of fruit-bearing Libya.

    ἔνθεν δ' ὔμμι Λατοί-
        δας ἔπορεν Λιβύας πεδίον
σὺν θεῶν τιμαῖς ὀφέλλειν, ἄστυ χρυσοθρόνου
διανέμειν θεῖον Κυράνας . . . (259-61)

To you did Leto's son grant Libya's plain for increase, with honors from the gods, that you may govern the divine city of Cyrene . . .

The repeated matronymic of the god reinforces the connection (Λατοίδαισιν, 3; Λατοίδας, 259).

[31] For the theme of *xenia*, see 30, 35, 78, 97, 128, 233, 299; in general, Schadewaldt, 314f.; Gundert, 32ff.; Ruck-Matheson, 20ff.; Gianotti, 14ff.

LANGUAGE OF GODS AND MEN

Pelias' oracles are appropriate to his character. Unlike the elaborately described prophecies given to Battus and Jason (59-63, 189-202), his have an austere brevity appropriate to their grim contents:

θέσφατον ἦν Πελίαν
ἐξ ἀγαυῶν Αἰολιδᾶν θανέμεν χεί-
ρεσσιν ἢ βουλαῖς ἀκάμπτοις. (71b-72b)

It was prophesied for Pelias to die from the hands of lordly descendants of Aeolus or from their unbending counsels.

ἦλθεν δέ οἱ κρυόεν πυκινῷ μάντευμα θυμῷ,
πὰρ μέσον ὀμφαλὸν εὐδένδροιο ῥηθὲν ματέρος. (73f.)

There came to him in his densely crafting mind an oracle spoken beside the omphalos placed in the middle, navel of the well-treed mother.

Though this "chill prophecy" is "spoken at the navel of the well-treed mother (earth) at Delphi" (74), no voice or messenger is mentioned, in contrast to the Pythia at 59-63 and Pindar's praise of the good messenger in 277-79. Nor is there a prayer for divine aid. Instead, the prophecy (*manteuma*, a rather neutral word) merely came (*ēlthen*). The content of the oracle too is negative rather than positive: it tells him to keep a sharp lookout (75), an action for which this calculating ruler needs little encouragement. The oracle suits its recipient.

When Pelias himself describes the oracle's command to lay the ghost of Phrixus, the element of divinity is still further reduced, and his language has a matter-of-fact practicality:

ταῦτά μοι θαυμαστὸς ὄνειρος ἰὼν φω-
    νεῖ. μεμάντευμαι δ' ἐπὶ Κασταλίᾳ
εἰ μετάλλατόν τι· καὶ ὡς τάχος ὀτρύ-
    νει με τεύχειν ναῒ πομπάν. (163f.)

45

CHAPTER 2

> *These things did the wondrous dream in its coming speak to me. And I have consulted the oracle at Castalia to see if anything further is to be sought out; and speedily it urged me to fashion a voyage with a ship.*

The poet's third-person narration called the prophecy *thesphaton*, something "divinely spoken" (71b); but Pelias' *ipsissima verba* contain no explicit word for divinity: the gods have little place in his oracular world. There is no inspiration, immortal mouth, or spontaneous utterance from the god's chamber, no aura of mystery, no sense of the numinous. The dream that visits Homer's Agamemnon in the second book of the *Iliad* is a "divine Dream," *theios Oneiros* (2.22 and 56); but Pelias' dream, though "wondrous," is not "divine." Unlike the traditional dreams of early Greek poetry, it lacks a personal shape, human or divine.[32] The Argonauts, on the other hand, receive urgent and immediate divine messages. The first of these (in the narrative, not the chronological order) comes to Euphamus, the second to the seer Mopsos (23f., 197f.). The unnamed divinity, presumably Triton, who approaches Euphamos in the eddies of Lake Tritonis "puts on the shining countenance of a man of reverence" (28f.).

Pelias' only mention of gods is a brief reference to Zeus Genethlios in his last quoted line (167). For the command to lay Phrixus' ghost he cites only the authority of the dead man himself, not that of the gods: κέλεται γὰρ ἐὰν ψυχὰν κομίξαι / Φρίξος ("For Phrixus bids me to lay his ghost," 159f.).[33] The gods will intervene directly in Jason's behalf to make Medea fall in love with him (213-23), but they make her the instrument of Pelias' death (250).

Apollo's oracular compensation to Battus for the "misspeaking voice" of his stutter brings together speech, ora-

---

[32] On the human form in the Homeric dreams, with a useful bibliography, see Jan Bremmer, *On the Soul* (Princeton 1982), 19.

[33] For the meaning of this passage, see below, chap. 4, note 5.

cle, and the exchange between god and man (59-63). The scene contains the plainest oracular utterance in the ode, and its clarity complements the rather mysterious contact of men and gods in the first section, the "friendly words" between Euphamus and Eurypylus-Triton (29). In Apollo's vigorously forthright answer at Delphi, Battus' deformity of speech calls forth a more effective meeting with divinity than the face-to-face exchange in the heroic past. "Stutterer" Battus has better communication than "Good-speaker" Eu-phamus.

In that pre-Delphic setting on the remote sea the essence of the exchange takes place through sacred signs and the gift of tokens: the divine stranger bestows the mysterious clod, and the recipient "presses hand to hand" (χειρί οἱ χεῖρ' ἀντερείσαις / δέξατο βώλακα δαιμονίαν, 37). This hand-to-hand touch marks a privileged contact between a mortal and divine power: we may compare Parmenides' journey to Being, where "the kindly goddess *received* me and touched *my right hand with her hand*" (ὑπεδέξατο, χεῖρα δὲ χειρὶ / δεξιτέρην ἕλεν, 28 B 1.22f. DK). Yet Pindar's divine form is concealed behind the deceptive appearance of "likeness" (θεῷ ἀνέρι εἰδομένῳ γαῖαν διδόντι, 21). Only the god-sent omen, Zeus' thunder, indicated the real significance of the meeting (23f.). With the presence of the Delphic god later the truth, spoken out loud and clear, replaces deformity with straightness or uprightness of speech (σὲ δ' ἐν τούτῳ λόγῳ / χρησμὸς ὤρθωσεν, "You, Battus, in this account did an oracle raise up," 59f.). The close juxtaposition of Apollo and the Muse in the proem connects the emerging clarity of oracular speech and the inspired discourse of poetic language. Elsewhere Pindar speaks of his poetry as a kind of oracular utterance.[34] His favorite hero, Heracles, "speaks

[34] E.g., *Pae.* 6.1-6; *Nem.* 9.50; frag. 83 Bo.=94a Sn.; frag. 137 Bo. = 150 Sn. See in general Gundert, 62; Maehler, 98; Duchemin, 32ff.; Gianotti, 64f.

CHAPTER 2

like a prophet" when he interprets an omen of Zeus for Telamon in *Isthmian* 6.51ff.

Within the first section of *Pythian* 4 there is an increasing explicitness in the gods' communication with men. The Pythia's inspiration and Medea's "immortal mouth" bring the divine will directly into mortal life (5-11). The exchange between man and god continues in the "hand-to-hand" greeting (37) and the tangible gift of the clod between Triton and Euphamus (34ff.). That first access to the divine, however, is mediated by "semblance" and disguise (21, 29). Later the mortal heroes' "forgetfulness of wits" (41b) postpones the fruition of the god's gift (41-49). In this early time the divine will remains obscure. The disguise of divinity here (21, 29) corresponds to the "pretext" of the god's visit (*prophasis*, 32). God and hero may exchange friendly words (29), but the burden of communication between them is carried by eager gestures (35-37) and appearances (21-29) which prove ultimately less effective than the spoken words of prophecy (9, 57).[35]

As the poem continues, contact with divinity becomes surer. The gods send their sons to participate in the expedition (170-83). Hera and Aphrodite bestow their respective gifts to help the voyage toward success (184-87, 213-23). Zeus gives clear omens from the heavens (197-201), and Poseidon helps them through the Symplegades (207-11). Euphamus' earlier reception of a god who appears in the guise of a man (21ff.) is balanced by the Thessalians' conjecture that the mortal stranger in their midst is a god (87ff.).

---

[35] For the privileged character of verbal prophecy, as opposed to other modes of foretelling the future, in Greece, see J.-P. Vernant, "Parole et signes muets" in Vernant, ed., *Divination et rationalité* (Paris 1974) 18f. Later in the myth, however, the Argonauts "obey signs" (*samasin peithomenoi*, 199f.), although these also have a quasi-verbal component (*phthegma*, 198; cf. 23).

LANGUAGE OF GODS AND MEN

At the critical moment of departure Pindar highlights the clarity of the signs from the gods and the efficacy of sacral gestures. The seer Mopsus "divines with birds and sacred lots" (μάντις ὀρνίχεσσι καὶ κλάροισι θεοπροπέων ἱεροῖς, 190). Zeus the Father caused to resound back (ἀντάυσε) to the priest a voice of destiny from the clouds, a voice of thunder, with lightning flashes accompanying:

ἐκ νεφέων δέ οἱ ἀντάϋσε βροντᾶς αἴσιον
φθέγμα· λαμπραὶ δ' ἦλθον ἀκτῖ-
νες στεροπᾶς ἀπορηγνύμεναι. (197f.)

As good omen a voice of thunder resounded back in reply from the clouds, and there came bright flashings of lightning breaking forth.

The close parallel with the thunder at Euphamus' meeting with Triton in the first account of the journey reinforces the connection between the two passages:[36]

αἰσίαν δ' ἐπί οἱ Κρονίων
Ζεὺς πατὴρ ἔκλαγξε βροντάν·
ἀνίκ' ἄγκυραν ποτὶ χαλκόγενυν
ναῒ κριμνάντων ἐπέτοσσε, θοᾶς 'Αρ-
γοῦς χαλινόν. (23-25)

And as good omen Father Zeus, son of Cronos, roared out to him in thunder when he found them hanging out the bronze-cheeked anchor for the ship, the swift Argo's bridle.

In the later scene too the Argonauts are weighing anchor:

---

[36] Note too the repetition of Zeus as "father" in both passages: Κρονίων Ζεὺς πατήρ (23); πατέρ' Οὐρανιδᾶν ἐγχεικέραυνον Ζῆνα, (194). Father Zeus who "wields the sword of thunder" here also prepares for the martial atmosphere of the expedition, in contrast to the dangerless life "beside the mother" in 186. Cf. also the implication of Zeus's authority for prophecy in line 4.

CHAPTER 2

ἐπεὶ δ' ἐμβόλου
κρέμασαν ἀγκύρας ὕπερθεν. (191f.)

When they hung the anchors down from the prow.

Here, however, the omens are deliberately sought by a *mantis* (190) with holy rites (*hiera*, 191) and with libations from a golden cup (193). These prayers and omens also have greater fulness of detail (195-98). Instead of the inarticulate "fated thunder" of the earlier scene (*aisian brontan*, 23), there is a "fated *voice* of thunder" (*brontas aision phthegma*, 197). This utterance in response (*ant-aüse*) makes Zeus' reply seem something more specifically like a human voice than the earlier *eklanxen* (23). In the earlier passage there was sound only; now "there came brilliant flashes of lightning breaking forth" (198), clear and visible signs from the god (*theou samata*, 199), and at these the heroes feel a breath of relief (*ampnoan*, 199).[37] This joyful physiological response of the vital functions in the *ampnoan* of 199 implies the same direct contact with the force of divinity as Medea brought into the mortal world in her inspired prophecy at the beginning (*apepneuse*, "breathed forth," 11).[38]

The omens of 23ff. are followed by an arduous passage overland, as the heroes carry their ship on their backs (25-27).[39] Mopsus' omens, however, are followed by "insatiable rowing from swift oars" (202) and the winds on the open sea (203f.). The scene of Mopsus' prophecy is chronologically anterior to Euphamus' meeting with Triton, but it comes later in the poem. The rearrangement of the order of events enables Pindar to reinforce the feeling of a pro-

[37] On the syntax of 198, see Duchemin, ad loc., who also comments on the reinforcing effect of "la valeur visuelle et la valeur auditive de l'image."

[38] For a somewhat similar play on this root, cf. ἀμπνοάν, ἀμπνεῦσαι, ἐνέπνευσεν in *Ol.* 8.7, 36, 70.

[39] On this passage, see Giannini (1976) 77-81.

gression towards that fuller communication with the gods that follows from the spontaneity of Apollo's oracle in 59-63 and from the greater clarity of heroic achievement at Jason's appearance. This increasing clarity of oracular utterance in the ode also corresponds to the poet's increasing power to escape the deceptive potential of language and to reveal the (true) workings of divinity in human life.

Pindar's recasting of the order of events implies an interpretation of what the myth means.[40] Through their common features of oracles and omens from the gods and the recovery of a lost kingdom, the tales of Battus and Jason mutually illuminate one another. Hidden behind the sequential order that ordinary mortals perceive is the larger pattern of the gods' will. The poet's break-up of chronological sequence follows from a wider perspective on events that is, in effect, that of gods rather than of mortals. Its parallels, contrasts, analogies are discernible only when chronological order is ignored. This larger pattern, outside of time, is what the poet makes visible in the ode, just as he reveals to the present celebrants of the *kōmos* (cf. 2b) the perspective of eternal things in which emerges the true meaning of the victory.[41]

[40] Some of this rearrangement, of course, is a matter of practical necessity. The landfall at Lemnos, for example, usually comes very early in the Argonauts' travels, and there Jason's union with Hypsipyle results in the birth of two sons (cf. Apollodorus 1.9.17), an obvious embarrassment to a version in which the marriage to Medea is a major event. On Pindar's handling of the legend (probably still quite fluid in his day), see Farnell, 2.144-48; Van der Kolf, 71-76. The differences between the chronological order and Pindar's narrative order are set out in tabular form by Hurst, 157f.

[41] See below, chap. 10.

3. Trials of the Hero: Sexuality, Generational Passage, and the Seeds of Creation

I. EROS

IN *Pythian* 4, as in early Greek literature generally, sexuality is a magical power and a divine force. In dealing with it the heroes of the odes require special aid from the gods. Even Apollo, albeit with a playful irony, needs the advice of the wise centaur Chiron in unlocking the "secret keys" of Aphrodite's "sacred" realm (*Pyth.* 9.36ff.).

For both Jason and Euphamus, landfall among dangerous females on a foreign shore moves from seduction or dangerous sexuality to marriage and political stability. Jason wins a bride (223) who also conveniently removes the usurper of his throne (250). Euphamus founds the royal line of Cyrene (254-56), which will continue to enjoy prosperity and honor through Apollo's favor (256-62). Correspondingly, the erotic magic that one expects in a poem about Medea does not hold the hero in thrall on a remote island, as in the *Odyssey*, but rather speeds him directly on his successful return.[1] Pindar suppresses the baneful

---

[1] The story of Medea in literature prior to Pindar's ode is not well documented. In Hesiod, *Theogony* 992-1002, we have the bare outline of the story that Pindar tells us here; Medea is a colorless figure whom Jason "makes his blossoming bride," and she bears him a son named Medeios. On the other hand, the ominous associations of her witchcraft, in the killing of Pelias, are attested in the art of the archaic period. See Duchemin, *Pythiques*, 104; Robert, 792ff., 865ff.; D. L. Page, *Euripides, Medea* (Oxford 1938), xxiff.

SEXUALITY AND CREATION

side of Medea's *mētis* (to which he in fact alludes elsewhere); but the drugs that save Jason (221, 233) will kill Pelias (250).[2]

Here, as in Euripides in part, Medea is the victim, not the agent, of erotic magic (213-19).[3] Events in Colchis begin with her falling in love. And of course it is all magical and supernatural, far removed from the prosaic details of secret meetings, promises, and go-betweens that occur in the tragedians and later in Apollonius of Rhodes.[4] Pindar does not even attribute her love directly to physical attraction to the handsome male body described in 82ff. and 123, but her longing (*pothos*) is only for Greece (218). Sexual desire is bent to the divine purpose of heroic achievement; female longing is subordinated to a collective embodiment of Hellenic glory (218), as if Hellas should naturally awaken the desire of a young Colchian girl. The parallel between the desire that Hera "burns" into the Argonauts to leave Greece on their quest and the desire that sets Me-

---

[2] In *Ol.* 13.49-54 the *mētis* of Medea is paired with that of Sisyphus: she "set forth a marriage for herself in opposition to her father, savior of the ship Argo and of its crew" (53f.). Pindar also suppresses any reference to Medea's killing of her brother Apsyrtus, which was related by Sophocles in his *Colchian Women* (frag. 319N = 343P; schol. ad Ap. Rhod. 4.223-30d) and by Pherecydes: see Apollodorus 1.9.23f., with Frazer's note ad loc. in the Loeb Classical Library edition; also Farnell, 2.145-48; Robert, 799-802. Medea's magical powers seem already established in the *Iliad*, assuming the (very probable) identification of Agamede with Medea in 11.740f.: she "knew as many drugs (*pharmaka*) as the broad earth nurtures." See Walter Leaf, *The Iliad*, ed. 2 (London 1900-02), ad 11.740; also Beye, *Epic and Romance in the Argonautica*, 49.

[3] E.g., Euripides, *Med.* 8: ἔρωτι θυμὸν ἐκπλαγεῖσ' Ἰάσονος, "smitten in her soul with desire for Jason."

[4] In Sophocles frag. 315 N = 339 P (*Colchian Women*), Medea seems to be alone with Jason and to be extracting a promise from him; cf. also Apollodorus 1.9.23. The motif of go-betweens and attendants is fully developed by Apollonius of Rhodes: cf. 3.475ff., 609ff., 661-743, 891ff. See in general Robert, 793.

CHAPTER 3

dea "burning" for Hellas reinforces this working together of the heroic and the erotic:

τὸν δὲ παμπειθῆ γλυκὺν ἡμιθέοι-
    σιν πόθον ἔνδαιεν Ἥρα
ναὸς Ἀργοῦς . . . (184f.)

Hera burned into the demi-gods a sweet all-persuasive desire for the ship Argo.

ποθεινὰ δ' Ἑλλὰς αὐτὰν
ἐν φρασὶ καιομέναν δονέοι μάστιγι Πειθοῦς (218f.)

that desire for Hellas might whirl her about, ablaze in her heart, with the whip of Persuasion.

As the erotic mystery is displaced from love to war and from women to heroes, the sweet all-persuasive desire that burns in the hearts of the Argonauts is sent not by Aphrodite but by Hera:

μή τινα λειπόμενον
τὰν ἀκίνδυνον παρὰ ματρὶ μένειν αἰ-
    ῶνα πέσσοντ', ἀλλ' ἐπὶ καὶ θανάτῳ
φάρμακον κάλλιστον ἑᾶς ἀρετᾶς ἅ-
    λιξιν εὑρέσθαι σὺν ἄλλοις. (185-87)

so that no one, left behind, remain by his mother coddling a life without danger; but rather find a most noble drug of his valor even against death with the other companions of his age.[5]

---

[5] For the meaning of this dense phrase, see Farnell, ad loc. The "drug" would serve to protect their *aretē* (objective genitive) from death through the immortal glory that may be expected to result from their great exploits. Gildersleeve, ad 186, following Boeckh, construes *aretas* as a defining genitive, so that the whole phrase means "a lovely drug that induces valor, even at the price of death." But Farnell convincingly refutes this view of the passage.

SEXUALITY AND CREATION

This magic does not keep the hero languorous with a seductress (again, like Odysseus with Circe or Heracles with Omphale), but rather counters possible idleness among women (186f.). "In the heroic world, a man's love affair is always with adventure."[6]

The negative side of the alternative is framed in terms of the mother ("to remain beside mother coddling a dangerless life"), whereas the positive side involves commitment to males of the heroes' own age (ἅλιξιν σὺν ἄλλοις, 187). This god-sent drive toward glory on a sea-voyage into the unknown is a generalized and heroized expansion of Jason's first journey (cf. ὁδόν, "road," 115), when, as an infant, he left his house amid danger (109-115). That first passage took him from women inside the house ("mingled with the wailing of women," 114) to Chiron in wild nature on Mt. Pelion (115; cf. 102). When Jason introduces himself at the beginning of his speech, he begins with his teaching from Chiron (φαμὶ διδασκαλίαν Χίρωνος οἴσειν, 102); but he goes on to speak of his nurture (θρέψαν, 103) from Chariclo and Philyra, pure daughters of the Centaur (ἵνα Κενταύρου με κοῦραι θρέψαν ἁγναί, 103). The context of this autobiographical detail of family life is his own dutiful behavior, for he is a son attempting to defend the rights and honor of a father (106-8), a role analogous to that of Orestes and Telemachus in the *Odyssey*. Some ten lines later, in his flashback to the circumstances that brought him from Iolcus to Pelion, he repeats the motif of "nurture," but says nothing of the daughters. Instead, he gives Chiron the significant epithet "son of Cronus": Κρονίδᾳ δὲ τράφεν Χίρωνι δῶκαν ("they gave me to Chiron, Cronus' son, to be nurtured," 115). The epithet underlines Chiron's role as a substitute father-figure and con-

---

[6] Beye, *Epic and Romance in the Argonautica*, 48. Compare *Ol.* 1.81-84 and 6.9-11; see Burton, 162f.

CHAPTER 3

nects Jason's salvation with the continued influence of the father-figure in the ode, ultimately the great father of heavenly gods, Zeus (194).[7]

Later, as Jason moves to a new stage of life, he acquires another "teacher," namely Aphrodite, "mistress of the sharpest shafts" of love. She instructs him in the magical power that inflames Medea with love (213-17; cf. *didaskalia*, "teaching," 102 and *ekdidaskēsen*, "taught," 217). Barbarian Colchis, at the end of a perilous sea-journey, requires the instruction of Aphrodite rather than the nurture of Chiron's pure daughters. As in other myths of the youthful hero, sexual initiation and passage to maturity accompany a journey overseas.[8] Jason steals a girl away into his ship, after the manner of the pirates and other ne'er-do-wells in the *Odyssey* and the later Greek romances. Chiron and his family are not likely to have approved, but Jason now needs the lessons appropriate to his young manhood.

The motifs of sexual desire, danger, quest for honor, and sea-travel are regular features of myths of generational passage. They constitute a kind of archaic *Bildungsroman*, condensed into the exemplary form of myth. Pindar's narrative, particularly in Jason's account of his life story, education, and the embarcation of the *Argo*, highlights the crises of transition from one stage of life to another.

Encoding the cultural patterns of generational passage

[7] Cf. Zeus' epithet "father" in the closely parallel passage, 23, and see above, chap. 2, note 37. Note the epithet *Kronidēs* also in 171.

[8] Cf. the gift of a robe for the time of his marriage that Helen gives to Telemachus after his journey from Ithaca, *Odyssey* 15.126f. See in general my "The Myth of Bacchylides 17," 32ff. and now (with a somewhat different view) Anne Pippin Burnett, *The Art of Bacchylides*, Martin Classical Lectures 29 (Cambridge, Mass. 1985), 26. Like Theseus in Bacchylides 17, Jason's trial involves both a martial test (the confrontations with Pelias and Aeetes) and an erotic initiation (the union with Medea).

SEXUALITY AND CREATION

into mythical narrative, the ancient poet weaves together the parallel strands of where one is, both in physical space and in the natural order; how one behaves to men and to women; what one wears, and so on. The individual details function as pointers to aspects of cultural and personal identity. Thus Jason's hair, uncut and flowing down his back (82f.), is a mark of the hero's still adolescent status.[9] This detail occurs just at the point when he "makes trial of his unfrightened resolve" as he "takes his stand" in the agora of Iolcus (84f.). Jason leaves the half-beast centaur who reared him in the mountains beyond the civic space (cf. αἰπεινῶν ἀπὸ σταθμῶν, "from his steep dwelling-place," 76) and enters the agora as the life of the town begins ("in the agora, as the crowd fills up," 85). Wearing the hair-style of adolescence, he not only makes his first test of a manly spirit (82-84) but also lays claim to the rights of citizenship and to his patrimony (106ff.).

The panther skin over his shoulders marks his affinities with the savage realm of the hunt, which in Greek myth often functions as the in-between place of the ambiguously civilized adolescent, not yet securely placed in the community.[10] Yet he also wears the local dress of Thessaly (80). Combined with the skin of the wild animal, this constitutes a "double garb" (ἐσθὰς ἀμφοτέρα, 79), which in turn corresponds to the doubleness of his "liminal" status, between the wild and the city, between being a total outsider and being the king of the city.[11]

---

[9] See P. Vidal-Naquet, "Le chasseur noir et l'origine de l'éphébie athénienne," *Le chasseur noir* 155. Jason doubtless has long hair throughout his adventures, but Pindar chooses to mention it at this crucial moment of his return to the kingdom that he is now to claim as his rightful inheritance.

[10] See Vidal-Naquet, *Le chasseur noir*, 154f. and 169ff.; Fontenrose, *Orion*, chap. 7 and pp. 252f.; Detienne, *Dionysus Slain*, 24ff. my *Dionysiac Poetics*, 169ff. and *Tragedy and Civilization*, 31f., 300-303.

[11] Cf. ξεῖνος αἴτ' ὢν ἀστός, "stranger or townsman," 78. On the "lim-

CHAPTER 3

The panther skin also has erotic associations, for that feline is the most seductive creature of the ancient Greek bestiary.[12] Jason's combination of panther skin and two spears (79, 81) suggests an association with another ambiguous hero famed for his powers of erotic seduction, Paris at his first appearance in the *Iliad* (3.17f.). Wearing the skin and carrying the unheroic bow, Paris also brandishes two spears and "challenges all the best of the Argives," only to leap back into the crowd of his companions in fear when he sees Menelaus (3.30ff.).

At this point of initiatory transition, then, Jason faces both forward and back; he is, as Vidal-Naquet calls him, "homme double."[13] He is both an outstanding "man" (ἀνήρ, 79) and a youth of twenty years (104); both a potential warrior-hero (the two spears) and a potential seducer (the panther skin); both a nameless stranger who has no rank whatsoever in the community and someone "outstanding," a king (cf. ἀνὴρ ἔκπαγλος, 79). But this hero, destined to succeed, will resolve all this doubleness into a firm unitary identity. The key detail of the single sandal marks him out as distinct from others, an anomaly.[14] But it also designates him as the one chosen by the gods as the winner, the true king.

It is instructive to compare Jason with another youthful hero of double identity as he approaches a martial trial,

---

inality" of the passage between states (Victor Turner's term), see my *Dionysiac Poetics*, 170; Crotty, 112 and 117. The centaurs, fluctuating between wise educators and drunken brutes, between culture and nature, are the appropriate figures for this liminality: see Page duBois, *Centaurs and Amazons* (Ann Arbor 1982), 28ff.

[12] See Detienne, *Dionysus Slain*, 36-40, with figure 3 on p. 29.

[13] Vidal-Naquet, *Le chasseur noir*, 155.

[14] The "singleness" of the sandal (μονο-, 75) seems to be played off intentionally against the "doubleness" of the two spears and the dress (δί-δυμαι, ἀμφοτέρα, 79). As in the Oedipus myth, the emphasis on the feet associates movement and locomotion with generational passage: cf. Sophocles, *Oed. Tyr.* 800ff.

SEXUALITY AND CREATION

Aeschylus' Parthenopaeus in the *Seven Against Thebes* (527-49). This youth, one of the would-be ravagers of Thebes, is a "man-boy" (*andropais anēr,* 533) of ambiguous origins and "raw spirit." Come to overthrow a ruler who has usurped power in a city by expelling a kinsman, he bears on his shield the emblem of a "raw-feasting Sphinx." In a brilliant analysis of this passage Froma Zeitlin describes him as follows:

> *He is an* andrópais anḗr *(533), undefined somewhere between boy and man, having no place in the clear hierarchical structure of age differentiation. As* anḗr *[adult male], he is entitled to participate in warfare, as* paîs *[boy] he is not. He is an alien, a* métoikos *in Argos, an outsider who behaves as an insider, repaying his nurture to his adopted land. [. . .] He is more specifically a man from the mountains of Arcadia, the world of wild nature, who has cast his lot in with that of the city and fights with spear and shield. He is also an amalgam of male and female qualities, and in this patronymic world, he is the child of his mountain-roaming mother, Atalanta (532). Finally, he bears the name of Parthenos [unmarried girl], a sign of benign femininity, but that name is belied . . . by the ferocity of his Gorgon eye (536-37).*[15]

Jason in every respect succeeds where Parthenopaeus fails. He emerges from an undifferentiated state to a well-defined status in the city, from potential savagery among the mountains and its half-bestial inhabitants to full civility within Iolcus, from a virginal upbringing (cf. 102f.) to marriage, from irregularity to exemplary status as a cultural ideal. Instead of destroying a city by unleashing savage violence (the raw-eating monster, Sphinx), he exhibits re-

[15] Zeitlin, *Under the Sign of the Shield,* 99.

CHAPTER 3

straint (*aidōs*) and brings both moral and political order to a disordered realm.

In successfully passing his trial, Jason moves from the hunt (the panther skin of 81) to agriculture (plowing with Aeetes' bulls), from adolescence to marriage, from an anomalous, marginal status to being the "king" at the head of his peers (βασιλεὺς ὅστις ἄρχει ναός, "You king who rules the ship," 229f.). His successful establishment of his adult male identity, then, is overdetermined by the multiplicity of tests in different areas and by the doubling of the same test (e.g., challenge from two older and powerful males, Pelias and Aeetes). It is overdetermined in another way too, for it is established both by Apollo's oracle and by Jason's own heritage. It is fated in the sense that it is part of a foreordained, prescribed pattern for every young male.

Jason's two departures from Iolcus, first as an infant and then as a young hero-to-be, are sequential in chronology but homologous in narrative function: both are rites of passage along the male road of life. Thus Jason's journey in 109ff. recapitulates the hero's earlier passage from the darkness of birth amid wailing women to heroic "nurture" (like Achilles) by a wise beast-man in the liminal space of house and forest.[16] In the similar tale of the birth of Iamus in *Olympian* 6 divinely appointed, non-human creatures (here the two "grey-eyed serpents") provide the nurture (53-61). Here too there is a progression from a secret journey attended by the mother at birth to a second journey at adolescence involving water and presided over by father-figures (43-47 and 57-62), with a resultant founding of a line of prophets who stand in close relation to the highest father, Zeus (70ff.).[17]

[16] Cf. also the education of Achilles and Asclepius by Chiron also in *Nem.* 3.43-55, where the motif of the hunt also plays an important role.

[17] On the motifs of birth in *Ol.* 6, see Stern, "*Olympian* 6," 335ff. and below, chap. 5, sec. II.

SEXUALITY AND CREATION

Jason's still wider journey at the next crucial passage of his life also stands under the aegis of the father, "Zeus, father of the heavenly gods, who wields the sword of thunder" (πατέρ' Οὐρανιδᾶν ἐγχεικέραυνον Ζῆνα, 194). It is Zeus who speeds the ship on its way; and his martial epithet, ἐγχεικέραυνος, "with the sword of thunder" or "whose spear is the thunderbolt" (Slater), anticipates the active heroism of the journey. After founding an altar to Zeus' brother, Poseidon, they "impel themselves forth into deep danger" (ἐς κίνδυνον βαθὺν ἱέμενοι, 207), proof that they have in fact escaped the inertia of the "dangerless life beside mother."

This first trial is a passage through a narrow opening guarded by female monsters, the Symplegades. These figures resemble devouring sea-monsters like Odysseus' Scylla and Charybdis.[18] They too, like Oedipus' Sphinx on land, block the hero's advance and are the first obstacle on his progress to kingship and marriage.[19] Success causes the "end" or death of the Symplegades ("That voyage of the demigods brought an end to them," τελευτὰν . . . αὐταῖς, 210). As in the tale of Perseus and Medusa that Pindar tells in *Pythian* 12 or in the version of Oedipus and the Sphinx told in Apollodorus, the hero's first exploit brings death to the monster that opposes him.[20] After the Symplegades, the way lies open straight to Colchis (ἐς Φᾶσιν δ' ἔπειτεν ἤλυθον, 210-12).

From this point potentially dangerous female power is on their side. Aphrodite helps with her love-charm, the

---

[18] For such female powers of the dangerous sea, see Gilbert Durand, *Les structures anthropologiques de l'imaginaire* (Paris 1969), 103ff.

[19] For passage through the rocks as an initiatory journey, see Beye, *Epic and Romance in the Argonautica*, 44, citing Jack Lindsay, *Clashing Rocks* (London 1965), 10f. Cf. the narrow, rocky defile in Gustave Moreau's painting of Oedipus and the Sphinx in the Metropolitan Museum, New York, and Ingres' version in the Louvre, Paris.

[20] Apollodorus 3.5.8. Of the same type are the stories of Theseus and the Minotaur, Heracles and the Nemean Lion, Meleager and the boar.

CHAPTER 3

iynx, invented expressly for this occasion (213ff.). The language of drugs and fire recurs for Medea; the effect, again, is to aid, not hinder, the heroic quest:

σὺν δ' ἐλαίῳ φαρμακώσαισ'
  ἀντίτομα στερεᾶν ὀδυνᾶν
δῶκε χρίεσθαι. (221f.)

With oil she fashioned drugs as antidotes to hard pains and gave it to him as an unguent for his body.

πῦρ δέ νιν οὐκ ἐόλει παμ-
φαρμάκου ξείνας ἐφετμαῖς. (233)

Thanks to the behests of the foreign woman, all-deviser of drugs, the fire did not press him.

The literal fire (*kaiomenon pur*, 225) from which Medea's *pharmakon* protects Jason recalls both the fiery desire for the voyage that Hera "burns" into the Argonauts (*endaie*, 184) and the figurative fire of love with which Medea herself is "aflame" thanks to a "desire" and a "persuasion" very different from Hera's (218f.).

In offering the erotically tinged aid of persuasion, desire, drug, and fire in Jason's support, Hera also functions to neutralize the erotic seduction that one expects from a figure like Medea. Hera is also the goddess of legitimate marriage. When she borrows Aphrodite's power in the form of the irresistible *kestos* in Homer's *Dios apatē*, the seduction is still exercised within the sphere of marriage.[21] So here, the help of Aphrodite that follows upon that of Hera brings not just sex, but marriage (*koinon gamon*, 222), albeit a marriage anomalously founded on the girl's loss of *aidōs*. The positive direction of Aphrodite's intervention has been anticipated by Hera; and the latter's erotic-sounding "desire" and "drug" in 184-87 prove to be not

[21] *Iliad* 14.198-213.

SEXUALITY AND CREATION

love-magic but war-magic. Just as Medea's "dense craft" in 57f. stands under the sign of Apollo's wisdom and prophecy, so Aphrodite's seductive iynx and dangerous fires of passion stand under the sign of Hera's marital stability.[22]

The neutralization of Aphrodite's seduction by Hera and by marriage, then, exactly parallels the neutralization of the dangers of Medea's *mēdea* and *mētis* by the directly Apolline prophecy of the virginal Pythian priestess.[23] Hence the potentially sinister immobilizing effect of Medea's "dense craft" is followed by the spontaneous voice of the Pythian "bee," associated with the good feminine virtues of industry and chastity.[24] In both cases, as also in the case of Euphamus and his *androphonos* Lemnian bride, female sexuality is rendered innocuous by Olympian intervention so that it may subserve the patriarchal aim of founding a stable succession of rulers.[25]

This complementation of the two goddesses who intervene in Jason's behalf, Hera and Aphrodite, is worked out in a number of verbal details. Erotic persuasion (*peithō*, 184, 219), desire (*pothos*), and the imagery of sweetness appear in both passages (185, 222f.). Near the end of the

[22] Giannini (1977-80) 143 observes that "il rapporto tra due intellegenze astute di cui la prima, sia pure con la mediazione di Giasone, riesce a prevalere sulla seconda"; but he does not explore the further complementarities between Hera and Aphrodite. On iynx and the opposition of marriage and seduction in Greek notions of eros, see Detienne, *Les jardins d'Adonis*, 141-72, 215-26, 237-39, and his *Dionysus Slain*, 40-52; J.-P. Vernant, *Mythe et société en Grèce ancienne* (Paris 1974), 173-76.

[23] This motif reflects, of course, Pindar's exaltation of Delphi in the odes for the games there (cf. in general Gerhard Nebel, *Pindar und die Delphik*, Stuttgart 1961; Gianotti, 54f. with note 45, for further bibliography); but it has, none the less, a function in the design of the ode as a whole.

[24] On the Pythia as "bee," see above, chap. 1, note 6. Cf. also the bee-woman of Semonides, 7.83ff. West.

[25] For this aspect of the ode, see below, chap. 9. Even Aphrodite is enlisted in the cause: 213ff.

CHAPTER 3

myth, the erotic sense of mingling (*meixai*, 223) is combined, in a strong zeugma, with the heroic achievement of the quest as the Argonauts "mingle with the red sea and with the race of man-killing Lemnian Women":[26]

ἔν τ' Ὠκεανοῦ πελάγεσσιν μίγεν πόντῳ τ' ἐρυθρῷ
Λαμνιᾶν τ' ἔθνει γυναικῶν ἀνδροφόνων. (251f.)

Jason's erotic mingling with Medea is also balanced by the martial mingling of force with the Colchians when the Argonauts first arrive (212f.):[27] ἔνθα κελαινώπεσσι Κόλχοισι βίαν / μεῖξαν Αἰήτᾳ παρ' αὐτῷ ("Then they mingled force with the dark-visaged Colchians in Aeetes' very presence"). When Euphamus' descendants "mingle with the men of Lacedaemon" at the very end of the myth, it is also for the heroic enterprise of masculine action, in this case the colonization of Thera (257-59):

καὶ Λακεδαιμονίων μειχθέντες ἀνδρῶν
ἤθεσι τάν ποτε Καλλίσταν ἀπῴκησαν χρόνῳ
νᾶσον

And mingling with the ways of the men of Lacedaemon, they colonized in time the isle Most Lovely [i.e., Thera].

If Jason owes his victory to the love-magic of Aphrodite's *poikila iunx* (214ff.), Pindar is also careful to give credit to the hero's physical strength (*bia*, 212), which he mentions immediately before Aphrodite's love-charm. To

---

[26] Pindar seems to be playing on the sexual connotations of the verb for "mingling," *migen*, here. The lines can mean, "On the Ocean's flood and on the Red Sea and (among) the race of Lemnian Women they (Jason and Medea) mingled," and also, "They (the Argonauts) mingled among (i.e., travelled on) the Ocean's flood." On Pindar's range in the use of the notion of mingling, see Thomas J. Hoey, "Fusion in Pindar," *HSCP* 70 (1965) 236ff.

[27] On the suggestion of aggression in βίαν μεῖξαν, see Farnell, ad loc. (2.148).

SEXUALITY AND CREATION

the "sweetness" of love and marriage (222f.) he sharply juxtaposes the trial of the fiery bulls, with the ominous details of the adamantine plow, tawny jaws, and brazen hooves (224-31).[28] Medea's drugs are indispensable to Jason's success (233), but Pindar's vivid participles carefully highlight the effort of "dragging" the plow, forcing their necks "by necessity" to submit to the harness, and "laying on their form of massive flanks the goad relentless":[29]

σπασσάμενος δ' ἄροτρον, βοέους δήσαις ἀνάγκᾳ
ἔντεσιν αὐχένας ἐμβάλλων τ' ἐριπλεύρῳ φυᾷ
κέντρον αἰανὲς βιατὰς
   ἐξεπόνησ' ἐπιτακτὸν ἀνὴρ
μέτρον· ἴυξεν δ' ἀφωνήτῳ περ ἔμπας ἄχει
δύνασιν Αἰήτας ἀγασθείς. (234-38)

Dragging the plow, binding by constraint the bull necks in their harness, and throwing upon their strong-flanked form the goad relentless, the man of force accomplished the appointed measure. And Aeetes, astounded at his might, cried out in grief, unspeakable though it was.

Now Jason is no longer a youth but a man (*anēr*) and a man of force (*biatas*; cf. *bia*, 212) and of courage (*karteron andra*, 239). He performs a difficult labor (*ponos*, 236b; cf. 243) and exhibits a power (*dunasis*) that leaves his regal taskmaster amazed (238). The repetition of *anēr*, "man," in 236b and 239 fulfils the promise implicit in the phrase "outstanding man," *anēr ekpaglos*, at the beginning of the myth (79) and rounds off the narrative in characteristic ring composition.

The end of Jason's story brings together the winning of Medea and the winning of the fleece:

[28] On the style of 224ff., see Méautis, 245f.
[29] On the vividness of the style here, see Burton, 165f. The details of color are particularly striking (225, 231f.).

CHAPTER 3

κτεῖνε μὲν γλαυκῶπα τέχναις ποικιλόνωτον ὄφιν,
ὠρκεσίλα, κλέψεν τε Μήδειαν σὺν αὐ-
 τᾷ, τὰν Πελίαο φονόν. (249f.)

By devices he killed the grey-eyed snake of the glittering back, O Arcesilaus, and stole away Medea, Pelias' murderer, with herself (joining in).

This conclusion helps define Jason's success not merely as a victory of seduction (cf. 218) but as the heroic capture of the prize of valor.[30] As in folktale, the hero wins both the bad king's Magical Object and his Beautiful Daughter. The early part of the ode, moreover, has helped to establish Medea's role not as a sexual object but as a divinely appointed instrument for achieving the quest (cf. 10ff. and 57f.). By carefully phrasing the details of Jason's sexual triumph and by enframing it between the martial encounter with Aeetes (213 and 224) and his violence (*bia*, 212 and 236), Pindar mutes the aspects of the hero's success that Euripides, a generation later, will brutally expose; and he stresses the steady complementation between masculine directness and more devious feminine arts (Medea's and Aphrodite's).

In this perspective we can better understand the collocation of Apollo and Aphrodite in 87f. The citizens of Iolcus wonder at Jason's presence among them:

οὔ τί που οὗτος Ἀπόλλων,
 οὐδὲ μὰν χαλκάρματός ἐστι πόσις
Ἀφροδίτας.

Is this then not Apollo? Is he not Aphrodite's lord, (Ares) of the brazen chariot?

The handsome stranger has a mildly Aphroditic aspect: he might be "the bronze-charioted husband of Aphrodite."

---

[30] On the text of 250, see Duchemin, *Pythiques*, ad loc., who, however, rather glozes over the clash between the two sides of Jason's "conquest."

SEXUALITY AND CREATION

Appropriately, the martial aspect of Aphrodite's spouse, Ares, predominates ("bronze-charioted husband"). Both of these tentative recognitions identify Jason as a figure of masculine order. Aphrodite herself has a lord or husband, the potent war-god Ares. But the more negative side of the erotic theme emerges in the next lines, when the townspeople combine the two warning examples of Tityos and the Aloades. The former illustrates the importance of "desiring the loves in one's power" (92); the latter are precocious adolescent giants who attempt to scale Olympus:

ἐν δὲ Νάξῳ φάντι θανεῖν λιπαρᾷ
Ἰφιμεδείας παῖδας, Ὦτον καὶ σέ, τολ-
 μάεις Ἐπιάλτα ἄναξ.
καὶ μὰν Τιτυὸν βέλος Ἀρτέμιδος θήρευσε κραιπνόν,
ἐξ ἀνικάτου φαρέτρας ὀρνύμενον,
ὄφρα τις τᾶν ἐν δυνατῷ φιλοτά-
 των ἐπιψαύειν ἔραται. (88-92)

And in radiant Naxos they say that Iphimedeia's sons met their deaths, Otus and you, the man of daring, Lord Ephialtes. Artemis' swift arrow hunted down Tityos too as it surged forth from its invincible quiver, so that one may yearn to touch the loves that are within the realm of the possible.

The brief allusion to Tityos implies the violence of uncontrolled sexual desires, forcefully punished by the "swift missile" of an Olympian. Artemis, chaste huntress, defeats unbridled lust.[31] In the conjectures about Jason's identity Apollo and Ares balance and cancel out the Aloades and Tityos, who are, in fact, envisaged only as the *defeated* enemies of the Olympian order. Jason's adolescent energies will take the form of Apolline healing and

[31] The metaphor of her arrow "hunting" down its victim (θήρευσε, 90) is perhaps the negation of the violence of the unruly "hunter," a figure of incompletely civilized energies: see above, note 10.

CHAPTER 3

moderation rather than the Aloades' overreaching aggression;[32] and his masculine strength will, like that of Ares, find expression in marriage rather than seduction or rape.

Given the importance of Apollo in the first section of the ode, it is natural that the Iolcans should first identify Jason with that god. Given Hera's prominence at the start of the journey (184ff.) and the nature of Aphrodite's help with Medea later, it is also significant that the love-goddess is paired with her bronze-charioted husband. In this small detail, as in the role of Medea, Pindar takes pains to balance the erotic component of his hero's good looks (80ff.) by martial associations.[33] Jason stands between Aphrodite and Medea on the one hand and between Apollo and Hera on the other. This collocation of seduction and "drugs" with more traditional heroic acts, as I suggested above, is analogous to the place of Pindar's poetry between the ambiguities of its *sophia* and *mētis* and the "truth" it has to convey.

II. THE SEEDS OF CREATION

Throughout Pindar's odes the imagery of fertility and birth describes both heroic achievement and the positive effects of poetry.[34] Early in the ode the future Libya is to be

---

[32] Note the emphasis on the adolescent beauty of the Aloades in *Od.* 10.319f., and see above, note 8. In a more limited vein, Méautis, 233, thinks that the reference to the Aloades here implies the negative feelings of the crowd and therefore suggest Jason's courage in showing himself to the mob; but this explanation does not account for Apollo and Ares in the same context.

[33] The beauty of the victorious athlete, as of the mythical young hero, however, is a regular feature of epinician praise, e.g., *Ol.* 8.19, 9.94, 10.103-5; *Nem.* 3.19f. and 11.13f.; *Isth.* 2.3-5 and 7.21f.; see Young, *Isthmian 7*, 40, citing Tyrtaeus, 6-7.27-30; Bernadini, *Mito e attualità*, 25f.; Donlan, *Aristocratic Ideal*, 106f.

[34] E.g., *Nem.* 7.1ff., and see my remarks, "Pindar's Seventh *Nemean*," 456ff., 465ff. On Pindar's vegetal symbolism in general, see Norwood, 141 and 152; Duchemin, 238ff., 264 ("cet élan vers les forces et les mystères de la vie," 228); Young, *Three Odes*, 96f; Bresson, 123ff.

SEXUALITY AND CREATION

"planted" as a root or a seed from the sea (e.g., 14f., 42; cf. 144). The birth of a new land from the sea closely resembles the creation of Rhodes in *Olympian* 7.62-71.[35] Birthlike emergence from the sea is an image that Pindar also uses for his own poetic creation in *Nemean* 7.77-79, where his Muse fashions an elaborate work of art from the "smooth flower" which she "takes from the sea's dew."[36]

The cosmogonic sexuality of Thera's birth here is taken up, with the same generality of tone, in the seasonal metaphor that describes the "blooming" of the Cyrenean royal line and the "planting" of god-sent honors for the Argonauts (64f.; *phuteuthen*, 69; cf. *phuteusesthai*, 15). Later the sexual implications are fully realized in the power of Aphrodite's iynx and the passion of Medea (213-23). The end of the myth, modulating back to the founding of Cyrene and the ancestry of Arcesilaus, makes the motif of sexual union again explicit. What is planted here are not the metaphorical god-sent honors of the beginning (69), but a seed from which the future race of Cyrenean kings is descended:

καὶ ἐν ἀλλοδαπαῖς
σπέρμ' ἀρούραις τουτάκις ὑμετέρας ἀ-
κτῖνος ὄλβου δέξατο μοιρίδιον
ἆμαρ ἢ νύκτες· τόθι γὰρ γένος Εὐφά-
μου φυτευθὲν λοιπὸν αἰεὶ
τέλλετο. (254-57)

And then in foreign plowland did the destined day or the nights receive the seed of your prosperity's radi-

[35] On this passage, see Nancy Rubin, "Epinician Symbols," 76ff.

[36] On this passage, see my "Seventh *Nemean*," 460ff., and now Boedeker, 92ff., who emphasizes the connotations of procreative energies in the word *eersa*. Drawing on the 1982 University of California (Berkeley) dissertation of D. Petegorsky (which I have not seen), Boedeker believes that this "flower" of the Muse is not coral but sea-purple dye, and that the Muse's creation is "a woven headband of cloth dyed purple and ornamented with gold and ivory" (p. 94).

CHAPTER 3

ance. For then the race of Euphamus, planted, arose, as lasting forever more.[37]

The familiar analogy between legitimate marriage and agriculture in Greek literature moves us away from the Aphroditic themes of seduction in the winning of Medea (213-23) to the stability of founding a dynasty through procreation in marriage.[38] In the first tale a vague "seed" of earth is poured forth prematurely and without issue into the water (cf. κατακλυσθεῖσαν, 38; κέχυται, 42). Now, at the culmination of that story, male seed impregnates a woman in fields (*arourais*, 255) to sire the line of Cyrenean kings whose wealth has a radiance (*aktis*, 255) like that of the sky or the sun. The lost piece of plowland (*aroura*, 34b) at the beginning is recuperated in the "foreign plowlands" at the end of the myth when the future of Cyrene is assured.

As plowing the earth replaces the watery setting of Triton's gift early in the poem (20ff.), so fruitful sexual union replaces a fruitless pouring forth of seed (43). The motif of plowing, like that of marriage (cf. 223) also intertwines Euphamus' success with Jason's. After yoking the fire-breathing bulls, Jason is to break up the clods of earth with the plow (228). For both Jason and Euphamus the winning of a kingdom is associated, figuratively or literally, with the land-based stability of fruitful agriculture. Procreation in marriage, male domination, patriarchal sovereignty, and agrarian productivity form a cluster of interrelated themes. Unlike the tragedians, however, Pindar mutes or suppresses the dangers of feminine seduction, domestic

[37] With the majority of recent editors, I follow Hermann's emendation (supported by the scholia) of σπέρμ' for the περ of the MSS. in line 255. For recent discussion, see Duchemin, *Pythiques*, ad loc.

[38] On marriage and agriculture, see M. Detienne, *Les jardins d'Adonis*, 215ff.; J.-P. Vernant, *Mythe et pensée chez les Grecs*, ed. 3 (Paris 1974), 1.140f.; *Mythe et société*, 191ff. Vidal-Naquet, *Le chasseur noir*, 41ff.

and political chaos, and women who have killed their husbands, with threats of matriarchy or gynaecocracy in the background.[39]

An edge of danger, however, remains. Jason's union with Medea moves beyond seduction (213ff.) to marriage (222) but not to procreation.[40] It suffices for Jason's role as youthful hero that he win the bride; he does not have to become a father. Mention of children by Medea might introduce an ominous note. For Euphamus, as we have seen, bed and offspring go together, necessarily for the future of the Cyrenean monarchy (252-57). Jason's tale, however, ends on an unresolved note, not with children, but with death. He "kills" the dragon (*kteine*, 249) that guards the Fleece; but his "mingling" at this point (251, μίγεν πόντῳ τ' ἐρυθρῷ, "they mingled with the Red Sea"; cf. 223) is framed by women who kill men. Medea is the "killer of Pelias,"[41] and the Lemnian Women are "killers of their husbands" (Λαμνιᾶν τ' ἔθνει γυναικῶν ἀνδροφόνων, 252).

The ode, however, passes quickly over this dark strain in Jason's victory. Colchis, after all, lies on the other side of the world, subject to barbarian ways. Pindar ends the narrative portion of his ode not with this distant sea-world but with the secure planting of the future Battiad dynasty (254-61).

[39] On these relations in tragedy, see Zeitlin (1978), passim; Vidal-Naquet, *Le chasseur noir*, 286ff.

[40] As early as Hesiod, Jason does have children by Medea later: *Theogony* 1000-1002 (a son, Medeius, whom Jason gives to Chiron to be brought up "on the mountains"). Cf. also Pausanias 2.3.9f. (based on Eumelus of Corinth) and of course Euripides' *Medea*. As early as Eumelus Medea kills her children, although accidentally; the strong emphasis on the motif is probably Euripides' innovation, although there are some hints in earlier poetry: see Page (above, note 1), xxiii-xxv. In the two other places where Pindar mentions Medea, she is only the bride won on the Argonautic expedition (*Ol.* 13.53f.; frag. 155.4f. Bowra = 172.6f. Snell).

[41] It is tempting, after Didymus, to read Πελιαοφόνον as a single word, rather than τὰν Πελίαο φονόν preferred by most editors (with Wackernagel's correction of the accent in *phonón*). See Duchemin, ad loc.

4. Mythic Patterns I: Wandering and Foundation

I. NARRATIVE STRUCTURE: SEA, LAND, AND TIME

THE structure of *Pythian* 4, like that of the *Odyssey*, is both centrifugal and centripetal. It circumscribes wide exploratory adventures on an outward voyage; but it never loses sight of the homeward return and stable settlement as the certain goal. The richness, complexity, and impression of an open world of vast and varied experience derive in large part from the working together, in harmony and in counterpoint, of these two modes of narrative organization.[1]

The most vivid part of the myth, the Argonautic expedition, is a quest for a mysterious object, associated both with death (Phrixus' ghost) and with the imperishable quality of eternal things (cf.159-61 and 230f.), in a remote land of magic and the fabulous. Interwoven with this story of adventure in far-flung places is the colonization of Libya, with the extension of Battiad kings through to the present ruler. The foundation legend and the Argonautic adventures not only stand in causal and temporal relation to one another but are also thematically parallel.[2] Both follow a circular as well as a linear rhythm. Jason's story begins as a return to Iolcus (78ff.), and, in its turn, contains another circular movement back to origins (109ff.), the tale of his birth. His goal is defined as the recovery of a lost

---

[1] For the multiple orders of time in the ode, see Hurst, 159f.

[2] For the relation of the two narratives, with a review of previous discussions, see Giannini (1979) 37ff.

kingdom (106ff., 148ff.). That involves both return and progress: reclaiming his rightful patrimony and moving from the passivity of infancy (109-15) to action, success, and adult status as king and husband. Pindar breaks off in the midst of the Jason story (247ff.), just as he began by plunging us *in medias res* of the Libyan story (9ff.). But the brief reference to Pelias' death at the end of the myth (250) does effect a closure of Jason's tale. It also takes us back to the myth's point of departure, Pelias' fear of an oracle that prophesied his death, whether by force or (as Medea's presence at the end confirms) by guile (71f.).

The account of Cyrene's origins that spans the poem has also the form of a return to a familiar, settled place. Its fluid beginnings in the shifting, metamorphic realm of Triton (20ff.) are succeeded not only by the solidity of the agricultural image of 255 but also by the divinely given stability of legitimate power (260f.).

Battus, the Argonauts, and Jason all "leave" a homeland (cf. *lipōn*, 8 and 185f.; 111-115) only to gain or regain their home under more stable conditions.[3] Jason demands and (as 250 implies) eventually wins back the "sole-ruling scepter and the throne" that Pelias wrested from his brother, Aeson (152f.). To found Cyrene, Battus must first abandon the "sacred isle" of Thera (6f.); but later he obtains a "divine city" and a "throne of gold" (260f.). Arcesilaus, in the present, is to retain that godlike stability of legitimate authority as a builder and healer (270-74). For the future, Damophilus, the exile, has won the moral basis for his return home, having learned just and peaceful ways on his overseas journey (284-87, 293-99).

Taken together, the two myths of the ode form a progression toward order: there is a movement from Triton's

[3] In 125f. Pheres and Aeson's other brothers "leave" their homes to welcome Jason back to Iolcus.

CHAPTER 4

metamorphic sea-realm of divine disguise and mortal forgetfulness and loss (cf. 41f.) at the beginning to the victories of Jason, the union of Euphamus, and the founding of the Battiad dynasty in Cyrene at the end. The story of Euphamus, the clod, and Battus is circular and discontinuous.[4] The tale of Jason has a more linear mode of narration. It runs from the beginning of the Argonaut voyage (70f.) straight through to his completion of the quest. Even his flashbacks to his birth and education directly serve his goal: they establish his rights to the throne and also show the traits of character that insure his success.

The story of Cyrene, first told within an oracle (6ff.), has the elusive quality of oracular narrative: truth flashes out in fitful moments, is lost again in darkness, and then appears clearly once more. We glimpse the fulfilled future, move back into the past, which itself contains another projection into the future in Medea's prophecy (cf. 14ff.), and then, after another moment of oracular illumination (59-66), we leave this story altogether, only to return to it after all, almost unexpectedly, in close conjunction with the longer tale of Jason near the end of the ode.

This discontinuous narrative structure in the tale of Cyrene's origins corresponds exactly to its most striking detail, the clod of earth. This magical object is handed from god to man, lost, and then recovered, like Medea's own oracular word, at a later time (*epos ankomisai*, 9). This staccato movement of oracular time, with its several leaps of generations—seventeen from Euphamus to Battus (10), four from Euphamus to the lost earlier colonizers of Libya (47), and eight from Battus to Arcesilaus (65)—parallels the spatial movement of the clod, regained "in time" (cf. 55 and 258) when it has solidified into the Libyan main-

---

[4] For some good remarks on the discontinuous spatial and temporal structure of the ode, see Albert Cook, *Myth and Language*, 118-21.

WANDERING AND FOUNDATION

land. Similarly Jason has lost the throne of his native land, but then suddenly, unexpectedly, re-emerges there, almost as a divine apparition (78-92); and behind this recovery too stand "time" (78) and oracles from Apollo (71ff.; cf. 163ff.).

Jason's story, then, parallels that of Euphamus and Battus in the task of recovering a prerogative given of old but now lost:

ἀρχαίαν κομίζων
πατρὸς ἐμοῦ, βασιλευομέναν
οὐ κατ' αἶσαν, τάν ποτε Ζεὺς ὤπασεν λαγέτᾳ
Αἰόλῳ καὶ παισὶ τιμάν.   (106-8)

recovering the ancient honor of my father, now ruled over in contravention of due apportionment, which once Zeus granted to Aeolus leader of his people and to his children.

καὶ τὸ Μηδείας ἔπος ἀγκομίσαι   (9)

and to recover the oracular saying of Medea.

The first part of Jason's quest is to "bring back the soul of Phrixus" (ψυχὰν κομίξαι, 160), in the sense (probably) of laying the ghost of a man who died abroad:[5]

---

[5] This is the explanation of the scholiast, ad loc. (281a), citing *Od.* 9.64-66. Schol. 281b, paraphrasing Pindar's text, stresses also the second part of Phrixus' request, the recovery of the fleece because it saved his life, thereby interpreting 161b-62 as part of Phrixus' thought ("the Fleece through which he was once saved from the sea and from his stepmother's godless weapons"). This latter seems to be the view adopted by Beye, *Epic and Romance in the Argonautica*, 47: "the urgent desire of Phrixus' ghost that the fleece come back to Iolcus so that his soul can be at rest." This interpretation, however, goes beyond what Pindar actually says. See also Robert, p. 768, note 1; Méautis, 239; Duchemin, 271; David Claus, *On the Soul* (New Haven 1981), 68. Gildersleeve (ad loc.) thinks that the reference may be to erecting a cenotaph. The similar expression at *Nem.* 8.44 implies restoring the dead to life: see below, chap. 5, note 3. Farnell sees an allusion to actually bringing back the body, "which the soul

CHAPTER 4

δύνασαι δ' ἀφελεῖν
μᾶνιν χθονίων. κέλεται γὰρ ἐὰν ψυχὰν κομίξαι
Φρίξος ἐλθόντας πρὸς Αἰήτα θαλάμους
δέρμα τε κριοῦ βαθύμαλλον ἄγειν ... (159-61)

You have the power to take away the wrath of the dead. For Phrixus commands (us) to go to the halls of Aeetes and recover his shade and fetch the deep-fleeced skin of the ram.

In fulfilling this task too, Jason is to regain something that has been lost to death in a foreign land. This retrieval of a divinely promised gift brings together three major elements in the narrative of the ode: the recovery of a lost kingdom, oracles, and time.

The oracles are the mechanism through which the ode spans the wide gaps of time between the events it narrates. Medea's oracle about the loss of the clod ends with her prophecy of another oracle in later time (*chronōi husterōi*, 55f.) when Battus' visit to the "Pythian shrine" produces another journey in ships to the African coast (56). This second voyage will bring possession of the land whose "seed" was planted in the earlier expedition of which Medea's speech was itself a part (10-59). A similar structure of loss and recovery governs Jason's story: the bright light of his birth (111, 144f.) is at once concealed, "hidden away" by secrecy in the night of his escape from Pelias' treachery (*krubda ... nukti*, 114f.; cf. *kalupsai*, 146); but oracles bring him back (71b, 73), in time (ὁ δ' ἦρα χρόνῳ / ἵκετ' αἰχμαῖσιν διδύμαισιν ἀνὴρ ἔκ-/παγλος, "And in time he came, a man extraordinary, with his twin spears," 78f.).

---

would follow." The motif of appeasing the wrath (*mēnis*, 159) of the dead also suggests an affinity with the frequent aetiological myth of appeasing a heroized mortal who meets with a violent death: see Fontenrose, "The Hero as Athlete," 73-104; also Rohde, *Psyche*, 129ff. B.M.W. Knox, *The Heroic Temper*, Sather Classical Lectures 35 (Berkeley and Los Angeles 1964), 56ff.

WANDERING AND FOUNDATION

"Brilliant" in youthful beauty (cf. *aglaoi*, 82), he has regained even greater luminosity after the darkness attending his birth.[6] Finally, Euphamus' arrival at Lemnos, during the Argonautic voyage, produces the family line that "in time colonized the Loveliest Isle (Thera), and from there Leto's Son granted you Libya's plain to increase with honors from the god and to govern the divine city of golden-throned Cyrene":

τάν ποτε Καλλίσταν ἀπῴκησαν χρόνῳ
νᾶσον· ἔνθεν δ' ὔμμι Λατοί-
   δας ἔπορεν Λιβύας πεδίον
σὺν θεῶν τιμαῖς ὀφέλλειν, ἄστυ χρυσοθρόνου
διανέμειν θεῖον Κυράνας ... (258-61)

These lines at the end recall Medea's prophecy in 50-53 about honor from the gods (σὺν τιμᾷ θεῶν, 51) and the destined ruler over dark-clouded (Libyan) plains (κελαινεφέων πεδίων δεσπόταν, 52f.). The verbal echoes imply a parallel between events that belong together in the unitary shape of things contained in *chronos*, time from the perspective of the gods. Medea's prophecy in 50-53, like that of 259, has behind it the oracular authority of Apollo (54f.) operating "in time" (55, 258). When Pindar, at the end of the ode, holds out to the exiled Damophilus the hope of return as the sea-weather changes "in time" (*en chronōi*, 291), his context is the even vaster mythical scope of Zeus' design, the temporal perspective of the centuries that hold the eventual release of the Titans from their dark prison in Tartarus (291).[7]

Jason achieves in a single linear thrust the destined goal

[6] The pattern of light emerging from darkness is a recurrent one in the odes: cf. below, chap. 5, note 18.

[7] Gildersleeve, ad 291, notes that each of the four times that *chronos* occurs it comes at the end of the verse (55, 78, 258, 291). On *chronos*, see below, chap. 10.

CHAPTER 4

that in the case of Cyrene is divided between the two kings, Euphamus and Battus, who are separated by many generations. His clear and tangible success in obtaining the fabled prize of the Golden Fleece, a single magical object conspicuous by its radiance (231), is the ideal paradigm to clarify the unitary shape of events in the complex story of Cyrene, with its several stages over the centuries, from Iolcus to Lemnos to Thera to Cyrene. His success takes him, like Euphamus, from sea to land; but in his case the vague prophecy by a mortal in a marine setting changes to sure omens, of a fiery and celestial nature, from "father Zeus, ruler of the sky-dwellers" (193-202; cf. 10 and 23). The fleeting appearance of an unnamed god in disguise is completed by the direct interventions of Zeus, Hera, and Aphrodite.

Jason's story, like the Cyrenean founding legend, brings together sea and earth: the clod and Lake Tritonis on the one hand, plowing the earth (228, 234) and defeating a monster that rivals a penteconter in size (245) on the other.[8] In both stories Greek heroes venture over barbarian seas to establish, or re-establish, possession of a Hellenic city on land. Apollo will send Battus to bring ships to Zeus' temenos of rich soil in Africa (56) to be lord of the dark-clouded plains (52f.: φῶτα κελαινέφεων πεδίων / δεσπόταν). To restore the throne of Iolcus to Jason, Zeus speeds the Argonauts over the seas, where they achieve a victory over the dark-faced Colchians: ἔνθα κελαινώπεσσι Κόλχοισι βίαν / μεῖξαν (212).[9] In the Cyrenean myth this combination of land and sea points to a still remote future (254-59; cf. 42-49), whereas for Jason the victory brings an

[8] Note the verbal echoes involving clod, plowland, sea, and growth in 15 and 257, 26 and 228, 34 and 254, the *bōlax* of 37b and 228. There are numerous other echoes between the beginning and the close of the myth, e.g., 51 and 260, 3 and 259 (*Latoidaisin, Latoidas*).

[9] In an image-pattern common in Pindar (as in other Greek authors) the darkness of the danger at sea contrasts with the radiance of the success: cf. *Ol.* 1 and 6; frag. 98b Bo. = 108b Sn.

immediate and tangible reward: the hero carries off in his ship both the Golden Fleece and the king's daughter. The thematic parallelism of the two myths is reinforced by their coming together at this point in the ode (254-62). This juncture is also the intersection of the syntagmatic and paradigmatic axes of the narrative. In other words, the forward movement of the narrative in chronological sequence from the Argonauts to the founding of Cyrene (the syntagmatic or diachronic line) comes together with the underlying thematic pattern that cuts across sequential narrative: this is heroic success leading to the reacquisition or the establishment of legitimate kingship (the paradigmatic or synchronic line).

The use of oracles as an organizing device of the narrative facilitates the ring-form of the composition.[10] The description of the Lemnian Women at the end of the myth, when the oracle's fulfilment is assured, brings us full circle with the announcement of the oracle when the future still seems remote and uncertain:

καὶ ἐν ἀλλοδαπαῖς
σπέρμ' ἀρούραις τουτάκις, ὑμετέρας ἀ-
 κτῖνος ὄλβου δέξατο μοιρίδιον
ἆμαρ ἢ νύκτες. (254-56)

And then in foreign plowlands the destined day or night received the seed of your prosperity's radiant beam.

[10] On the ring-composition in the structure of the ode, see Illig, 65ff., 76-78, 87f.; Ruck-Matheson, 26-31; Greengard, 17ff. and 23ff. Cf. the echo between 13, κέκλυτε, παῖδες ὑπερθύμων τε φωτῶν καὶ θεῶν ("Hear, sons of high-spirited heroes and gods") and 58, ἥροες ἀντίθεοι . . . κλύοντες ("heroes equal to gods . . . hearing"). Compare also 68f., μετὰ γὰρ / κεῖνο πλευσάντων Μινυᾶν, θεόπομ-/ποί σφισιν τιμαὶ φυτεύθεν ("for when the Minyans *sailed* in search of that [Golden Fleece], the god-sent honors were *planted* for them [the descendants of Battus]") with the "planting" of the Battiad family "with the honors of the gods" (γένος Εὐφάμου φυτευθέν . . . σὺν θεῶν τιμαῖς, 256, 260), after remote travel at sea (*Okeanos, pontos*, 251).

CHAPTER 4

νῦν γε μὲν ἀλλοδαπᾶν κριτὸν εὑρήσει γυναικῶν
ἐν λέχεσιν γένος. (50f.)

Now he will find a distinguished race of foreign women in the bed (of marriage).

Yet the displacement of some of the motifs in this prophecy from Euphamus to Jason—the meeting of god and man, celestial omens, sexual union, and plowing—creates an overarching movement that draws both tales together. The recovery of both the clod and the Golden Fleece involves plowed earth, marriage, and winning back a lost kingdom.

Medea's role in the ode also exemplifies this complementary structure of circularity and linearity. At the beginning her homonymous *mēdea* or "counsels" (27) make possible the ship's anomalous passage over land:

δώδεκα δὲ πρότερον
ἀμέρας ἐξ Ὠκεανοῦ φέρομεν νώ-
   των ὕπερ γαίας ἐρήμων
ἐννάλιον δόρυ, μήδεσιν ἀνσπάσσαντες ἁμοῖς. (25b-27)

And, for twelve days before, we carried the sea-faring vessel forth from Ocean over the land's barren back, dragging it in accordance with my counsels.

But later, when the ship is fully reimmersed in its sea-journey, that same Ocean is the scene for Jason's success, both sexual and heroic (250f.). The phrase νῶτα γαιάς, "back of the earth" (26), recurs when Medea's magical "drugs" enable Jason, also in a mysterious and remote place, to cut his way through "the back of the earth" (ἀνὰ βωλακίας δ' ὀρόγυιαν σχίζε νῶτον / γᾶς, "and for a fathom he split the back of the clodded earth," 228f.).[11] The literal, if magical,

---

[11] There are some minor textual and metrical problems in 228f., but they do not greatly affect the meaning: see Farnell and Duchemin, *Pythiques*, ad loc.

WANDERING AND FOUNDATION

cutting through the earth here marks another progression from the watery realm of the first section to the terrestrial firmness and solidity of the ruling house of Cyrene, founded, as we have noted, in another context of plowing (254-57).

Medea's prophecy in the first part of the ode stresses the fluid interchange of land and sea. Thera, the place where she speaks (9f.), is to be the "root" from which the cities of the Libyan mainland will grow (15f., cf. 19f.); but it is a land that still belongs to the sea (τᾶσδ' ἐξ ἁλιπλάκτου ποτὲ γᾶς, "from this sea-beaten land," 14),[12] and the marine setting dominates her speech (20ff.), particularly in the vividly evoked meeting with Triton. From a sea-tossed land a root of cities will be planted (14f.). Its heroes will exchange horses for dolphins and reins for oars (17f.). The *Argo's* anchor is the "bit" or "bridle" of the ship (24), and the heroes will have to carry overland what belongs to the sea (literally, "the wooden sea-vessel," ἐννάλιον δόρυ, 26). The clod of earth, destined to become the mainland of a city rich in crops (cf. 6b), will be washed away from the ship to become a thing of the sea:[13]

πεύθομαι δ' αὐτὰν κατακλυσθεῖσαν ἐκ δούρατος
ἐναλίαν βᾶμεν σὺν ἅλμᾳ
ἑσπέρας ὑγρῷ πελάγει σπομέναν.   (38-40)

I learn that this (clod), washed overboard from the ship, went off into the sea at evening with the brine following the watery expanse.

Now the clod, which is a piece of the land, has taken on the marine attribute that previously belonged to the ship,

[12] On the imagery, see Bowra, *Pindar*, 218. The manuscript variants in the epithet for "land" in 14 do not affect the basic connection with the sea.

[13] For these interchanges of sea and land, see Duchemin, ad 17ff; Giannini (1976) 77-81; Farenga, 24-28.

81

CHAPTER 4

itself a piece of wood artificially made into something of the sea (cf. ἐννάλιον δόρυ, 27; ἐκ δούρατος / ἐναλίαν, 39f.).

The main narrative stresses the land-based settings of Delphi and Iolcus, with their trees, mountains, Chiron's cave (74-78, 85, 102). The "fruit-bearing" plowed land of Libya's plains (6f., 52; cf. 259f.), the agora that gradually fills with the crowd of citizens (85), the houses of Jason's kinsmen and of Pelias (133f.), the spring of Apollo in the heart of Cyrene (294),[14] and perhaps even the hall of the regal palace (cf. 267) give specific, local support to the emergence of cities and civic life from the wastes of water or desert (19ff.).[15] These local references serve to reinforce the land-based stability of Battiad rule, which doubtless needed all the support it could get.[16]

At the end of the myth the boundaries between sea and land are reinstated. The heroes combat the sea in strong rowing (202) and are helped by Poseidon "of the sea" (*ennaliou*, 204b), to whom they dedicate a holy temenos. In the first section of the narrative they meet a disguised divinity who *pretends* to be the son of the sea-god, Poseidon (33). Phrixus, whose ghost Jason was to lay, was saved by the ram "from the sea" (*ek pontou*, 161). The dragon that guards its fleece "surpasses in width and in length a fifty-oared ship which the blows of iron have made" (245f.).

After leaving the potential shelter of the "dangerless life," the Argonauts pray for successful travel over the "roads of the sea." The first concrete act is the founding of an altar to Poseidon of the sea (Ποσειδάωνος ἔσσαντ᾽ ἐν-

[14] On the reference to the Kura of ancient Cyrene, see Farnell on 294; on the local setting in general, see Burton 135f.

[15] Note the importance of the theme of cities (7f., 56, 19f., 260, 272) closely connected with the theme of rule and kingship (e.g., 106, 152, 165f.).

[16] See below, chap. 7, sec. I.

WANDERING AND FOUNDATION

ναλίου τέμενος, 204), after which they pray to the lord of ships (δεσπόταν λίσσοντο ναῶν, 207). Poseidon's altar in 204-6 is but a momentary refuge. The first trial comes at once, and it belongs to the essence of the sea, the twin rocks of the Symplegades, whose terrible "movement" would put an end to their own advance (συνδρόμων κινηθμὸν ἀμαιμάκετον πετρᾶν, 208). These rocks that should be stationary have a monstrous capacity for swift movement: they can "roll together more swiftly than the columns of deep-roaring winds" (209f.).

The heroes' first encounter with the terrors of the sea takes the metaphorical form of a plunge from the surface into dangerous depths. The word θέναρ in 206 of the dedication to Poseidon at the first landing denotes properly the hollow at the surface of the altar,[17] so that when they "hurl themselves into deep danger" in the next line (ἐς δὲ κίνδυνον βαθὺν ἱέμενοι, 207), it is as if they abruptly leap into the god's dangerous element.[18] The marine flavor of this first heroic danger confirms the young heroes' rejection of the dangerless life on land beside mother (cf. ἀκίν-

[17] "Un creux sur une surface plane," comments Duchemin, *Pythiques*, ad loc.

[18] Pindar uses the word θέναρ again of Heracles' explorations of the sea in *Isth.* 4.62: βαθύκρημνον πολιᾶς ἁλὸς ἐξευρὼν θέναρ ("finding out the deep-cragged *thenar* of the hoary sea"). The connotation seems to be of troughs in the waves at the surface rather than the deep water below, as some understand it ("hollow bed," Slater; "abyss," Lattimore). The notion of surface rather than depths is all the more likely as the next phrase refers to "taming" the sea for shipping, i.e., for safe movement across its surface (ναυτιλίαισί τε πορθμὸν ἁμερώσαις). Farnell, ad loc., takes the phrase to refer to "the whole basin of the Mediterranean closed in by high land" (2.355). With the MSS. reading βαθυκρήμνου (instead of Heyne's widely accepted βαθυκρήμνον) the meaning will be "the cupped surface" of both land and sea; so Thummer, 1.175: "die Fläche der ganzen Erde und des grauen, mit steilen Ufern umrandeten Meeres." Cf. also the leap into the sea at the trial of the young Theseus in Bacchylides 17, on which see Segal (1979) 33f. and below, chap. 5, note 21. See also above, chap. 3, note 8.

CHAPTER 4

δυνον, 186; βαθὺν κίνδυνον, 207). Yet the successful completion of the quest requires a return to the land and to the agrarian-aristocratic values of family continuity and stably transmitted property implied in the imagery of planting and fields.

Medea's spatial movement from barbarian Colchis to Greece has both a causal and an exemplary relation to the hellenization of Libya. It is a causal result because Jason's success and marriage with Medea (222) lead directly into the union of Euphamus with the "man-slaying women of Lemnos" (252). It is related paradigmatically because the Lemnian Women's foreignness and murderousness are a displaced form of Medea's potential danger (*androphonoi*, 252; *allodapai arourai*, 254f.; cf. Medea's *phonon*, 250). As in the case of Medea, their possible threat is neutralized and incorporated into a patriarchal monarchy by a sexual conquest at sea.

In the closing lines of the ode the dangers of the sea reappear for a moment metaphorically (the sea-change and falling wind of 292f.) but are allayed by the prayer that Damophilus will reach land, as it were, and see his home (*oikon idein*, 294). The theme of recovery (9), and especially the recovery of lost earth (initially, the magical clod, later Jason's home of his fathers in 117), now moves from the remote mythical past to the personal and concrete present. Atlas, at the end, has toiled far from his fatherland in 290. The closing movement brings us from the metaphorical springs of song and Damophilus' place of hospitable entertainment in the poet's own home-city of Thebes to the geographically "real" springs of Apollo in Cyrene and Damophilus' symposiac festivity there (294-99). The entertainment of the exile as stranger in a place not his own, ξενωθείς, is the last word of the ode (299). We recall Jason's victory over ostensible foreignness in the myth. He firmly asserted, "I have come home" (ἱκόμαν οἴ-

WANDERING AND FOUNDATION

καδε) in 105 and declares that he has reached a land that is not foreign to him (οὐ ξείναν γᾶν ἱκάνω) in 118.

This last section again links Greece and Libya and constitutes another journey from the Greek mainland in search of the longed for but elusive earth of Cyrene. This too is a passage between sea and land, as the exiled Damophilus hopes to "bilge out" *diantlēsais* (293), the "destructive sickness" of the discord that caused his exile[19] and find the springs of fresh water in his native land (294). This final recapitulation of the spatial movement of the ode also completes the formal ring-composition in harking back to the themes of Apollo, celebratory *kōmos*, and song in the proem:

ἐπ' Ἀπόλλων-
ός τε κράνᾳ συμποσίας ἐφέπων   (294)

at Apollo's spring supervising festivals of shared drinking.

κωμάζοντι σὺν Ἀρκεσίλᾳ
... Λατοίδαισιν ὀφειλόμενον ... οὖρον ὕμνων   (2b-3)

(joining) with Arcesilaus in his festive revel, ... a breeze of songs owed to the children of Leto.

Though located "at the springs of Apollo," these symposiac activities also suggest the interior setting of a house appropriate to a social gathering; and here too we may think of the palace of the king at the beginning, from which the *kōmos* would set out.

II. FIXITY, MOVEMENT, AND POETRY

The spatial and thematic movements in the ode, from Triton to Apollo, from the dense guile of Medea to Delphic wisdom, from loss to stable foundation, are also, as often

---
[19] For the image of 293, see Péron, 147f.

CHAPTER 4

in the Epinicia, parallel to Pindar's clarification of his poetic discourse. This too participates implicitly in the change from formlessness to form, from potentiality to actuality, from disguise and guile to truth, from wandering to firm implantation.

As the clod shifts from its unstable sea-world to the solidity of the Libyan land-mass and the stability of a line of kings who have "found a *mētis* of upright counsels" (262), so Pindar's poetic craft finds its way from an art of variegated, daedalic mobility to the permanence of monumentalizing kings. The poet begins in the concrete moment of the celebratory *kōmos* in the house of Arcesilaus where he stands "today" with his Muse (1-3). But he at once addresses the Muse to "swell a wind of songs" that would waft us on wide journeys over the sea, between Delphi and Libya and between mainland Greece and the remote barbarian northeast.[20]

The juxtaposition of fixity and movement established in the proem ("standing beside a friend" and swelling "winds" of song) is a microcosm of what happens throughout the ode. The "sailing Minyans" and "sea-voyage" (*pleusantōn*, 69; *nautilias*, 70) introduce the myth of the Argonauts' expedition; but the next image is one of fixity (71): "What danger with strong nails of adamant bound them fast?" To speak of "binding" in the case of a far-flung voyage is a bold oxymoron. The paradox is expressive of the situation: the "danger" at this point lies precisely in being immobilized by fear. This is what Hera's "all-persuasive longing" for the sea has to counteract (184), so that each one "may not remain (*menein*) by his mother coddling a lifetime without danger (*akindunon aiōna*)" (185f.).

[20] Note also the reference to the remote Colchians in 11b and 212. For a similar movement from the specific moment of the celebration to the locale of the mythical events cf. *Ol.* 6.22ff.

WANDERING AND FOUNDATION

Once launched on his voyage, Jason himself overcomes the danger of being immobilized by the paradoxically mobile rocks of the Symplegades. These inanimate objects are anomalously living creatures (ζωαί, 209), stones that have the rapidity of airy winds (210).[21] After this success, Jason receives the magic that wields power over motion and immobilization: the iynx "yokes" its victims in an "unloosable circle" (215). With the iynx he sets Medea's heart "whirling" with passion (δονέοι, 219).[22] When Aeetes plants the "adamantine plow" firmly in the midst of the assembled host (ἀδαμάντινον ἐν μέσσοις ἄροτρον σκίμψατο, 224), he confronts Jason with another potentially immovable object. In his success Jason is now overcoming those "strong nails of adamant" that "rivetted" him to his task (κρατεροῖς ἀδάμαντος δῆσεν ἅλοις, 71). In the sequel, Jason himself succeeds in immobilizing the object of his attack, "binding by necessity" the necks of Aeetes' bulls to the plow (dēsas anankāi, 234).[23] The final stage of his sojourn in Colchis brings him to the thicket of the fleece and its guardian dragon, which is itself described in terms of sea-travel (245f.). Pindar's own "broad" journey of song follows at once (247).

Jason's part of the myth ends at sea, "in Ocean's stretches and on the Red Sea" (251), whereas the race of Euphamus, as we have noted, has the agricultural stability of plowlands and planting (254-61). The gnomic transition

[21] For Bowra, Pindar, 369, treating the Symplegades as living creatures was "a reasonable conclusion" on Pindar's part. In Homer and Euripides the rocks are rather less magical: cf. Odyssey 12.69f.; Euripides, Med. 2, 432f., 1263f. and Iph. Taur. 124f., 241f. See D. L. Page, Euripides, Medea (Oxford 1938), 61f.

[22] Duchemin, Pythiques, ad 219, notes the "vocabulaire très violent" of passion here.

[23] On the association of anankē with the notion of immobilization, see Heinz Schreckenberg, Ananke. Untersuchungen zur Geschichte des Wortgebrauchs, Zetemata 36 (Munich 1964), especially 2-11.

CHAPTER 4

that follows, with its parable about the wisdom of Oedipus, implies the interior, stable setting of a kingly palace (cf. especially 267), like that of Arcesilaus' *kōmos* in the proem. The brief marine images point to return and security rather than departure: in a wise government the god "becomes the steersman for the leaders" (274) and the exile returns home, with a change of sail "as the wind drops" (292f.).[24]

This last phrase, λήξαντος οὔρου, harks back to the "increase of wind" at the beginning as the poet set out on his figurative journey of song. Now he looks to the end of travel (cf. also 247f.) as he hopes to bring Damophilus back on a final sea-voyage from mainland Greece to Libya. There he will recreate the scene of the ode's opening, festive song in a Cyrenean dwelling (3 and 295f.). The theme of stability takes a political turn in the assurance of "calm" or "peace" in Damophilus' hopes (*hēsuchia*, 296b).

The glance back toward Thebes in the ode's last verses offers full closure to the motif of travel, both spatially and temporally. Damophilus' entertainment as a guest-friend there (*xenōtheis*, 299) is a thing of the past; it is a tale that he can recount (*muthēsaito*, 298) to Arcesilaus and his fellow countrymen now that he is once more settled in Cyrene. The interweaving of the travel themes of the two myths (Cyrene's foundation and the Golden Fleece), the restoration of Damophilus to his homeland, and the prominence of song elegantly pull together the poem's expansive material.

[24] For this sea-imagery for a hopeful change of fortunes, see *Ol.* 7.94f.; *Isth.* 4.16ff. and 7.25-27. See Young, *Isth.* 7, 26; Péron, 113 and 134f.

5. Mythic Patterns II: The Voyage Beyond and Primordial Beginnings

I. *NOSTOS*: TRITON AND HADES

THE motifs of hospitality, travel, and return owe much to one aspect of the ode's occasion, the poet's friendly intervention in behalf of a guest-friend, Damophilus, an exile seeking restoration to his native land.[1] Pindar, however, characteristically incorporates the historical circumstances into a larger vision of the victory as an interchange between mortality and divinity, transience and eternity. This transfiguration of the present particulars is part of his conception of his task as a spokesman of the Muses of immortal Truth.

Within the mythical portion of the ode *nostos*, the return home, is a central theme and is closely associated with encountering death or the near threat of death.[2] Eu-

---

[1] Pindar, of course, is emphatic about his friendship with Arcesilaus, asserted strongly in the opening line. Establishing a rapport of *philia* between patron and poet is a familiar convention of the Pindaric epinician: e.g., *Pyth.* 10.66, *Nem.* 1.19f., 3.76, 7.62. See in general Schadewaldt, 314f. and Bowra, *Pindar*, 387f.

[2] For the centrality of the *nostos* motif in the poem, see Burton, 167f. and 173; Robbins, 206f., with further literature in note 2, p. 207; cf. also Gildersleeve, 281, and Ruck-Matheson, 19ff. Crotty, 106ff., stresses the ambiguity of the *nostos* as a point of critical transition, holding possible danger as well as joy for the hero and the community (111ff.). Commentators generally overlook a playful variation on the theme in line 5: as the poet is poised for his metaphorical voyage on the "wind of songs" (3), Apollo "happens not to be away from home" when the Pythia gives her prophecy (*ouk apodamou tuchontos*). Relevant to Pindar's association of the *nostos* motif and the threat of death is also Douglas Frame, *The Myth of Return in Early Greek Epic* (New Haven 1978), who argues for early connections of this theme and the journey to and return from the land of the dead.

89

CHAPTER 5

phamus' meeting with Triton early in the ode itself contains the theme of a *nostos* (32); but this hero fails to bring his gift of the clod on its fated passage "near the underground mouth of Hades" at Taenarus (43f.). Jason's *nostos*, however (cf. 196), brings him into closer contact with the Underworld, for Pelias' command to "lay the ghost of Phrixus" has as its aim "removing the wrath of those below" (*chthonioi*, 159f.; cf. *chthonion stoma*, "mouth to the underworld," 43f.).[3] This motif gives Jason's voyage the familiar mythical component of a journey to the Other World, like that of Odysseus in the *Nekyia*, Gilgamesh, and Heracles.[4] At the same time the allusion to Taenarus and Hades in the context of Euphamus' voyage in 43f. establishes a parallel with Jason's journey. Both heroes sail to the ends of the earth, one to the Libyan wastes in the eastern ocean in the far south, the other to the dangerous land of enchantments in the far north and west. Both stories contain the mythical pattern of the quest that carries the hero to the limits of the world.

Pindar is the first to relate and may even have invented Euphamus' meeting with Triton. This trial by water has a mood of friendship and hospitality. But encounters with the Old Man of the Sea are not always so easy. In the *Odyssey* Menelaus needs far greater effort to wrest from Proteus the knowledge that he needs to complete his voyage (4.413-25, 456-61). Pindar's version may be a deliberately

---

[3] The phrase ψυχὰν κομίξαι in 159 occurs in *Nem.* 8.44, with the clear meaning of bringing the dead shade or ghost back to life. That meaning does not seem appropriate here, but some transaction with the shade of one below seems to be involved: see above, chap. 4, note 5.

[4] For this motif, see Fontenrose, *Python*, 485-87; Duchemin, *Pythiques*, 103, and *Pindare*, 271 and 303ff., especially 307f. For Heracles' journey to the West in Stesichorus, see Walter Burkert, "Le mythe de Géryon: Perspectives préhistoriques et tradition rituelle," in B. Gentili and G. Paioni, eds., *Il mito greco* (Rome 1977), 273-84. Wilamowitz, 390, suggested that Hypsipyle was the "Mistress of High Gates" that lead to Hades.

VOYAGE AND PRIMORDIAL BEGINNINGS

softened form of an ancient Near-Eastern story pattern wherein a seeker after supernatural wisdom must consult a sea-god of oracular power on or over his native element of water; and this watery quest usually constitutes a dangerous test or trial.[5] Pindar, however, suppresses the dangerous side of the quest. Whereas Menelaus has to exert force upon his reluctant marine informant, Pindar's god of the deep comes unbidden and gives the knowledge and the token of future success as a friendly gift.[6] It is characteristic of epinician myth that the heroic deed is envisioned as fulfilment rather than struggle. Pindar always looks to the success at the end rather than to the effort in the middle.

The poet, as well as the hero, has a magical voyage and a homeward return: he spreads his sails to the winds of song (3) and later makes his journey homeward (247). Even Damophilus partakes of the wondrous voyage. The "spring of ambrosial words" that he has found as a guest at Thebes (298f.) adapts to the epinician motif of hospitality the ancient pattern of mythical quest: the hero, after a perilous sea-crossing, attains a fountain of immortal life or some other token of immortality.[7] Similarly, in *Olympian* 2, the poet's eschatological vision comprehends the great voyage after death. In the Other World the just reach an island in the remote Ocean (cf. 71f.), a place of calm and bliss where grow mysterious plants of gold, some on land and some in waters of life:

---

[5] For the narrative pattern, see Detienne, *Maîtres de vérité*, 34ff., with a brief reference to *Pyth.* 4 in note 41, p. 36. Cf. Gilgamesh's meeting with Utnapishtim in the *Epic of Gilgamesh*. Aeneas' meeting with Charon in *Aeneid* 6 may owe something to the same pattern.

[6] Similarly in Herodotus 4.179.2 Triton appears to Jason (without disguise) and shows him the route, in return for a bronze tripod that Jason has on board. Cf. also Ap. Rhod. 4.1552. For other versions, see also Robert, 859-61; Van der Kolf, 76.

[7] Cf. Heracles and the apples of the Hesperidae and Gilgamesh's search for the plant of immortality.

CHAPTER 5

ἄνθεμα δὲ χρυσοῦ φλέγει,
τὰ μὲν χερσόθεν ἀπ' ἀγλαῶν δενδρέων,
ὕδωρ δ' ἄλλα φέρβει . . . (72-74)

Blossoms of gold are ablaze, some on land from radiant trees, but others the water nourishes.

The theme of bringing perishable mortal life into contact with the immortal substance of the gods (the *aphthiton sperma* of the clod, 42; cf. 230b) also draws on the myth of first beginnings. Many rituals (and their reflections in myth) symbolically re-enact the moment of creation, *in illo tempore*, when men stand especially close to the energies of creation.[8] Here we renew the victory of cosmos over chaos in mythical time. For this contact with the energies of original creation Pindar draws on the age-old imagery of birth from the primordial waters.[9]

Euphamus' encounter with Triton took place in an obscure setting of unclear boundaries: between land and sea (20f.), between promise and failure, between achievement and loss. This meeting involves "likeness" rather than truth (θεῷ ἀνέρι εἰδομένῳ, "a god in the likeness of a man," 21); change of form (φαιδίμαν ἀνδρὸς αἰδοίου πρόσοψιν θηκάμενος, "putting on the radiant appearance of a man worthy of respect," 28f.);[10] the mysterious visitation of divinity; travel hemmed in by inland lakes (20f.); and the anomalous passage of a ship over the earth (25-27). This watery realm belongs to what Mircea Eliade calls the

---

[8] See Eliade, *Cosmos and History*, 34ff., 73ff.; also Pépin, 57-60; and for Pindar, see Rubin, "Epinician Symbols," especially 76ff. See also below, chap. 10. I hope to develop elsewhere these remarks on myths of primordial beginnings in *Pyth.* 4 and other odes.

[9] The Mesopotamian creation-epic, *Enuma Elish* is the most important early document. For a recent translation and lucid account, see Thorkild Jacobsen, *The Treasure of Darkness: A History of Mesopotamian Religion* (New Haven 1976), 168ff.

[10] For the associations of "likeness" with potential deceptiveness (and hence also with art and poetry), see Pucci, *Hesiod*, 9ff. and 91ff.; Kahn, *Hermès*, 73ff.

VOYAGE AND PRIMORDIAL BEGINNINGS

"undifferentiated formless modality of pre-Creation."[11] From this point the creative energies of heroism—and also of poetry—will shape chaos into cosmos. We view this mysterious exchange between land and sea through a somewhat ambiguous medium, the eyes of a barbarian enchantress whose potentially sinister arts of *mēdea* and *mētis* ("counsels" and "craft") have been brought into the service of Apolline destiny by Pindaric skill.[12]

The initially fruitless meeting between Triton and Euphamus leads eventually from marshy swamp (20) and empty ridges of earth (26) to fruit-bearing Libya (6b; cf. 259f.). The mysterious power of Medea on the Argo at the beginning (cf. 10f. and 57f.) is traced back to Jason's success in winning her from the black-faced Colchians (212ff.; cf. 11b), thanks to the mistress of (love's) sharpest missiles (213).[13]

As the ode progresses, it gradually equates sexual and political conquest. Thus Pindar makes the hellenization of Medea parallel to the hellenization of Libya.[14] In both cases the hero's victory over barbarians is an aspect of order emerging from chaos. The verb *dianemein* in 261—"arrange," "make orderly distribution," and in this context "govern" Cyrene—follows immediately after the myth and marks the transition from the creation of order in the remote tale to its present realization in the political life of Cyrene and in Pindar's song.[15]

[11] Eliade, *Cosmos and History*, 9.
[12] For the potentially dangerous meaning of *mēdea*, cf. the epithet *thrasumēdēs* of Salmoneus in 143, one of the evil-doers punished in Hades for imitating Zeus' lightning: cf. the schol. ad loc. (citing Hesiod, frag. 10 M-W); also Hesiod, frag. 30.16ff. M-W, and Norden on Virgil, *Aeneid* 6.587ff. See above, chap. 1, note 11.
[13] Compare also the mastery over "dark-clouded plains" that is to mark Battiad success in 52f.
[14] Cf. also the myth of Cyrene in *Pyth.* 9, where the agency of hellenization, mythically, is also that of sexual union: see Finley, 109f.
[15] *Dianemein* occurs only one other time in the Epinicia, to describe Apollo's governance of his shrine at Delphi (*Pyth.* 8.62).

CHAPTER 5

II. BIRTH AND CREATION

Three epinician myths illuminate the birth of Cyrene from the sea-wandering clod: the birth of Iamus in *Olympian* 6, the birth of Rhodes in *Olympian* 7, and the founding of the Olympian games in *Olympian* 10.[16] According to an "ancient tale," the island of Rhodes was "hidden" in the ocean (*pontos*, the sea as unmarked, pathless waste), and was "not yet visible" to the light:[17]

φαντὶ δ' ἀνθρώπων παλαιαὶ
ῥήσιες, οὔπω, ὅτε χθόνα δατέοντο
Ζεύς τε καὶ ἀθάνατοι,
φανερὰν ἐν πελάγει Ῥόδον ἔμμεν ποντίῳ,
ἁλμυροῖς δ' ἐν βένθεσιν νᾶσον κεκρύφθαι . . .

(*Ol.* 7.54-57)

The ancient sayings of men recount that when Zeus and the immortals were apportioning the earth Rhodes

---

[16] For Rhodes' watery birth, see Norwood, 141; Young, *Three Odes*, 88f.; Rubin, "Epinician Symbols," 76-79; Bresson, 23ff. On the myth of creation from the primordial waters, see J. Rudhardt, *Le thème de l'eau primordiale dans la mythologie grecque* (Bern 1971); Vernant-Detienne, *Cunning Intelligence*, 140ff. (on Alcman 5 *PMG*).

[17] On *pontos*, see E. Benveniste, *Problèmes de linguistique générale* (Paris 1966), 297f.; Rudhardt (preceding note) 24ff.; Vernant-Detienne, *Cunning Intelligence*, 151ff. and 221f. In *Ol.* 7 there is a gradual shift towards more creative associations in the words for sea as we approach the moment of Rhodes' emergence. Πέλαγος πόντιον ("ocean's vast expanse," 56) and ἁλμυρὰ βένθεα ("salt depths," 57) stress the formless, concealing mystery of the deep waters. Later πολιᾶς ἔνδον θαλάσσας ("within the hoary sea," 61) juxtaposes the barrenness of the sea as a container of growth with the fertile land that is soon to arise from it. Finally the phrase ἐξ ἁλὸς ὑγρᾶς ("from the moist sea," 69) emphasizes the lifegiving moisture of the sea at the moment of birth (βλάστε) and at the point when the rays of the generative father "hold it" firm in his allotment. Perhaps, then, the juxtaposition of "briny sea" and "moist expanse" in *Pyth.* 4.39f. looks ahead to the fertility contained in this pouring forth of seed (42), especially when one considers the vitalistic associations of "pouring" in Pindar (e.g., *Ol.* 7.7, *Pae.* 15.8.=frag. 52p Sn.); cf. *Pae.* 7.9.

VOYAGE AND PRIMORDIAL BEGINNINGS

was not yet visible in the sea's expanse but was hidden in the salty depths.

Helios perceives it in its embryonic state of "growing" from its place in the ocean floor "within the sea" (ἔνδον θαλάσσας αὐξανομέναν πεδόθεν, 62) and causes it to be "sent forth into the brilliant aether" (φαεννὸν ἐς αἰθέρα νιν πεμφθεῖσαν, 67). From the watery depths issues forth "earth of much nurture to men and kindly to flocks" (63). These origins have the form of a movement from the obscure ("hidden," 57) to the luminous (56, 67), from the subaqueous to the celestial, from water to fire, from unformed seed to the creative and ordering energy of the Father:

βλάστε μὲν ἐξ ἁλὸς ὑγρᾶς
νᾶσος, ἔχει τέ νιν ὀξειᾶν ὁ γενέθλιος
   ἀκτίνων πατήρ,
πῦρ πνεόντων ἀρχὸς ἵππων. (69-71)

It sprouted from the moist sea, an island, and the ancestral father of the sharp rays holds it, the ruler of the horses that breathe forth fire.

In *Pythian* 4 the celestial fire is remotely present in Zeus' omens at the exchange of guest-gifts between Euphamus and Triton (23f.); but it is much more prominent later in the watery journey of the Argonauts (197ff.). Eventually the cosmogonic theme of the seed of earth is transferred to the mortal seed and radiance of Cyrenean genealogy (254ff.).

The story of Iamus in *Olympian* 6, though restricted to an individual life history, uses the same underlying mythical structure. Iamus, like the clod and like Rhodes, emerges from concealment in a dark place of the "unlimited" (κέκρυπτο γὰρ σχοίνῳ βατιᾷ τ' ἐν ἀπειρίτῳ, "for he was hidden in the rushes and the thicket limitless," 54). This magical place, though on land, also contains the op-

CHAPTER 5

posing elements of liquid and fire. It has features both of a sea of life or nurturant waters and of celestial radiance. Here Iamus' "soft body is *drenched* with the yellow and the all-crimson *rays* of violets" (ἴων ξανθαῖσι καὶ παμπορφύροις ἀκτῖσι βεβρεγμένος ἁβρὸν σῶμα, 55). Later a watery passage brings him into contact with divinity as he "descends to the middle of the Alpheus" (58; cf. Euphamus' descent to meet Triton in the marshy waters of the lake, *Pyth.* 4.22). Iamus then journeys to a lofty place associated with paternal Olympian power ("the rock of high Cronion," 64), where he founds a lasting "treasury" of prophecy (65f.) and wins fame and radiance (*kleos*, 71; *phaneran hodon*, 73).[18]

In *Olympian* 6 the infant's "drenching" in the darkness of the "limitless thicket" replaces the primordial waters of cosmogonic birth in *Olympian* 7 and *Pythian* 4. But in all three odes this parturient emergence from darkness and chaos—what Norwood called the "awful vista of slowly opening centuries"[19]—is the grand mythical model for the human creation of political order, heroic deeds, victory in the games, and the immortalizing power of poetry.[20] In all three cases emergence from a dark, watery place of origins parallels a movement from formless and nameless obscurity to the radiance of great achievement: kingship, monuments of song, heroic fame.[21]

---

[18] On the pattern of birth and creation here, see Rubin, 81-86; Stern, 333-37; Stern, "*Olympian* 6," 333-37; Laura Nash, "*Olympian* 6: *Alibaton* and Iamos' Emergence into Light," *AJP* 96 (1975) 113ff.

[19] Norwood, *Pindar*, 38.

[20] Compare also the emergence of poetry from the "sea's dew" in *Nem.* 7.79, discussed above, chap. 3, note 36. Note too that in *Ol.* 7 Rhodes' watery birth follows immediately upon a gnomic generalization about the superiority of guileless art (*sophia adolos*, 53), which certainly applies to Pindar's own *sophia* as a poet.

[21] Rubin, "Epinician Symbols," p. 77, note 37, cites Eliade's *The Sacred and the Profane* (New York 1959), 130: "Immersion in water signifies regression to the pre-formal, reincorporation into the undifferentiated

VOYAGE AND PRIMORDIAL BEGINNINGS

In *Olympian* 10, finally, Pindar tells the myth of Heracles' foundation of the Olympian festival. Heracles consecrates the sanctuary by delimiting its sacred area (45-49). Parallel to this ritual dimension of his creative act is his naming the hitherto nameless place: "For previously it was without a name, as long as Oenomaus ruled it, and it was covered in the wetness of much snowfall" (πρόσθε γὰρ / νώνυμος, ἇς Οἰνόμαος ἆρχε, βρέχετο πολλᾷ / νιφάδι, 50-52). The energy of the hero has divine sanction from the female powers of birth, for here at this "festive rite of first birth" (πρωτόγονος τελετά) the Moirai, goddesses connected with childbirth, "stand nearby" (52f.). Accompanying the Moirai is Time, Chronos, the only test of Truth, *alatheia*, that which saves from "oblivion" or *lēthē*:

ταῦτα δ' ἐν πρωτογόνῳ τελετᾷ
παρέσταν μὲν ἄρα Μοῖραι σχεδὸν
ὅ τ' ἐξελέγχων μόνος
ἀλάθειαν ἐτήτυμον
Χρόνος. (52-55)

In this first-birth ritual the Moirai stand near and also Time, who alone tests what is really truth.[22]

---

mode of pre-existence." Anne Burnett, *The Art of Bacchylides* (Cambridge, Mass. 1985), 28-37, also views the plunge of Theseus into the sea in Bacchylides 17 as a motif of primordial creation. See also above, note 16.

[22] Note the juxtaposition of "forgetting" and "Truth" in the proem (ἐπιλέλαθα, Ἀλάθεια, 3f.). Cf. also *Ol.* 2.15-18, where "Time, father of all things," has the inexorability of what cannot be made "undone"; but a happy "forgetting" (λάθα) of suffering may yet be possible. This passage is complementary to *Ol.* 10.52-55. In both cases, Chronos, Time, is closely associated with truth as the negation of forgetting (*a-latheia*); but in *Ol.* 2 that inexorability of Time is relaxed if the "god's allotment sends lofty wealth" (*Ol.* 2.19-22). Note too the reference to the etymological meaning of *alatheia* as "non-forgetting" in the phrase ἀλάθειαν ἐτήτυμον (*Ol.* 10.54), on which see Norwood, *Pindar*, p. 252, note 43; also Gretchen Kromer, "The Value of Time in Pindar's Olympian 10,"

CHAPTER 5

The act of uncovering a waiting potentiality here does not take the explicit form of birth into the light, as in *Olympian* 6, but is displaced upon the giving of a name and then upon the radiance of the festival itself. This latter appears only at the end of the myth, after the list of the first victors in the newly founded games (73-77): "The lovely light of the fair-faced moon blazed upon the evening. And the whole of the sacred precinct was full of the songs of festive banquets, in the mode of victory-revels." Here, then, the founding act combines the bestowing of a name with the emergence of the future site from a formless covering into the light (the moon in 73-75) and a public, musical festival (76). To close this portion of the myth, Pindar, in ring composition, harks back to the motifs of "beginnings" and "naming" (ἀρχαῖς προτέραις, ἐπωνυμίαν χάριν, 78; cf. 51).

What corresponds here to the unformed sea surrounding Rhodes in *Olympian* 7 and the clod in *Pythian* 4 is the extraordinary detail of the "abundant snow" that "drenched" the hill of Kronus at Olympia. *Olympian* 10 takes only three words for this detail of the quiescent, liquid envelopment of the place before Heracles' arrival; but it is significantly combined with its "namelessness," and structurally it has an importance greater than its length.

Pindar repeats the verb for "drenching," *brechein*, at the end of the ode to describe his praise of the victor's city ("drenching with honey this city of noble men," 98f.). The repetition suggests a parallel with the hero's creative act of founding and naming the sanctuary. This "drenching" with the "honey" of song, however, unlike the snowy

---

Hermes 104 (1976) 425f. J. H. Quincey, "Etymologica," *RhM* 106 (1963) 146 would locate the *etymon* (in the sense of "etymological truth") in Chronos / Kronion rather than *alatheia—latha*, but the word order and the importance of truth in the ode as a whole strongly favor Norwood's interpretation.

VOYAGE AND PRIMORDIAL BEGINNINGS

"drenching" of Olympia in its pre-Heraclean anonymity, rescues the victor's deeds from the obscurity of Hades and gives them the "wide glory" that is "nurtured" by the Muses (91-96), another image associated with birth and growth.

If such passages reveal something of Pindar's conception of his creative process, they do so not as the subjectivizing, individualistic personality of the Romantic poet, but as a microcosm of poiesis projected into the myths of divine creation. The poet has before him the model of an ordering, shaping power that extends from the energies of nature to the civilized life of man. New forms emerging from the waters of a still unsettled world are analogous to the new verbal forms that the poet's voice brings forth from the deep well of his mind (cf. *Nem.* 4.8; *Nem.* 7.78f.). They are analogous too to the new words that enter human consciousness when the nameless receives a name (*Ol.* 6.56f. and *Ol.* 10.50f.). Through the myths of cosmic creation, the poet participates in the ode's process of tracing life back to the freshness of its beginnings. He recovers the divine impulse of the first moments of being. His Muse stands "today," *sameron*, the first word of the ode, at the specific moment of Arcesilaus' festivity in Cyrene and then sets out, on the swelling "wind of songs" (3), to a figurative journey into the mythic past whose first feature is divinely inspired prophetic speech (5-11). Across the vast journey of the ode (cf. 247f.), as the wind swells and then lets up (3 and 292), the poet again touches the magical origins of song in the spring of ambrosial words that Damophilus has found at Thebes (299).[23] While Pindar has journeyed back from Cyrene (2) to Thebes (299), Damophilus will hopefully have travelled in the opposite direc-

---

[23] Gildersleeve, ad 299, comments, "This fountain that he had found in Thebes was the ode that P(indar) composed for him in honor of Arkesilas, the ode we have before us."

CHAPTER 5

tion, from the metaphorical spring at Thebes to the real spring of Apollo at Cyrene (294); and, like an Argonaut returned, he will have a tale to tell (*muthēsaito*) of the ambrosial realm he found (298f.).

The quest for the clod, as we have seen, involves the cosmogonic motifs of the seed coming forth from the limitless waters near an entrance to the realm of the dead (42-44). Jason's journey is marked by the active power of a "beginning" that "received" the heroes (70). It includes Jason's moment of birth, when he "saw the first light of all" (ἐπεὶ πάμπρωτον εἶδον φέγγος, 111).[24] Jason soon after reminds Pelias of the binding force of those first origins when men at birth "see the golden force of the sun" (ἄμμες αὖ κείνων φυτευθέντες σθένος ἀελίου χρύσεον λεύσσομεν, 144f.)

The *Argo's* crew includes Orpheus, "father of songs" (176); and the voyage contains the building of a sacred temenos (204) where they come upon a "newly founded" shrine (206). This latter motif links Jason's story to the Cyrenean theme of "founding" cities (*ktizein*: cf. 7, 258).[25] His adventures also include the invention of the iynx, "first of all among men" (*prōton anthrōpois*, 217),[26] and breaks off with the "blows of iron" that built a pentecontar (τέλεσαν ἂν πλαγαὶ σιδάρου, 246). The lines may remind us, perhaps, of the tradition that the *Argo* was the first ship (attested, however, only in Hellenistic literature).[27] In any case these ringing blows of the axe, very dif-

[24] The adjective *pamprōtos* has only one other occurrence in the Epinicia, namely *Isth.* 6.48, which also describes a solemn moment of birth: Heracles, predicting the birth of an heroic son for his companion Telamon, takes an oath by the skin of the Nemean lion, the spoils of "the very first of (his) trials" (πάμπρωτον ἀέθλων).

[25] Note too the architectural imagery, discussed earlier, of Jason's "foundation" of gentle words in 138; cf. also 15, 56, 273.

[26] See Norwood, 41.

[27] Cf. Schol. ad Ap. Rhod. 1.4; Catullus 64.1ff; Robert, p. 770, note 4, and p. 771, note 9. Apollonius has the *Argo* built by Athena Tritonis

VOYAGE AND PRIMORDIAL BEGINNINGS

ferent from the quiet "fitting together" of Homeric shipbuilding, vividly convey the energy of construction.[28]

To understand more fully how Pindar's myth of origins connects the individual hero's life with the larger context, sacred and divine, of all life, we must return to Jason's account of his birth:

πεύθομαι γάρ νιν Πελίαν ἄθεμιν λευ-
    καῖς πιθήσαντα φρασὶν
ἁμετέρων ἀποσυλᾶ-
    σαι βιαίως ἀρχεδικᾶν τοκέων·
τοί μ' ἐπεὶ πάμπρωτον εἶδον φέγγος, ὑπερφιάλου
ἁγεμόνος δείσαντες ὕβριν, κᾶδος ὡσ-
    είτε φθιμένου δνοφερὸν
ἐν δώμασι θηκάμενοι, μίγα κωκυτῷ γυναικῶν
κρύβδα πέμπον σπαργάνοις ἐν πορφυρέοις,
νυκτὶ κοινάσαντες ὁδόν, Κρονίδᾳ
    δὲ τράφεν Χίρωνι δῶκαν.   (109-115)

For I learn that lawless Pelias, obeying thoughts bloodlessly white, stripped away (this honor) by force from my parents who had the just rights of rule. And when I looked on the very first light, they feared outrage from the overweaning ruler and made dark mourning in the house as if I had perished, and sent me forth secretly amidst the wailing of women, in my purple swaddling-clothes, making night only the sharer in their road, and they gave me to Chiron, son of Cronus, to be reared.[29]

(1.551 and 721). Fontenrose, *Python* 483-85, observes that builders, like pilots, of the *Argo* have associations with the primordial elements of earth and water and also have "manifold connections with demonic powers of sea, land, and underworld" (p.485). Thus the eponymous creator, Argos, is the son of Argeia, who is in turn the daughter of Ocean and Tethys and the mother of the culture-hero Pelasgus.

[28] On this passage, see Duchemin, *Pythiques*, ad loc. Wilamowitz, p. 391, note 3, regarded this phrase as an idle addition, mere filler. See above, Introduction, note 7.

[29] On Chiron and his epithet "son of Cronos," see above, chap. 2, note 36, and chap. 3, note 6.

CHAPTER 5

Jason's special reverence for the wonder of birth in this passage has a moral component: it places the vital energies of life on the side of justice. The "concealment" of the new-born child in the darkness of night (114f.) is the necessary defense against the "force" and "outrage" of an "overweaning" and "lawless" ruler.

The narrative pattern follows the folktale motif of the concealed birth of the hero. We have already noted the close similarities with the birth of Iamus in *Olympian* 6, probably not far in date from our ode.[30] But in *Olympian* 6 the figure corresponding to Pelias proves to be the good father-figure, Aepytus. Deception by hiding the new-born infant, Iamus, thus proves to be neither successful nor necessary, for this king duly consults Apollo's Delphic oracle (36ff.) and obeys the god rather than his own emotions of anger or resentment (contrast *Ol.* 6.37f. and *Pyth.* 4.109). Thus he turns the concealment motif to a happy outcome, setting the stage for the babe's miraculous emergence into the light, a symbolic rebirth or re-enactment of birth (*Ol.* 6.47-57).[31]

Jason's second speech, which is introduced by a markedly conciliatory tone (136-38), extends the wonder of birth to include Pelias in the sacred ties of kinship:

ἄμμες αὖ κείνων φυτευθέν-
τες σθένος ἀελίου χρύσεον
λεύσσομεν· Μοῖραι δ' ἀφίσταντ' εἴ τις ἔχθρα πέλει
ὁμογόνοις αἰδῶ καλύψαι. (144-46)

Planted from those in the third generation do we look upon the golden force of the sun. But the Moirai stand

---

[30] Cf. *krupse* and *kekrupto*, *Ol.* 6.31 and 54, with *krubda* in *Pyth.* 4.114; cf. the "all-crimson rays" of *Ol.* 6.55 and "seeing the first light" and the "crimson swaddling clothes" of *Pyth.* 4.111 and 114.

[31] For the light-dark contrasts in *Olympian* 6.54f. and 60ff., see Nash (above, note 18), 113ff. Compare the nocturnal setting of *Pyth.* 4.115 and Jason's return to the house of his "fathers of the white horses" in 117; cf. also Pelias' *leukai phrenes* in 109.

VOYAGE AND PRIMORDIAL BEGINNINGS

apart if any enmity comes to cover up respect among those who share kindred birth.

Instead of the vivid personal details of 109ff. Jason here stresses the reverence due to the ties of blood that of course result from birth. The repetition of the root *gon-* ("birth") in *gonais* (143) and *homo-gonois* (146) underlines the importance of kin ties. In the first passage he had given Pelias the epithet "lawless" (*athemis*, 109), whereas here he urges that both of them ("you and me," *eme kai se*, 141), act together in accordance with the lawful ordinances (*themissamenoi*, 141).[32] So too he adds the Moirai's repugnance at violating kin ties (145f.). Whereas the Moirai "stand beside" or "stand near" a birth sanctioned by the gods as the sign of the numinous energies of creation flowing into human life, here they "stand away" (ἀφ-ίστανται, 145).[33]

Jason's metaphor of "beholding the sun's golden strength" (144) for birth is not merely a strong variant on the conventional "coming into the light"; it also elevates the principle of birth to quasi-divine status and places human life in the midst of divine powers. Here, in contrast to Pelias in 109ff., he speaks not of human guile but of the eternal elements of the world, gold and sunlight. In his opening speech too he described his birth as "seeing the very first radiance" (πάμπρωτον εἶδον φέγγος, 111). His breadth of view, association with creative processes, and instinctive reverence for eternal things already contain the basis for his victory and Pelias' defeat.

The ode, finally, works its way back to cosmogonic myth in the reference to Atlas holding up the heavens and

---

[32] So in 54 *themites* is the word for the oracular authority of Apollo that establishes the Battiad line of succession, parallel to the oracle that establish Jason's rightful succession to the kingship of Iolcus (cf. 73ff. and 161f.).

[33] For the "standing near" of the Moirai at birth (a form of παρίστημι), cf. *Ol.* 6.42 and 10.52; cf. also *Nem.* 7.1.

CHAPTER 5

Zeus pardoning the Titans (289-91). As in the case of Typhos in *Pythian* 1, cosmic creation is a mythical analogue to political order (Arcesilaus' kingship and Damophilus' return, 271 and 293f.) and to the shaping power of poetry, poetry as *cosmos*.[34] The sovereignty of Zeus is the ultimate model and justification for stable kingship and law in Cyrene (cf. 260-62). It includes the Hesiodic themes of subduing unruly monsters, establishing authority over an older generation of divinities, and distributing the functions and prerogatives of power in the world (*Theogony* 881-85). Yet, as we shall see later, Zeus' defeat of the Titans is also a double-edged model, for it implies conflict and violence at the very core of the formation of the world order.[35]

The cosmogonic myth implicit in 289-91 is an ancient forerunner of the story of the clod, with its implications of creation from a watery chaos, the seed washed away into a remote ocean. We may again recall the creation of Rhodes from hidden, watery sea to Helios' bright sky and fire-breathing horses, with explicit cosmogonic, political, and artistic parallels (*Ol.* 7.53-76). In *Pythian* 4's myths of both Thera and Titans the order reaches eventual fulfilment in *chronos*, the divinely supervised "time" of the gods' design (cf. 258 and 291; also 55 and 78).[36] In contrast to this divine fulness of time stand the limited seasonal rhythms of spring and winter (cf. 64 and 265f.). This alternating, rhythmical time governs human events: the season (*hōra*) when it is right or not right for the creative act to take place (cf. 43 of the clod and Libya) or the "fated day" of the

[34] Cf. frag. 184 Bo. = 194 Sn.: κεκρότηται χρυσέα κρηπὶς ἱεραῖσιν ἀοιδαῖς. / εἶα τειχίζωμεν ἤδη ποικίλων / κόσμον αὐδάεντα λόγων ("With sacred songs a golden foundation has been beaten out. Come, let us build up a resounding structure of variegated words").

[35] See below, chap. 7, sec. IV, ad fin.

[36] For the meaning of *chronos*, see below, chap. 10. For another aspect of the Titan myth, see below, chap. 7, sec. IV, ad fin.

"planting" of the Cyrenean dynasty (*moiridion amar*, 255f.).³⁷ The poet's energies too should be governed by the rhythms of the *hōra*, for he must discern the right moment when he should end his journey of song and turn back (247f.). In the following sections of the ode both Oedipus' wisdom and the Titans' release are parallel exemplars of waiting for this right time or the fated day that is part of the divinely appointed order. It is the lesson of the clod's postponed arrival that Pindar would teach the exiled and waiting Damophilus.

³⁷ For mortal life and seasonal alternation, see *Nem.* 6.9ff. and 11.37ff.; *Isth.* 4.19f.

6. The Wisdom of Oedipus

For Pindar, as for early Greek poets in general, man is defined by his mortality, in contrast to the gods who are "deathless and ageless forever."[1] From Homer to tragedy the heroic figure works out this definition by spanning the extremes between doom and immortal glory and by exemplifying in his own great sufferings the inescapable necessities of the mortal condition. It is appropriately the hero of tragic doom, Oedipus, rather than the bright-haired young leader of the Argonauts who opens this darker area of the heroic pattern:

γνῶθι νῦν τὰν Οἰδιπόδα σοφίαν· εἰ
   γάρ τις ὄζους ὀξυτόμῳ πελέκει
ἐξερείψειεν μεγάλας δρυός, αἰσχύ-
   νοι δέ οἱ θαητὸν εἶδος,
καὶ φθινόκαρπος ἐοῖσα διδοῖ ψᾶφον περ' αὐτᾶς,
εἴ ποτε χειμέριον πῦρ ἐξίκηται λοίσθιον,
ἢ σὺν ὀρθαῖς κιόνεσσιν
   δεσποσύναισιν ἐρειδομένα
μόχθον ἄλλοις ἀμφέπῃ δύστανον ἐν τείχεσιν,
ἐὸν ἐρημώσαισα χῶρον. (263-69)

Know now the wisdom of Oedipus: for if one with sharp-cutting axe slash away the branches of a great oak and defile its lovely form, even so in the withering of its fruitfulness it gives a vote for itself if ever it comes at the last to the wintry fire or if, giving support with upright lordly pillars, it performs wretched toil in other halls, leaving abandoned its own place.

[1] See William G. Thalmann, *Conventions of Form and Thought in Early Greek Poetry* (Baltimore 1984), chap. 3, especially 80ff.; also J. S. Clay, "Immortal and Ageless Forever," *CJ* 77 (1981-82) 112-17.

THE WISDOM OF OEDIPUS

The lopped branches of the tree in "Oedipus' wisdom" (263f.) recall the most famous hero of epic as he enters the ambiguous space between mortality and divinity. Achilles' act of hurling down the scepter after his fateful defiance of Agamemnon sets him on the path of separation from his immortal mother and of confrontation with the inevitability of his own death (*Iliad* 1.234-38):

ναὶ μὰ τόδε σκῆπτρον, τὸ μὲν οὔ ποτε φύλλα καὶ ὄζους
φύσει, ἐπεὶ δὴ πρῶτα τομὴν ἐν ὄρεσσι λέλοιπεν,
οὐδ' ἀναθηλήσει· περὶ γάρ ῥά ἑ χαλκὸς ἔλεψε
φύλλα τε καὶ φλοιόν· νῦν αὖτέ μιν υἷες Ἀχαιῶν
ἐν παλάμῃς φορέουσι δικασπόλοι, οἵ τε θέμιστας
πρὸς Διὸς εἰρύαται· ὁ δέ τοι μέγας ἔσσεται ὅρκος
. . .

By this scepter, which will never again put forth leaves and bark ever since it has left its cutting-place in the mountains, nor will it let them bloom; for the bronze has stripped it all around of leaves and bark; and now the sons of the Achaeans who administer justice and keep the lawful ordinances from Zeus bear it in their hands. And this will be a great oath.

At this point Achilles begins the process of converting his mortal nature, by a self-chosen death, into the imperishable glory or *kleos aphthiton* that escapes the necessity of mortal decay.[2]

The myths of birth and creation that we have examined in chapters 3 and 5 all involve the "perishable" side of mortality, which, as often in archaic literature, is juxtaposed with the immortality of the gods. Euphamus' gen-

---

[2] The Homeric parallel of the scepter has frequently been noted, though not generally brought into connection with the main themes of the ode as a whole: see Schroeder, *Pythien*, 47; Burton, 169f.; Ruck-Matheson, 22; Carey, 145. For the interplay of mortality and the imperishable fame in Homer, see Nagy, *The Best of the Achaeans*, chap. 10.

CHAPTER 6

erative "planting" of the mortal race of Cyrenean rulers assures the arrival, after all, of the "immortal seed" of Libya (cf. 255 and 43). This interplay between the immortal achievement and the perishable material of which it is made—men, plants, seeds—is carried into the ode's closing section by the tree in the "wisdom of Oedipus." The implications of this motif too extend from the myth to Pindar's conception of his poetry.

As Pindar nears the end of the work, he slows down the tempo from colorful narrative to parable. *Mētis* is no longer the ambiguous dense craft (*pukinos*, 57, 73), but is called *orthoboulos*, "of upright counsel" (261). The repetition of the word *mētis* takes us full circle in the narrative (cf. 58) and thus helps modulate from storytelling to solemn advice about knowledge (262): "Come to know the wisdom of Oedipus." Such knowing already exists, Pindar implies, on the side of Damophilus: Cyrene knows of his just thoughts (ἐπέγνω, 279b), and Damophilus himself knows the right measure of things (εὖ νιν ἔγνωκεν, 287). Earlier in the ode the disguised Triton "knew" that the Argonauts were in haste (34); and the eyes of a loving father "know" the true identity of a son (ἔγνον, 120), as ordinary citizens do not (τὸν μὲν οὐ γίνωσκον, 86).

In Oedipus' wisdom, a tree of perishable fruit, or withered in its fruit, *phthinokarpos* (265), will prove itself even in the wintry season of life's end (265-69).[3] The tree's strain and "harsh toil" when, as a column, it supports the roof of a lordly hall (267f.) parallel Atlas' efforts as he "wrestles" to sustain the vault of the heavens (289f.). Both tales involve suffering; but the tree, unlike the imperishable (*aphthitos*) god, enters fully into the mortal process of *phthinein*, ripening, decay, and death (265).

The doomed hero of epic—Achilles, Memnon, Mele-

---

[3] See Burton, 168-70, and Carey, 151f. and also 144ff. for a survey of recent scholarship on "Oedipus' wisdom."

THE WISDOM OF OEDIPUS

ager—meets his death in all the splendor of his youthful prime.⁴ The expense of youth's beauty in premature death is the price for winning the fame imperishable. Achilles' choice in *Iliad* 9 is the great epic paradigm.⁵ Pindar exploits the pathos of the pattern in *Isthmian* 7, where he juxtaposes the "greatest fame" with the young warrior who "breathes out" the life of his early manhood as he dies of a fatal wound.⁶

Pindar's Jason has all the youthful glow of such figures: his wondrous limbs (80) and radiant, unshorn hair (82f.), in appearance like a god (87ff.). But no shadow of mortality crosses his brilliant beauty. Instead, the ugliness of old age and deterioration dominates the great oak of Oedipus' wisdom. The tree, a full participant in the mortal cycles, suffers the disfigurement of its wondrous form (αἰσχύνοι δέ οἱ θαητὸν εἶδος, 264), as Jason does not (cf. his "wondrous limbs," θαητοῖσι γυίοις, 80).⁷ Instead of the heroic success of a toil (*ponos*, 236b, 243) that regains a hero his home, the tree suffers wretched labor (μόχθον δύστανον, 269) in which it loses its abode and indeed its life. The beautiful Jason proudly asserts his rights to kingly rule (106f.) over his own "place," a city which is not the land of others (Αἴσονος γὰρ παῖς ἐπιχώριος οὐ ξείναν ἱκάνω γαῖαν ἄλλων, 118). The tree, subject to an alien "master" of a sort (cf. δεσποσύναισιν, 267b) and deprived of its "place" (ἑὸν ἐρημώσαισα χῶρον, 269), performs its labor "in other walls" (ἄλλοις ἐν τείχεσιν, 268).

In *Pythian* 4, as in many other odes, poetry seeks to overcome death, in part by reminding us of the moments

⁴ See Nagy, 174-95.

⁵ *Il.* 9.413ff.; cf. also 18.56ff.; Bacchyl. 5.151-60, the death of Meleager at whose shade even Heracles weeps.

⁶ *Isth.* 7.27-36: μέγιστον κλέος (29); εὐανθέ' ἀπέπνευσας ἀλικίαν (34). See also Young, *Isth.* 7, 20ff. and 40f.

⁷ The motif of the admirable or wondrous (*thaētos*) in 80 and 264 forms part of the epic "wonder" that characterizes Jason and his glorious quest: cf. 95, 163, 238, 241.

CHAPTER 6

of creative origins, while it also underlines the mortal processes of growth, planting, bloom, increase that tie us to the cycle of coming to be and passing away.[8] Hence the recurrence throughout this ode of words like *phuteuein, sperma, rhiza, thallein, auxanein.*

The "spring of ambrosial song" at Thebes, in the last line, alludes to poetry's immortalizing power. "Ambrosia" occurs twice in the Epinicia, in combination with nectar, as the divine food with which gods immortalize men, making them *aphthitous* (*Ol.* 1.61) or *athanatous* (*Pyth.* 9.62f.). In *Isthmian* 6 "nectareous libations" refer to the divinely inspired prophecy of the birth of a hero (*Isth.* 6.37).[9] In a celebrated fragment Pindar gives the epithet "ambrosial" to the "honied" water of the spring Tilphussa: μελιγαθὲς ἀμβρόσιον ὕδωρ / Τιλφώσσας ἀπὸ καλλικράνου ("ambrosial water, delighting like honey, from Tilphussa of the lovely springs," frag. 188 Bo. = 198b Sn.). The same vitalistic imagery characterizes the beginning of *Olympian* 7, where Pindar identifies his poetry with the wine's dew (*drosos*), with flowing nectar, and with Charis *zōthalmios*, the personification of the beauty of life-energy in poetry, nature, and human life.[10] Here the immortalizing power of poetry takes the metaphorical form of "nectareous outpourings" (7).

[8] For a recent study of this theme in Pindar, see F. J. Nisetich, "The Leaves of Triumph and Mortality," *TAPA* 107 (1977) 258-64; see also Duchemin, *Pindare*, 238ff. Note also the contrast of wintry waning of life and bloom at the end of the companion-piece, *Pyth.* 5.120f. Cf. also *Isth.* 4.16-21 and my remarks in *Ramus* 10 (1981) 72ff., with further bibliography in note 20, p. 85.

[9] See also *Isth.* 6.63-66 and 74f., on which see now Boedeker, 95. For the motifs of ambrosia and nectar and the overcoming of mortality, see Duchemin, *Pindare*, 247ff.; also her chapters on the funerary symbolism of the odes and the gift of immortality, 269-96, 297-334, especially 313ff.

[10] *Ol.* 7.2, 7, 11. Cf. the Charites of *Ol.* 14.1-12, on which see Gundert, 30; Norwood, 100; Duchemin, 72-80; Kirkwood, 119f. See in general Young, *Three Odes*, 101; Gianotti, 110ff.; Rubin (1980-81) 75f.; Segal, "Messages," 204-6.

THE WISDOM OF OEDIPUS

Implicit in these images is the analogy between the ordering power of song and the energy of cosmic creation. Though not formally enunciated (as is the way of poetry), this analogy forms the conceptual underpinnings of some of Pindar's greatest odes, notably *Olympian* 7 and *Pythian* 1. The link between poetic creation and the primordial creation of the world as a *kosmos* or ordered construct of harmonious beauty, seems to have been explicit in a poem about the wedding of Zeus, preserved, unfortunately, only in a late prose paraphrase. Zeus asks the gods if they want anything, and they reply with a request that "he fashion for himself divinities who would adorn (*kosmein*) with words and with music these great deeds and his entire handiwork" (πᾶσάν γε δὴ τὴν ἐκείνου κατασκευὴν κατακοσμήσουσι λόγοις καὶ μουσικῇ, frag. 12 Bo. = 31 Sn., ad fin.).[11]

Pindar's "ambrosial words" are not only analogous to the immortalizing liquid of the gods, but they also counter the forgetting (41b) that lets the imperishable seed be swallowed up in the limitless waters of the unknown sea (38-43). Conversely, the fulfilment of the sun-god's prophecy about Rhodes' watery birth in *Olympian* 7 is a "falling into truth," *a-lētheia* as non-oblivion ("Then were brought to fulfilment the peaks of his words, falling in truth," τελεύταθεν δὲ λόγων κορυφαὶ ἐν ἀλαθείᾳ πετοῖσαι, 68f.). In *Pythian* 4 the potential danger of *epea* that arise from "dense craft" (57; cf. 9) is clarified into "ambrosial" words bestowed in the generosity of guest-friendship in the poet's native city (299). Pindar's poetic hospitality at Thebes realizes the brighter side of the myth, not the deceptiveness of "craft," but the exchange of "friendly words" (*philia epea*, 29b) in a context of *xenia* between men and gods.

The "spring of ambrosial words" that Damophilus

[11] On this passage, see Maehler 82f.

CHAPTER 6

"found" is the last in a series of immortal prizes sought and found by voyagers, among them Pindar himself (cf. also 247). Jason's quest for the imperishable fleece (*aphthiton kōas*, 230) impels him out of the "dangerless life" of ordinary mortality (186) into the realm of eternal things. In the process he passes through feigned death, perishing (*phthimenos*) as an infant (112); and he tells his life story with a special sense of the wonder of birth, as if reborn, after darkness, to seeing "the golden force of the sun" (144f.). To win this object of immortal life, however, Jason, like Achilles, must also touch the realm of death, for the prize of the fleece imperishable is coupled with appeasing the wrath of those below the earth (*manin chthoniōn*, 159).

The epithet *aphthitos*, "imperishable," is withheld from the fleece until the moment when Aeetes, in direct discourse, promises it to Jason as the reward for yoking the fire-breathing bulls: "coverlet imperishable, fleece radiant with tassels of gold" (ἄφθιτον στρωμνὰν . . . κῶας αἰγλᾶεν χρυσέῳ θυσάνῳ, 230b f.).[12] Pindar, in propria persona, anticipates the immortality-conferring quality of the fleece when he promises, just before the Argonaut myth, "To the Muses will I give him (i.e., Battus) and the all-gold fleece of the ram" (67f.)[13]

ἀπὸ δ' αὐτὸν ἐγὼ Μοίσαισι δώσω
καὶ τὸ πάγχρυσον νάκος κριοῦ.

The deliberate echo between the poet's promise in 68 and its fulfilment in Jason's performance of the task set him by Aeetes in 229-31 not only provides formal unity through the ring-composition (cf. also 65 and 229f., 95 and

---

[12] See above, chap. 2, note 20. For the occurrence of the fleece at critical points in the ode, see Mullen 95f.

[13] On the importance for Pindar of the poet's "gift" that brings the victor in touch with the mythical hero, see Köhnken, p. 212, note 99.

THE WISDOM OF OEDIPUS

238) but also shows the poet's self-conscious accomplishment of the task that he has set himself. When we arrive at Aeetes' splendid words near the end of the myth, we realize that Pindar has in fact fulfilled his promise to us, his hearers. Through his brilliant interweaving of the foundation of Cyrene with the Argonaut myth he has indeed "given over to the Muses," for immortal praise, the family history of Arcesilaus.

The gold of the fleece (68, 231) is also a sign of the brilliance of immortal fame that success confers on the hero.[14] As often in Pindar, gold attends the mortal encounter with divinity. Thus the Delphic temple that announces the divine will to men is adorned by the golden eagles of Zeus (4) and has the epithet "of much gold," *poluchrusos*, when Battus enters it to receive the oracle that will lead to Cyrene's foundation (53). The power of divine memory (ἀ-μνάσει, "remind," 54) will overcome the mortal "forgetting" that lost the clod (τῶν δ' ἐλάθοντο φρένες, 41b). When the seer Mopsos takes in his hands a goblet of gold (193), he establishes contact with the gods through the omens that in fact presage success, success for Cyrene's founders as well as for Jason.[15]

The goal of the voyage, from the Cyrenean point of view, is the permanence of kingship on Cyrene, and this too is something "golden," namely "to govern the divine city of golden-throned Cyrene" (*chrusothronou ... Kuranas*, 260f.).[16] The immortality of Jason, Euphamus, Battus, and

---

[14] On the atmosphere of "divine incorruptibilité" associated with the fleece, see Duchemin, *Pindare*, 224.

[15] Cf. the parallel thundering from Zeus in 197f. and 23. Cf. also *Ol.* 7.1ff., where the very similar description of taking up a golden goblet is parallel to the poet's libation of song: see Bresson, 164f.; cf. also *Isth.* 6.40f. and 61ff.

[16] For the meaning of gold in Pindar, see especially Duchemin, 193ff., and Bresson, chaps. 4-6, especially 103ff., who stresses its economic function of exchange and property.

CHAPTER 6

Arcesilaus, on the other hand, is bound up with perishable things: growth, the seasonal movements of plowing and fertilizing the earth (cf. 15, 69, 144, 257; 43 and 255), aging, and death. Immortality for them comes through the mediate form of "sowing" a seed of descendants. The youthful Jason setting out on his dangerous voyage is described in a metaphor of the swelling growth of flowers:[17] σὸν δ' ἄνθος ἥβας ἄρτι κυμαίνει ("Your flower of youth is just now swelling," 158), says Pelias, encouraging Jason for the voyage. The youthfulness of the several of the Argonauts is stressed, particularly the twin sons of Hermes "of the golden wand" (chrusorhapis, 178), who "swell with youth's bloom" (κεχλάδοντας ἥβᾳ, 179). Here again the gold of incorruptible, quasi-divine achievement stands next to the fragile, perishable substance of mortal life. All of the participants are young and need Hera's "drug of valor" to assure that they not remain with their mothers (186f.), but face the danger with others of their same age (ἄλιξιν σὺν ἄλλοις, 187).[18] Such is the "bloom of sailors" who come down into Iolcus (ἐς δ' Ἰαολκὸν ἐπεὶ κατέβα ναυτᾶν ἄωτος, 188).

Beside youth stand age and the cycle of mortal generations. The aged eyes of Aeetes fill with the tears of a father when he looks with joy on his grown son in the bloom of early manhood, "seeing his child as the handsomest of men, outstanding" (120-23).[19] Old age and youth recur as a

---

[17] Péron, 248, sees here a mixture of nautical and flower imagery, but the verb kumainein also carries the more general meaning of "swelling" as in the growth of plants and babies in the womb: see Gildersleeve, ad loc.

[18] The terms for "time" here, unlike chronos that expresses the perspective of the gods' design elsewhere in the ode, express the rhythms of mortal life: aiōn, halikes (186f.).

[19] Pindar nicely distinguishes between the "father's eyes," organs of perception, which "recognized" the son (τὸν μὲν ἐσελθόντ' ἔγνον ὀφθαλμοὶ πατρός, 120), and the "aged lids" on which the tears rise up to show

THE WISDOM OF OEDIPUS

principal concern in the encounter between Jason and Pelias. Here, however, instead of the spontaneous emotion of a father, there is the suspicion of cunning manipulation by the astute king as he alleges the weight of his years as an excuse for sending Jason on the perilous mission:

ἀλλ' ἤδη με γηραιὸν μέρος ἁλικίας
ἀμφιπολεῖ· σὸν δ' ἄνθος ἥβας ἄρτι κυ-
μαίνει. (157f.)

The aged portion of my lifetime surrounds me, but your fresh flower of youth is just now swelling in growth.

Pelias' injunction also sharply juxtaposes this lovely bloom of youth with the angry dead below the earth, for he goes on to suggest that Jason's youth gives him the capacity of appeasing those below: δύνασαι δ' ἀφελεῖν μᾶνιν χθονίων ("For you have the power to take away the wrath of those below," 158f.). The contrast, as the context intimates, is not so much the result of a wise overview of the generations of man as a cunning pretext to serve "tricky profit" (cf. 140).

Even when the myth has assured Arcesilaus of the continuity of the "seed of his prosperity's radiance" (255), the imagery combines the celestial with the earthy. Almost at once Pindar reminds the king of the "wisdom of Oedipus," a parable about a living growth of perishable fruit (265) that comes to its end in the season of winter (266). The implicit qualification of Arcesilaus' good fortune reminds us of its first blooming "as at the high-point of crimson-flowering spring" (64). The seasonal metaphor, from spring to winter, spans the ode and places even the godlike "radiance" (255) of this regal wealth into the alternating

---

the old man's emotion: ἐκ δ' ἄρ' αὐτοῦ πομφόλυξαν / δάκρυα γηραλέων γλεφάρων, 121). Note too the expressive alliteration of γηραλέων γλεφάρων, as if the quality of age is particularly visible in the eyes that both see the long-lost son and express the emotion of the event in their tears.

CHAPTER 6

rhythm of perishable things.[20] That mortal rhythm gives the succession of generations, from father to son, its full importance as the means by which men preserve their identity and their achievements over time. The connection between seasonal rhythm and patriarchal succession is explicit in the simile of the springtime for the passage from Battus I to his present descendant (64f., reading παισὶ τούτοι(ο) in 65);[21] and it is implicit in Jason's recovering his legitimate inheritance of the kingdom in Iolcus (cf. 106-8, 148-55, 165f.).

If the oracle to Battus in 59-66 stresses the continuity of patriarchal succession, the story of Oedipus has behind it the danger of discontinuity. In the founding myth of Cyrene a son discovers a beloved father in a scene of tender recognition (120-23) and saves his kingdom. In the tale of Oedipus, as Pindar relates it briefly in the Second *Olympian*, "the fated son killed (his father) Laius when he met him" (38f.), loses a kingdom, and has no joy in his sons, who die in mutual slaughter:

ἰδοῖσα δ' ὀξεῖ' Ἐρινὺς
πέφνε οἱ σὺν ἀλλαλοφονίᾳ γένος ἀρήϊον,
λείφθη δὲ Θέρσανδρος ἐριπέντι Πολυ-
νείκει. (41f.)

Seeing this [Oedipus killing Laius], the sharp Fury killed his warlike race through their murder of one another, but Thersander was left (as son) to the fallen Polyneices.

When Pindar relates this myth in *Olympian* 2, he turns its better face outward and goes on at once to the survival of

[20] For this "seasonal" qualification of human life, see *Nem.* 6.9-11, 11.37-43, *Isth.* 4.14-21, and my remarks on the last in *Ramus* 10 (1981) 69-86.

[21] See Illig, 78-80, who stresses the importance of the continuity of generations in the family.

the royal line in the only descendant, Thersander, to whom Theron, the victor celebrated in the ode, traces his ancestry (43-47). But, as in *Pythian* 4, the bright side of seasonal alternation cannot be thought of without its death and darkness too. Thus a gnomic passage on the uncertainties of human fortunes leads directly into the myth of Oedipus (*Ol.* 2.31-37).

It is not only the rhythm of the seasons that measures human life, but the rhythm of the single day, the appropriate limit for man the *ephēmeros*.[22] The recurrent collocation "day and night," at several points in the ode may convey the solemnity that attends a long-delayed fulfilment, as in the "destined day or nights" of 255 (μοιρίδιον ἆμαρ ἢ νύκτες). But it can also suggest the brevity that limits the high moment of festive joy, as in the account of Jason's banquet to celebrate his return in 129b-31:

πᾶσαν ἐϋφροσύναν τάνυεν
ἀθρόαις πέντε δραπὼν νύκτεσσιν ἔν θ' ἁμέραις
ἱερὸν εὐζοίας ἄωτον.

He stretched to the full all festivity for five days and nights together plucking the sacred blossom of well-being.

When the seer Mopsus prays for calm winds "during the nights and days of calm" (νύκτας ... ἄματά τ' εὔφρονα, 195f.), the phrase may also connote the uncertainty of men's subjection to the changing weather of each single day, which they must endure while it lasts.[23] The "kindly portion of return" in the seer's prayer (*philian nostoio*

---

[22] Cf. *Ol.* 2.30ff., *Nem.* 6.6f.; in general H. Fraenkel, "Man's 'Ephemeros' Nature According to Pindar and Others," *TAPA* 77 (1946) 131-45; E. Thummer, *Die Religiosität Pindars* (Innsbruck 1957), 103; Vivante, "On Time in Pindar," 111.

[23] Cf. *Ol.* 6.104: "In a night of storms good are two anchors to hang out from a swift ship."

CHAPTER 6

moiran, 196) lies in the hands of the gods and will come on the "destined day," *moiridion amar* (255b), a day that no mortal can foresee.[24] This last expression brings the appropriate gravity of closure to the Argonaut myth. For the "real" figure of Damophilus at the end of the ode the poet wishes a change of weather at sea, this time for the better.

Every epinician ode of Pindar places the moment of the victory into the perspective of eternal things and praises the victor's achievement as a privileged contact with the permanence of godlike being. In the myths of the odes the divine gifts that the hero receives from the gods are paradigms for the glow of immortality and the aura of power and achievement that come with (athletic) victory.

But Pindar is interested not merely in creating eternal monuments to the victor's prowess; he is also concerned to show the passage between mortality and immortality, the critical point of transition between the transient and the imperishable. Such, for example, is the moment when Polydeuces, watching the death-throes of his brother Castor, chooses to sacrifice a portion of his immortality (*Nem.* 10.73ff.). For this process Pindar finds a number of images or narrative analogues: the seasonal alternation of spring and winter mentioned above; the collocation of the divine gold and the swelling blossom of adolescence in the young Argonauts (177f.); the clod that is both lost earth and imperishable seed and is conferred in a context of metamorphic instability by a god who has assumed the mortal shape of a son of *aphthitos* Poseidon (33); a *mētis* that comes into play at the exchanges between man and god, where the very ambiguity of the instrument ("immortal mouth" and "dense craft") reminds us of the uncertainty and difficulty of that access to the divine.

[24] In *Nem.* 6.6f. mortals "do not know what course *by day or in nights* destiny has set down for us to run" (ἐφαμερίαν . . . μετὰ νύκτας).

THE WISDOM OF OEDIPUS

The poet's ambrosial words touch human life with the imperishable; but poetry also exists in an interplay between craft and wisdom, seduction and truth, good and bad drugs. It refuses to leave the ground of its mortality, and at every point it recognizes the complexity of its mediation between the divine and the human. This, perhaps, is the ultimate meaning of the wisdom of Oedipus that Pindar would teach Arcesilaus (263ff.) even as he irradiates his life with a light like the rays of sunbeams (255).

II

Cultural Models: Language, Writing, and Sexual Conflict

7. Poetry and/or Ideology

I. IS POETRY A SALABLE COMMODITY? THE
POSITIVE AND NEGATIVE HERMENEUTIC

ONE could scarcely ask for a better example of the paradigm shift in interpretive method than the contrast between Wilamowitz's reading of *Pythian* 4 in 1922 and the recent interpretation by Farenga in 1977.[1] Although Wilamowitz acknowledged the "chimaera-like" and "unclassifiable" quality of the ode, he looked for its unity "not in the work" but in the poet's life and in the historical circumstances of the work's origins.[2] Farenga's reading is semiological, deconstructive, and anti-ideological. He would abandon the permanence of the classical text as a meaning fixed forever at its privileged point of origins—the point which Wilamowitz would seek to recover and occupy for his reading of the ode—and instead open the text to all the precariousness and evanescence of a de-objectivized, de-originized re-writing, and hence re-reading.

On such a view, the poem is a text into which are inscribed all the absences of letters, the distances between the spoken and the written word, between words and things, and between the moment of creation and the moment of successive recreations and interpretations. Such a text exists (if that term may still be used) only as it is re-written in each subsequent realization of its meaning, only as it is subjected to the necessary violence of re-creation in each interpretation.[3] The historical reading, setting out solely from the perspective of the ode's overt intentions—the honoring of Arcesilaus as legitimate king of

[1] Wilamowitz, *Pindaros*, 383-93; Farenga, 3-37.
[2] Wilamowitz, 392.
[3] Farenga, 5f.

CHAPTER 7

Cyrene—cannot be the final or exclusive one. But before deconstructing the ode in its "poetics of absence" we have to grasp the complexity of Pindar's design as fully as we can. To understand the full range of the ode's meaning we need to follow the dialectic between the historical and the contemporary perspectives. We have no sure way of discerning to what extent Pindar himself identified with his ode's overt, ideological commitment to affirm the rightful continuity of Battiad rule; but we can trace the shifting currents in the text between the present circumstances and what Pindar views as the permanent laws and constraints of the mortal condition. In this effort we approach the core problem of Pindaric interpretation, the question of how, if at all, these poems transcend the limited historical occasions of their origin.

Pindar writes for aristocratic patrons at a time when in many parts of the Greek world they are embattled against a rising wave of democratic feeling. By the very nature of their occasion and the self-selection of the audience, the Epinicia aim at promoting the traditional aristocratic values of noble birth, class and family solidarity, and the rightful inheritance by blood of tangible property and of the intangible qualities of excellence.[4] We cannot reconstruct with any degree of certainty the intentions of the kings and nobles who commissioned Pindar to write odes celebrating their athletic victories; but clearly they expected productions consonant with their beliefs.[5] Tyrants like Hieron or Theron, or "kings" like Arcesilaus, whose precarious regime required the strongman tactics gener-

[4] See Bresson, passim, especially 18ff., 25ff.; Donlan, *Aristocratic Ideal*, 95-111, especially 108ff.; Rose, "First Nemean," 150-55. For the explicit concern of *Pythian* 4 with legitimizing the power of Arcesilaus, see Giannini (1979) 39 and Farenga, passim.

[5] For a lucid discussion of the question in a Marxist perspective, see Peter Rose, "Towards a Dialectical Hermeneutic of Pindar's Pythian X," 49-73, especially 63ff.

ally practised by tyrants,[6] probably hoped that some degree of legitimization would accrue to their reign by having their exploits included in the panhellenic cultural norms celebrated by the Pindaric epinician: prosperity as a gift of the gods, energetic action, good order, lasting glory, and the stable inheritance of name and property.

Through his victory ode Pindar expects to confer an aura of brilliance and largeness on events, institutions, and individuals of a certain kind; and he has an implicit principle of selection for what needs and deserves aggrandizing and embellishment. The underlying mythic patterns of the action, just because they are emblematic and paradigmatic descriptions of behavior and of expectations about life, are also affirmations of the cultural norms and social values that Pindar endorses.[7] In *Pythian* 4, for example, Jason's straightforward and open assertion of a legitimate claim to ancestral rights contrasts favorably with the deviousness of the usurper, Pelias. Pindar stacks the cards in Jason's favor (or, in less colloquial terms, overdetermines Jason's success) by endowing him with the positive moral values attaching to the youthful hero: good breeding, modesty, beauty, reverence, supernatural aid in love and war. This strategy of association and analogy enables him to invest Arcesilaus' reign with the legitimacy and stability of the ancient cultural traditions embodied in the myths, for we tend to associate the victor being praised (Arcesilaus) with the mythical hero whose tale is the ode's primary instrument for conveying praiseworthy attributes. As we noted earlier, Pindar's emphasis on the oracle which Bat-

[6] See H. Berve, *Die Tyrannis bei den Griechen* (Munich 1967), 1.126: "Die Geschichte der Battiaden bietet ein bemerkenswertes Beispiel für den Wandel einer traditionellen Königsherrschaft zur Tyrannis, den als historisches Phänomen schon Aristoteles bemerkt hat."

[7] For the importance of exemplary actions, whether of myths or of approved behavior, in Pindar, see Young, *Isth.* 7, 42ff.; Bernadini, *Mito e attualità*, 75ff.

CHAPTER 7

tus received at Delphi (59-66) also gives a divine validation to the royal line that he founds.[8]

Through the very explicitness of such attempts at Battiad legitimization, however, the ode peeks around the edges of its message, as it were, and shows its self-awareness of the conditioned, limited service that it is performing for its patron. By showing power and authority in the process of being constructed, it also shows the path of their possible destruction. Thus here, as elsewhere, Pindar returns again and again to the uncertainties of success in a world of change and mortality. Beside the achievements of the radiant young Jason stands the tribulation implicit in the "wisdom of Oedipus," the doomed son fated to kill, not defend, his father.[9] Beside the burgeoning seed of the future Cyrene stands the decay of the aged oak (262-65). Such parallels and contrasts are a constant feature of the Epinicia. The alternating fortunes of the great houses from generation to generation—the houses of Cadmus or of Aeacus—are a recurrent theme.[10]

Thus the poet's explicit commitment to the victor, at the surface level of encomiastic intention, stresses permanence, the solidity of weath, and the secure transmission of inherited virtues and inherited power; but the structure of the ode, with its open-ended mythical paradigms of loss amid prosperity, points up the precariousness of such acquisitions and the limitations of defining the human condition in terms of them. In *Olympian* 2, for example, Pindar confidently declares that "wealth adorned with virtues" is "a star conspicuous, truest light for a man" (*Ol.* 2.53-56). But his very next lines are about "the future," which holds death and judgment in the afterlife. Here a more mysterious and more elusive light, no

---

[8] See above, Introduction, ad fin.

[9] *Ol.* 2. 38-42; see above, chap. 6.

[10] See *Nem.* 6.8-11 and *Nem.* 8.37-44. For the line of Cadmus and of Aeacus, see *Ol.* 2.22-34, *Pyth.* 3.86-106, *Nem.* 5.7-39, *Isth.* 8.54-66.

POETRY AND IDEOLOGY

longer of a "star" in the sky, glows in a supernatural realm (72), and kingship and authority are beyond human control (75-77). The contrastive interplay between these two dimensions of the ode is essential for understanding the nature of Pindar's praise of the victory.

We can also discern the ideological basis of the odes through Pindar's pervasive concern to articulate the nature and difficulty of his poetic accomplishment. *Pythian 4*, like many of the Epinicia, is emphatic about its dissonances of language, the contrasting modes of communication and affirmation that it uses, and the different views of poetic speech that it implies.[11] The ideological elements in the odes become particularly visible at the points where Pindar tries to clarify what his art can and cannot do. The poet puts the victory in touch with the truth that endures throughout time; but like Hesiod's Muses he can also tell lies.

In his awareness that his art is potentially a poetry of falsehood and deception as well as of truth and eternizing commemoration, Pindar's work is open to what Peter Rose calls a double or "dialectical" hermeneutic, a deconstructive as well as a constructive potential.[12] The former calls attention to those negative features of guile or craft that we have discussed above in chapter 1. In thus underlining the fact that he practices an *art* of commemoration, Pindar also leaves open the possibility that poetic technique may, for a price, ennoble even unworthy objects. "Profit" is the danger that the poet must resist; it must not distract him from his discernment of what is noble and his

[11] With a rather different emphasis Farenga too stresses the ode's "concern over the language itself, its forms, its tangibility, the play of its production of meaning, its signification through the poetic function, in short" (p. 12).

[12] See Rose, "Pythian X," passim, especially 62ff. I am much indebted to Rose's clear and systematic formulation of the problem of ideology in the Epinicia. In the discussion that follows, I use the terms "positive" and "negative" in a sense different from Rose.

CHAPTER 7

celebration of this as "truth."[13] Hence he points out that the sweetness of Homer's song gave more honor to the crafty Odysseus than to the stalwart Ajax (*Nem.* 7.20ff.). This poetic self-consciousness of a "craft" or "art" of praise, however, applies not just to other poets as negative paradigms (Homer, Archilochus, Simonides) but to Pindar himself.

The epinician poet must write a different song for different victors on different occasions. The act of mental reorientation required each time finds its concrete, physical enactment in changes of place. In reality or imagination, the poet moves from Thebes to Syracuse, Aegina, Thessaly, Cyrene, and so on. To the spatial mobility corresponds a mobility of thought: to compose a song of praise is to understand and interpret poetically the new victory in its unique and present moment and against its specific local and family background. Each occasion, then, has a slightly different kind of truth as the poet adapts his song to the requirements and circumstances of different winners. Thus he is ever finding his way between a single underlying truth and a flexible and adaptable craft that can encompass changing terms.

What mitigates this division between the poet's unity of ideals and the different circumstances of the separate victories is the common values of the class to which nearly all the competitors belong. Conversely, the poet himself brings into consciousness this realm of shared class values or "Wertewelt" (to use Hermann Fränkel's term)[14] and fosters the solidarity implied by such unified concerns.[15]

---

[13] On payment for poetry and the dangers of such "profit," cf. *Pyth.* 11.41f.; *Nem.* 7.20-24; *Isth.* 2.6-11; in general Bowra, *Pindar*, 355-58; Bundy, 1.10ff.; Leonard Woodbury, "Pindar and the Mercenary Muse: *Isth.* 2.1-13," *TAPA* 99 (1968) 533ff.; Moses I. Finley, "Silver Tongue," in *Aspects of Antiquity*, ed. 2 (Harmondsworth 1977), 43-47, especially 44f.

[14] Fränkel, *Dichtung und Philosophie*, 558.

[15] For Pindar's creation of a unity of values and his interlocking of values, see Fränkel, 558ff., 566f.

POETRY AND IDEOLOGY

The poet has to be able, on the one hand, to identify sympathetically with men of different temperaments and pursuits (cf. *Pyth.* 2.83-89). On the other hand he has a commitment to a set of constant moral and religious principles, a body of attitudes, both cultural and personal, that pervade his every celebration of a victory. These he associates with the constancy and permanence of the divine, over against the instability and uncertainty of the human.[16] Here too, in this intersection between the recognition of human instability and the assertion of timelessness, the ideological activity of the poet becomes self-conscious and visible.

It is part of this ideological activity that Pindar clearly privileges one side of this polarity, although he does not thereby efface the other side. He presents himself as emerging ultimately as a poet of the One rather then of the Many, of the true rather than of the false, of the continuity of traditional *areta* and inherited *phya* rather than of rootless, infinitely adaptable Odyssean guile (*dolos*). But that poetic of the "always" is deliberately superimposed on a poetics of the "sometimes" (cf. *Pyth.* 2.85).[17] The poetry of a unitary Truth emerges only out of juxtaposition and conflict with the poetry of shifty "craft" (*mētis*). Each implies the other as its inseparable other side. This dialectical relation is a useful conceptual mechanism for grasping and analyzing this necessary coexistence of two antithetical

---

[16] See, for example, the implicit contrast between the adaptability of the "straight-tongued man" and the "god" against whom one may not "strive" in *Pyth.* 2.86-88. On the pervasive contrast in Pindar between the "volubilità della mente umana" and "la perenne certezza del Vero," see Gentili, "Lirica greca arcaica e tardo arcaica," 77, who also points out the contrast of this "conservative" world-view with Simonides' more "dynamic" acceptance of change.

[17] See Slater, *Lexicon*, s.v. ἄλλοτε and also s.v. ἄλλος, B 2 (p. 34). *Isth.* 3.19 is typical of this antithesis, with its contrast between the changeful "days" of mortal time (*aiōn*) and the invulnerable "sons of the gods": on this passage, see my remarks in *Ramus* 10 (1981) 71.

CHAPTER 7

directions in Pindar's self-description and self-presentation of his art.

II. ANALOGY, DISCREPANCY, AMBIGUITY

Another dimension of Pindar's double-faceted "art" of celebration derives not so much from the changing circumstances of each ode's respective *laudandus* as from the nature of the relational patterns that are a constant feature of all the odes. The parallels that Pindar establishes between the present and the past seek to lift every detail of the action into the realm of the potential timelessness of myth. They provide a multi-levelled affirmation of order pervading the individual life, the political and social community, the natural world, and the supernatural. Jason's life story in *Pythian* 4, for example, can be read in the register of myths of generational passage, of kingship and hierarchy, of cosmic creation, and, at the level of poetics, of form emerging from the formless.

The very density of the poetic weave, however, encourages the continual formation of analogies and parallels, even when they may operate in ways that call into question the specific situation that Pindar intends to praise. One cannot always predict where a certain train of connections, once set into motion, will come to rest. A richly analogical momentum of this nature cannot necessarily be halted within limits that are "safe" to the *laudandus*. As interpreters have occasionally speculated, Hieron may have felt the impetus of that momentum when, having received *Pythian* 1 two years earlier, he gave the commission for his Olympian victory of 468 not to Pindar but to Bacchylides.[18]

On the positive side we can trace how Pindar relates events to one another within these overlapping systems of analogies and how he imbues the specific details of the in-

---

[18] See Finley, 92ff.

POETRY AND IDEOLOGY

dividual life with the force of the exemplary and the universal. The negative approach leads us to explore the openness of such networks of analogies and to perceive their inherently dialectical potential. These analogies may lead to back-formations that are not necessarily flattering to the celebrant. Both *Pythian* 1 and 4, for example, offer paradigms of hybristic violence (Typhon, the Aloades) and cruel or illegitimate kingship (Phaleris, Pelias) that might be construed as a warning to the ruler who commissioned the poems. The equation Battus-Jason-Arcesilaus or even Arcesilaus-Zeus certainly works *ad maiorem gloriam Arcesilai*. But the equation Pelias-Arcesilaus remains a possibility, at least as a monitory paradigm in the negative hermeneutic. We cannot, of course, know whether Pindar explicitly or implicitly intended such a parallel or whether the initial Cyrenean audience would have detected it. But for the modern reader the momentum of such analogical associations cannot be halted short of at least raising the possibility.

The claims to universality and moral exemplarity in the myths and the reversibility inherent in the nature of Pindar's analogical thought-processes are, ultimately, what enable the odes to transcend the limited conditions of their production.[19] The surface aim of the odes is to set the present events into a world-order in which political, aesthetic, and cosmic harmony are all homologous with one another.[20] The poet thereby validates the athletic victories, along with the social class of the victors, as an extension of the heroic exploits of the kings and princes of myth to whom the aristocratic families trace their descent.

In relating the specific historical and political moment of the victory to this realm of permanent values, however,

[19] See Rose, "Pythian X," 64. Also above, chap. 2, note 6.

[20] To view this function of praise or encomium solely in terms of rhetorical conventions, therefore, as a Bundyist reading tends to do, is reductive.

CHAPTER 7

Pindar also opens the gap between the actual and the ideal, between the individual and the mythical exemplar. *Pythian* 4 at one level urges Arcesilaus to follow the model of Zeus who forgives and releases the rebellious Titans (291). But to adduce so lofty a model for the mortal king also invites recognition of the distance between the human city and the heavenly paradigm. The same potential discrepancies apply to the relationship between the kingdom of Hieron and the cosmic kingdom of Zeus in *Pythian* 1. In like manner, the models of kingship in *Pythian* 4 include the reverent Jason but also the incumbent of the throne of Iolcus, the proud and crafty Pelias. Arcesilaus has Jason's claims to legitimate rule, but structurally he occupies Pelias' seat of power.

Viewed another way, the dialectical interpretation makes us aware that the victor/hero occupies a position of ambiguity. He stands in the forefront of the community, but he is also isolated in his danger, at the godlike peak of his extraordinary success. He thus requires repeated warnings not to overstep the limits of mortal life. To return home after signal triumph is a dangerous passage, and to reintegrate the high intensity of that glory into the normal human relationships is a difficult task.[21] Pindar's contemporaries told several quasi-mythical tales of great victors in the games who, like Ajax in Sophocles or Neoptolemus in Pindar's own corpus, fail to bridge the gap and go on a rampage of berserk destruction, after which they become vengeful local deities.[22] The "danger" facing Jason and his companions on their voyage (186, 207) hovers over the success as well as the trial.

The Victory Odes, then, are not merely songs of praise for the *jeunesse dorée* of late archaic aristocracy, but explore the limits inherent in the mortal condition and the

[21] See Crotty, 122ff.
[22] See Fontenrose, "The Hero as Athlete."

risk and the necessity of reaching beyond those limits to attain the highest reward possible to a man. At every point ambiguities surround that endeavor. If life without these dangers is inglorious and mean (185-87), the yearning for what transcends the ordinary lures men to the places where only a god may dwell. Here the victor/hero stands ominously exposed to the chaotic desire for what lies beyond his powers.[23] Hence beside the ordering and creative impulses of founding heroes like Heracles, Pelops, or Iamus stand also the violence and destructiveness (of self or of others) in heroes like Neoptolemus or Ajax.[24] Pindar can celebrate the triumph of a hero like Bellerophon in *Olympian* 13, recipient of a divine gift and conqueror of monsters; but in another ode that hero's ambition, like the Aloades' audacity, is a warning against reaching beyond mortality (*Isth.* 7.44ff.; *Pyth.* 10.27-30). To these risks of the hero correspond those of the poet. He too treads a path hedged about with dangers; and he too, if he does not perceive and grasp the *kairos*, the opportune time and the right balance or measure, may plunge into darkness and disorder.[25]

It is characteristic of our time to perceive discrepancy and discontinuity where the ancient poet emphasized hierarchy and continuity. But however sensitive we are to the negative potential that inheres in the text and in the reversible analogies of Pindar's mythical and literary discourse, it is essential not to lose sight of what remains Pin-

---

[23] For the destructive course of such desires, cf. *Pyth.* 4.90-92; also *Pyth.* 3.19ff., and in gnomic form 59-62; *Nem.* 8.4f.; *Nem.* 11.47f. Cf. also *Ol.* 1.114. To label such statements merely formulas of the "ne plus ultra" motif is to miss their moral significance.

[24] For Heracles, cf. *Ol.* 3 and 10, *Nem.* 3; for Pelops, *Ol.* 1; for Iamus, *Ol.* 6; for Neoptolemus, *Nem.* 7 and *Paean* 6; for Ajax, *Nem.* 7 and 8, *Isth.* 4.

[25] E.g., *Ol.* 3.44f. or *Pyth.* 3.59ff. Cf. also *Nem.* 8.35ff.; *Isth.* 7.39ff. Such passages are to be taken as exemplary expressions of communal values and not just as personal utterances. See in general Crotty, 128ff.

CHAPTER 7

dar's dominant emphasis, the immortalization of great deeds in a framework of mortal limitations and moral order.

III. CONTINUITY, DISCONTINUITY, DECONSTRUCTION

In *Pythian* 4, as we have seen, Pindar views his art as something potent, mysterious, and ambiguous. Its power and effect partake of both craft and inspiration, disguise and divine presence, guile and truth, seduction and persuasion, medicine as enchantment and medicine as true healing.[26] Thanks to the double-edged forces that control the heroes' success and therefore control also the movement of the plot, these tensions are never fully effaced. Yet Pindar suggests a more or less positive resolution, on the side of the divine, truthful, and healing power of language, both in public and in private. This power is one of the enabling assumptions of the ode, a kind of latent myth in its own right. But it is a power asserted always against the threat of its opposite: the darkness of blame and slander, artifice practiced without a sense of reverence or wonder, elegant tales that charm but lack the moral substance of what Pindar means by truth.

Over the clarification of poetry as truth rather than deception presides Apollo. His presence is the counterweight to Medea's. He is the Olympian source of the peculiar strength of language in the ode, of which the final proof is the poem's power to reconcile men. Pindar is himself the mortal vehicle of that power, sending his composition from Delphi and Thebes to Cyrene to re-unite the exiled Damophilus and King Arcesilaus. The victory over the dark and destructive power of language (falsehood,

[26] The importance of language, persuasion, and drugs is recognized, to a greater or lesser degree, in recent studies of the ode, e.g., the essays of Giannini (1979 and 1977-80), Robbins, Sandgren, Carey, and Gigante.

guile, slander) is confirmed in the closing movement from the obscure riddle-form of the "wisdom of Oedipus" to the "spring of ambrosial words" (262ff., 299).

This optimistic forward impetus, however, is halted by a discontinuous rhythm in which a vital element is lost and then re-emerges into light and life. Jason, hidden away in the darkness of night because of the evil and guile of Pelias (114f.), returns as a youth with "radiant" hair (82) and talks of the light of birth (144f.). Sent to "recover a soul" from Hades (cf. 159), he returns with the "radiant" Golden Fleece.[27]

Submersion and re-emergence characterize both the content and the form of the ode. The oracular beginning is appropriate to the ode's mode of narration. The convolutions of imbedded prophecies (4-63) create an obscurity and complexity of discourse that will gradually unfold into the sharp details of Pindar's developed narrative style. The ode begins with the ambiguity of female prophetic voices (the Pythia and Medea), gradually finds the Apolline voice of choral and epic clarity, and ends with Pindar's own bardic voice, which blends with the Homeric (cf. 277f.) in a combination of lucidity, divine authority (cf. 291), and friendly, Apolline healing (cf. 294). To neglect this movement is to ignore or misread the signposts that Pindar has placed along his road of song.

The oracular speech of the ode's opening corresponds to the lyric poet's privileged power of selecting and ordering events in a non-linear, non-epic fashion. It marks the distinctive quality of his mode of narration. He is not bound to a chronological sequence in telling his tales. His mythical narration is an exemplar rather than an end in itself. He may sketch a myth in four words, as he does the story

[27] The same adjective of radiance, *aglaoi, aglaen*, describes Jason's hair at his arrival at Iolcus and the successfully won fleece: 82 and 231.

CHAPTER 7

of the Titans (291), or tell it in two hundred lines, as he does the story of Jason. His form may be the expansive breadth of the Ionic frieze or the discrete paradigm of the Doric metope. He may imply the end in the beginning, may obscure one-directional development by reversible time, and may threaten to lose the present in the future, and vice versa. It is among the risks of the poet's journey, parallel to his hero's, that he may wander among the details of the moment and stray from the clarity of the total design.[28]

IV. AMBIGUITIES OF THE PROPHET: MEDEA AND APOLLO

In the first lines of *Pythian* 4 poetry appears as immediate and effective communication. Language here has the power to evoke presence. The poet's Muse, addressed in the second person, is to "stand beside" his friend, Arcesilaus, today.[29] "Today," *sameron*, is the ode's first word. It anchors us concretely in the present, a present which the ode creates each time that word is pronounced in reading or recitation, and thereby gives us a clear point of reference for the backward movements into the various strata of the past. At the same time this is a present which is gradually lost to view as the ode weaves its way through its deep spirals of the obscure past. The poet's own movement from today to the remote yesterday of his myths will be repeated by the main narrators within his story.[30]

---

[28] Ruck and Matheson, 17, remark on Pindar's "skill in obscuring the germinal unity of his theme beneath the baroque elegance of his ornamentation."

[29] A vivid "standing" is also the mark of the hero's energy, confidence, and willingness to take risks: so Jason "stands" in the agora of Iolcus in 84, and he and his kinsmen "take their stand" in the halls of Pelias in 135. In both cases too, communication is powerful and effective as Jason makes an important speech.

[30] *Ol.* 6. 22-28 has a similarly self-conscious movement (cf. *sameron*, 28), but without as much attention to different narrative voices. Even

POETRY AND IDEOLOGY

Medea tells a story in which past, present, and future are all strangely mingled. Jason, so much a figure of the vivid present in the brilliant flash of the moment (78ff.), recounts his remote ancestry (142ff.). In all three narratives the procedure is a model of the poet's own freedom in weaving together, in his own artfully chosen sequence, the disparate elements that form his total design. He rearranges chronological order so that he may convey his own vision of a unity and a structure that goes deeper than the succession of isolated events in mortal time.[31]

Pindar, in his own person, will allude to a story that takes us all the way back to the beginnings of the world-order, Zeus' reconciliation with the Titans (291), which is, in turn, the hopeful model for a future event, Arcesilaus' pardon of Damophilus. Pindar reinforces the immediacy of the present in his poetic discourse by evoking the specific celebration of the victory in the *kōmos* ("revel," 2b) at which his Muse is to stand (*stamen*, 2) beside his friend, the King. As elsewhere, the physical and spatial arrangements of the singer(s) in performance, the actuality of their standing in a particular place and at a particular time, evoke the concrete reality of the festive occasion of which the song is a part.[32]

The immediacy and specificity of this festive moment, however, begin to recede at once before the spatial distance of the metaphorical "wind of songs" that the Muse will "increase" (3). From standing we pass to travel, from land to sea and wind. The present opens out into a temporal distance too, signalled by *pote*, "once" (4). With this word we enter the past, the story of old prophecies that tell

---

here, however, we may note the movement from *legetai* (29) to Apollo's speech mediated by Delphic prophecy and then the call of Poseidon to Iamos in the dark river (61ff.)—all in a context of names, omens, and signs from the gods.

[31] For Pindar's rearrangement of the mythical chronology, see Hurst, 157-60 and 162f.; Van Groningen, 44f.; Walsh, 47.

[32] Cf. *Nem.* 1.19-22; *Ol.* 7.1ff.; *Isth.* 6.1ff.

CHAPTER 7

us of distant events but also bind those events meaningfully to the present moment. The oracular discourse is itself a microcosm of the recessive movement of narrative in the ode, for within the Pythia's prophecy to Battus at Delphi is embedded Medea's prophecy to the Argonauts pronounced on their voyage seventeen generations before (10).

In space as well as in time this opening scene of divinely sanctioned speech—Pindar's Muse and the oracles from the wise women—creates a polyphony of contrasting realms that the ode seeks to encompass and unify: the inner chamber of the Pythia and the golden statues outside on the roof, Delphi and distant Cyrene, the solid temple at the earth's navel and the ship tossed by the winds at sea, Arcesilaus' festive hall with his male companions and the whole "well-charioted city" poised atop its female "shining breast."

The Pythia tells Battus that he is to "bring back" (*ankomisai*, 9)—that is, realize or fulfil—the prophecy that Medea told the Argonauts during their heroic voyage. The transition from Muse to poet in the invocation is parallel to that from Apollo to the Pythian priestess who is his mouthpiece. This movement appears as the recessive play of language stressed by Farenga. But in the surface structure of the ode it is more prominently an act of recovery or recuperation (9), a renewal of communication with a lost past. The oracle is an *epos* (9) whose fulfilment includes not just a deferral (the seventeen generations between the Argonaut Euphamos and the founder of Cyrene, Battus) but also a "bringing back" or "recovering" (*ankomisai*). The active force of the verb treats the "word" (*epos*) of prophecy as something solid and tangible: it is an object capable of attainment, and hence it is parallel to the city which that word's recipient will found (7-9). *Epos* is also a common word for poetry in Pindar,[33] and thus may suggest too the divine sources of poetic inspiration (cf. the *ambrosia epea* at the end of the ode, 299). The concrete achievement implicit in this "recovering" is then extended later to heroic action, for Jason is to bring back or recover the soul of Phrixus (ψυχὰν κομίξαι, 159). And yet this "prize," a *psychē*, is of a singularly elusive, immaterial nature. Behind the heroic success, the poetry, and the prophecy, however, stand the assurance and permanence of the god at whose festival the victory has been won and in whose honor the ode is, in some sense, being performed.

The complexity of this ode, as of most of the Epinicia, lies in the fact that it invites reading from both the human and the divine perspective. It is both a bulwark against the fragile transience of "today" and a monument solid in the eternal time of the gods. The two perspectives are also inseparable from the duplicity (and dialectic) of language and the duplicity of Medea.

Medea is not an Apolline figure; yet, as we observed above, her prophecy is included in the pronouncement of Apollo's priestess to Battus. Medea's words too, like the Pythia's, have divine authority. The Pythia gives her prophecy (*chrēsen*, the *vox propria* for oracular utterance) when Apollo "happens not to be away from home" (5). Medea speaks as the inspired (*zamenēs*) child of Aeetes and she "breathed forth" her words from "immortal mouth" (ἀπέπνευσ' ἀθανάτου στόματος). The verb suggests divine inspiration.[34] The adjective *athanatos*, "immortal," clearly associates Medea with the divine: her mouth, partaking of immortality, is the organ of messages

---

[33] See Gianotti, 86, citing H. Koller, "Epos," *Glotta* 50 (1972) 19f.

[34] Cf. Aesch. *Ag.* 1178-83; see Péron, 178. Méautis, 208f., also insists on the connotations of inspired prophecy in *zamenēs* ("plein d'une force prophétique," p. 209), but the word has a broader meaning: see below, note 36.

CHAPTER 7

from the gods.[35] Yet both her patronymic and the epithet *zamenēs* are potentially ominous.[36] Her addressees are the "semi-divine (*hēmitheoi*) sailors of Jason the spearman," and she calls them by the honorific epithet, "children of high-spirited mortals and of gods" (13). This remoter oracle, then, belongs to a time when the human world stands in close connection with the divine and is permeated by attributes of divinity.

When Medea finishes her prophecy, however, what these godlike heroes "hear" is not divine knowledge but something which sounds distinctly mortal. This is her "dense craft," and for a personage as ambiguous as Medea the phrase has a potentially ominous ring (*pukinan mētin kluontes*, 58; cf. *keklute*, "hear," 13). It is necessary to cite this passage at length:

> *So spoke the marshalled lines of Medea's words, and the godlike heroes crouched unmoving, in silence, hearing her dense craft. O blessed son of Polymnastus, in this account did the oracle of the Delphic bee-woman*

---

[35] For the problem of the epithet, see Farnell, ad loc., who suggests that she is so called because she is "inspired by a god" or because her words have a quality of immortality. Wilamowitz, p. 387, note 2, is much troubled by the word and inclines toward the notion of Medea's eventual divinity, as in Hesiod, *Theogony* 992.

[36] Note that the epithet *zamenēs* is also used of Chiron addressing Apollo in *Pyth.* 9.41 in a context that has much in common with the Medea passage of *Pyth.* 4, including the theme of *mētis* (see below, chap. 9, sec. II). In both cases the epithet marks a supernatural power enframed within the Olympian wisdom of Apollo: cf. *Pyth.* 9.42ff. and Woodbury (1972) 566. Elsewhere, however, *zamenēs* has associations of elemental forces: sun in *Nem.* 4.13; wind in *Pae.* 8.63f.; daring (*tolma*) in frag. 231 Sn. It is also used of Memnon, Achilles' foe, in *Nem.* 3.63 and of Silenus (frag. 156 Sn.). Of the four living beings described by the adjective, then, one is a centaur, one a silenus, and two are barbarians. The adjective has distinctly hostile or ominous connotations in *h. Merc.* 307 and Sophocles, *Ajax* 137. Medea's patronymic, "child of Aeetes," may also look toward Jason's success, as her loss of "respect toward her parents" (218) places her on Jason's side in helping him to defeat her father, King Aeetes.

> *raise you up straight with her spontaneous shout, she who, thrice crying out, "Hail," revealed you as Cyrene's destined king when you came to inquire what recompense there will be from the gods for your misspeaking voice. Afterwards and now too Arcesilaus blooms as the eighth part among his descendants, as at the peak of crimson-flowered springtime. To him Apollo and Pytho granted the glory of the horse-race from the Amphictyons. Him shall I give over to the Muses, along with the all-gold fleece of the ram, for when the Minyans sailed in quest of that prize, god-sent honors were planted for them.   (57-69)*

These lines reiterate the earlier movement of loss and recovery that was itself a basic constituent of oracular speech (5-12). The heroes addressed by a mortal woman "hear the dense craft" of her magical words, just as the audience hears the magical spell of Pindar's verses.[37] Both are encompassed in a discourse that combines divine inspiration with *mētis*.[38] But that human distance from divine discourse is at once recuperated in the multiple potency of divine presence in language.[39] As at the beginning, Medea's prophecy to the Argonauts and Apollo's oracular words to Battus are inseparably linked. Medea's *epea* are at once followed by a *chrēsmos* that has the active power of

---

[37] The model here is the poetic enchantment exercised by bards like Phemius (*Od.* 1.337-40). Farenga seems to have such a passage in mind when he compares the Argonauts' silence to the enchantment of Odysseus' men by Circe (p. 14); but in fact Odysseus' men are not "transfixed" or "enchanted" in this way. Eurylochus is speechless (*Od.* 10.210ff.), but only on his *return* from Circe. The speechlessness, moreover, is due to his personal grief, not to her magic (10.246-48). I cannot agree with Farenga's interpretation of this passage as signifying "the text's own rejection of what it, through Medea, has just presented: the mythic hypothesis of Cyrene's Argonaut origins" (14).

[38] For *mētis* as poetic craft, see *Ol.* 1.9 and 31; *Ol.* 13.50; *Nem.* 3.9. See in general Giannini (1979) 62.

[39] See the remark above on *epos* in line 9 (note 33).

CHAPTER 7

"raising up" and "revealing" (60, 62) through its "spontaneous sound" (*automatos kelados*, 60).

This second version of the prophecy adds a new emphasis on speech and language. Pindar thereby instructs us, again (cf. 9), to view the ambiguity of Medea's speech and prophecy against its Apolline background. This insistence shows him at his work of mythopoiesis, constructing his underlying *mythos* of the Apolline power of poetry and counteracting Medea's ambiguous "dense craft" by Apolline wisdom and Olympian purpose.

In the first strophe the Pythia "prophesied Battus as the founder of fruit-bearing Libya" (4-6). He is to leave (*lipōn*, 7) his own "sacred island," Thera, to "found" the new city and thereby "recover Medea's word" uttered seventeen generations before on the Argo. That combination of loss and regain, "leaving" and "recovery," in the first oracle is now restated in the second, but focussed more strongly on language. The first oracle made no mention of Battus' stammer. The initiative of the Delphic visit and what is said there seems to come entirely from the god (5f.; cf. also 53-56). When the oracle recurs in 59ff., we are given more details of the meeting between Battus and the Pythia, including her thrice-repeated greeting; and we are told that his purpose in approaching the god is to restore his maimed speech to full utterance. This added detail interweaves the heroic content of the myth, the founding of cities, with its poetic medium, the power of language.

In the potency of divine and oracular language the Pythia's address both reports and enacts the recovery of full speech. It does so both literally and figuratively and on the axes of both metonymy and metaphor. It is a literal "recompense" to Battus because it directly answers his request to heal the "misspeaking voice" of his stammer with a cry free of his impediment: her "spontaneous shout" bodes well for his own speaking. It is a figurative recompense because the oracle functions by metonymy for the lost land that replaces both Battus' lost voice and his ancestor's lost clod.

The scene at Delphi uses the mode of speech as a metaphor for the more difficult problem of the human voice speaking to or about the gods. For this brief moment the great heroic exploits told in the ode rest on a seemingly trivial matter of vocal articulation, producing *phōna* rather than *logos* (*dysthroou phōnas*, "ill-speaking voice," 63; *logōi*, "account," "tale," 59). The deficiencies and retardation of the flawed mortal stutter are made good by the "spontaneous utterance" of the divine speech of the Pythia that "raises up" the inquirer (60). The immediate juxtaposition of *logos*, "tale," and *chrēsmos*, "oracle," in 59f. calls attention to the interlocking of divine and human speech. The divine "prophecy" raises up the stutterer in both his "speech" (cf. 63) and in his "tale" (*logos*, 59).

Farenga rightly points out the ambiguities of oracular speech as a "disembodied, hidden voice transmitted through a patently false addresser (priestess or sibyl) in a notoriously problematic 'code' and self-conscious 'message' " (p. 13). But Pindar, as a poet of truth, knows how to discipline and master this code, how to operate within the ambiguities of such problematic utterances, and how to constitute a realm of truth as the other, divine side of this "disembodied, hidden voice." Before we de-construct Pindar's system of making truth in poetry (that is, of creating a myth which enables him to regard language as a locus of truth), we have to see how he con-structs that system. On the other hand, this very self-consciousness of the construction of meaning in a poetry of "truth" and "presence" leaves open the way to the negative hermeneutic discussed above. The poet has the power to impose his coherence upon the world, to remake reality in accordance with his own vision. But in so doing he is also forced to confront

CHAPTER 7

the artificiality of what he constructs. This is the artifice of superimposing the order of literary discourse upon the non-order of life.

Thus, to turn back from poetic to cosmogonic order, the myth of Zeus pardoning the Titans in 291 implies that the Olympian order is fixed and stable. It is a firm reference point for the poetic celebration of power exercised with compassion, and the mortal analogue is Arcesilaus forgiving the humbled and repentant rebel, Damophilus. The brief mythical allusion, however, also recalls the cosmogonic struggle between the Olympians and their predecessors, which culminates in the victory of the former and the imprisonment or immobilization of the latter in Tartarus (see Hesiod, *Theogony* 617-745). The firm and apparently timeless realm of Olympian Zeus, in other words, has an origin. Behind the present unity lies a primal division in the divine authority, behind order lies disorder, behind surface stability lies conflictual process.

Characteristically Pindar views this event from the retrospective vantage point of an already achieved victory, not from the precarious point of involvement in present effort and battle, like Hesiod in the *Theogony*. This perspective of achieved harmony closely parallels the perspective on Medea. The potentially disruptive force of the Other, the chaotic adversary, is seen only when its disruptive force has been neutralized and made into a part of the established Olympian order. Thus the Titans are already incorporated into the reign of Zeus, and their one function now in the ode is to illustrate its clemency. Likewise Medea exercises her magical power, as we have seen, only in close association with the Apolline prophecy of the Pythian priestess and only after she has already been removed from dangerous Colchis and made a part of the heroic expedition. She is thus co-opted into its purpose of founding a colony; and her voice is co-opted, alongside that of the Muse and the Pythia, into the ode's purpose of celebrating

POETRY AND IDEOLOGY

that founding act and the other male achievements which flow from it, including the present victory of the founder's descendant.

V. AMBIGUITIES OF THE KING: BATTUS AND OEDIPUS

The tale of Battus at Delphi has behind it another mythical construction. The "straightening up" of a man maimed in his voice is thematically parallel to the straightening of a man maimed in the foot. Behind the *logos* of Battus stands the mythical model of the life of the tyrant, a lamed king of remarkable prosperity but of unstable abode (homelessness, wandering, the quest) who may be restored to health and kingdom but who also, like Oedipus, has the dangerous qualities of excessive power, isolation, and marginality.[40]

For Battus, as for Oedipus, the mysterious deformity carries the risk of a destabilizing asymmetry for the social and natural orders. Both heroes are led to their throne by an oracle from Delphi. But Battus is almost the reverse of Oedipus. Instead of usurping power by an act of violence as *tyrannos*, he possesses the kingship as legitimate *basileus*.[41] Instead of being brought low from high places by irrational chance and divine malevolence, he is "set upright" by miraculous intervention from the gods.[42] Apollo is now the helper, not the destroyer. In Sophocles the god

[40] See J.-P. Vernant, "From Oedipus to Periander: Lameness, Tyranny, Incest in Legend and History," *Arethusa* 15 (1982) 19-38.

[41] Oedipus, of course, is also the legitimate *basileus* (tragically), but he does not know this until he has moved beyond the limits acceptable for the king. Oedipus' status as *basileus* is ambiguous and ironic in a way that Battus' never is. Arcesilaus, be it noted, is emphatically *basileus*, not *tyrannos* (*Pyth.* 4.2; cf. 62, 166, 229); see Bowra, *Pindar*, 137-39 and Méautis, 221f. Cf. also *Pyth.* 5.15f., 97; see above, chap. 2, note 19.

[42] One recalls, for example, the recurrent imagery of standing or setting "upright" (*orthos*) in Sophocles' *Oedipus Tyrannus*, where the implications extend also from the personal life of the King to the political, natural, and supernatural realms.

CHAPTER 7

exposes the anomaly of the tyrant, set apart by his mark on tongue or foot, "at once elect and cursed."[43] In Pindar the god "reveals a destined king" (61f.). Instead of a precarious succession, as limping as his gait or his stutter, this ruler, "blessed" in happiness (59), will found a continuity of generations whose regularity corresponds to the rhythmical order of nature and the stability of seasonal growth and agriculture (64f.).

Jason's winning a kingdom through upright action is also symmetrical with the felicitous correction of Battus' maimed speech. The "single-based" gait of Jason's one sandal (τὸν μονοκρήπιδα, 75) is structurally parallel to the deformity of King Oedipus' foot and King Battus' tongue. To Pelias (thanks to the warning oracle from Delphi) it signifies an anomalous walker whom he must fear. Jason, like Oedipus, returns to his native land with something peculiar about his feet; and in both cases Delphi looms large in the background. But in Jason's story the conflict with the Father is deflected into a legitimate direction, and the struggle between father and son is played out far from the narrow domestic world of Oedipal Thebes and with third-party surrogates for the father. Unlike Oedipus too, Jason is openly welcomed by a real father who rejoices in his mature beauty (120-23). This youthful hero's aggressive energies can be directed outward to lawful enemies, and he can make a marriage which is the very epitome of exogamous union. For both Jason and Battus the physical anomaly is turned by Delphi from a defect to an advantage. The Pythian priestess "straightens up" Battus' crooked speech (59-63). For Jason the old oracle validates the upright speech and manners of his education that will enable him to overcome Pelias' deviousness. In the verbal duel between them, Pelias uses "concealment" (96),

[43] Vernant, "From Oedipus to Periander," 33.

POETRY AND IDEOLOGY

whereas Jason "has done no deed or spoken no word out of the way" (*epos ektrapelon*, 105), a metaphor that unites straightness of speech with straightness of walk.

Whereas tragedy focusses on the asymmetries in the tyrant's situation and the resultant violence,[44] Pindar's choral lyric establishes a hierarchical framework that alleviates his remote position through a series of parallel mediations between human and divine. He places the king/victor/hero's superlative and therefore exposed exaltation (like the sun in the empty sky of *Ol.* 1.6) into a communal context that disarms the danger (cf. *Ol.* 1.97ff., 113ff.). The ode implicitly transforms the unique and the anomalous (like Jason's single sandal) into a set of moral alternatives that restores excessive wealth or extraordinary success to the norms and constraints of other men, both as citizens and as mortal beings. Binary mythical paradigms (e.g., Croesus versus Phalaris at the end of *Pythian* 1) guide the king to the side of order, harmony, and law.[45]

Battus is the subject of a "tale" and of an "oracle," of a poem by Pindar and of an oracle "by" Apollo. In both cases speech is itself the object of concern, and in both cases the efficacy of the divine word manifests itself in the renewed power of human speech. Battus himself seems to break clear of his handicap in the direct question, "What recompense will there be from the gods?" (ποινὰ τίς ἔσται πρὸς θεῶν, 63). So Pindar too breaks free of the "dense craft" of Medea's embedded prophecy when he moves from this complicated speech-within-speech to a direct second-person address to Battus: "You, O blessed son of Polymnastus, in this account (*logos*) did an oracle of the Delphic bee-woman, with shout spontaneous, raise up . . .":

[44] See my *Tragedy and Civilization*, 239.
[45] Cf. *Pyth.* 1. 10ff., 94ff.; *Ol.* 1.55-100. See Crotty, 128-30, for some good remarks on the treatment of godlike happiness in Pindar's myths.

CHAPTER 7

ὦ μάκαρ υἱὲ Πολυμνάστου, σὲ δ' ἐν τούτῳ λόγῳ
χρησμὸς ὤρθωσεν μελίσσας
Δελφίδος αὐτομάτῳ κελάδῳ . . . (59f.)

The resolution of verbal intricacy, from "dense craft" (58) to clarity on the level of style as well as of plot, paradigmatically lifts Pindar's own poetry closer to the penetrating communication of divine speech.

In the Pythia's first oracle the divinely sent *logos* contains its own deferral: the distance between the gods' *telos* and its mortal realization. The eight generations between Battus and Arcesilaus (65) parallel the delay of seventeen generations between Medea's word to the Argonauts and the Pythia/Apollo's speech to Battus (10). The eight generations, however, stand more directly under Delphic sanction. These form a continuity in time rather than an empty gap: this is a period solidly filled by the succession of Battiad kings. As the seasonal imagery of 64-65 implies, the generations are more firmly on land in every sense: the oracle is given in a temple (55) not on a ship; and the interval is filled by the continuous succession of rulers already ensconced in Libya and not (in part) still wandering over the seas.

At their point of juncture Medea's and the Pythia's prophecies are carefully dovetailed (53-56, 60-67); and the juxtaposition of "Pythian" and "Nile," "shrine" and "ships" in consecutive lines reinforces the connections (ναόν, νάεσσι, 55f.). Thus the divine voice, though transmitted through such different vehicles, appears as unified and continuous. Through the archaic ring-form (cf. 9 and 57, 6 and 60) the narrative device of repetition recovers the distance that the prophecies marked as postponement. Here, as often in Pindar, oracular speech functions as the sign of positive mediation between man and god. It parallels the discourse of the poet which, like prophecy, links

POETRY AND IDEOLOGY

the remote past with the present and the future. As the sign of genuine communication with the divine, oracles are a model for Pindar as poet, for the poet is also a "prophet of the Muses" (frag. 150 Sn. = 137 Bo.).

Medea's prophecy on the *Argo* is "breathed forth" "from immortal mouth" (11). Pindar's song is compared to a favoring wind at sea that is a gift of the Muse (3). As *epeōn stiches*, "ranks of words," and *pukina mētis*, "dense craft" (57f.), her oracle veers between the ethereal and the solid, between divine counsel and the guile that one expects from a barbarian enchantress.[46] Divine utterance has still another form, the Pythia's spontaneous shout (*automatos kelados*, 60b) by which Apollo makes good Battus' speech defect (60-63). Each of these acts of speech holds the threat of failure. Apollo might not "chance to be at home" when the Pythia answers Battus (5). The potent "mistress of the Colchians" might be practicing her "dense craft" for her own, not Apollo's, ends. Battus might receive no recompense for his stuttering.

The verbs "straighten up" and "reveal" here (*ōrthōsen*, *amphanen*, 60, 62) characterize the positive side of Pindar's poetry. Their opposite is the crookedness and darkness of a poetry of blame, falsehood, and deception.[47] Poetry is situated, potentially, between Medea and Apollo, between "dense craft" and "spontaneous shout," between

---

[46] The scholion, ad loc. (100a), paraphrases: "Hearing the dense (*pukinēn*) and solemn (*semnēn*) counsel of Medea," rather understating the ambiguity of Medea's *mētis*. Similarly Puech in the Budé translation, "en recueillant ses profondes pensées." Lattimore's "hearing the depth of her brooding thought" comes closer to the hint of danger in *mētis*. Duchemin, *Pythiques*, ad loc., rather blandly paraphrases *pukinan mētin* as "(l'expression d') une profonde sagesse," although she notes the parallel with the more sinister *pukinos thumos* of Pelias in 73. See above, chap. 1, note 7.

[47] E.g., *Nem.* 7.20ff.; *Nem.* 8.32ff.; cf. Bacchyl. 13.199ff. See above, chap. 1.

CHAPTER 7

dangerous, powerful, and potentially seductive "wiles" and the "upright," straightening effect of the chaste bee-woman at the holy center of the civilized world. By placing the "dense craft" of Medea's prophecy in the context of Apolline prophecy and its power to heal the broken voice of Battus, Pindar implies the efficacy of his own discourse as a poetry of truth, a poetry that overcomes human guile and dangerous blindness about the gods.

VI. COMMUNICATION WITH GODS: LOSS AND RECOVERY

The ode operates through a series of mysterious messages from the gods or from their surrogates, the Pythia and Medea.[48] The remotest and obscurest of these, the oracle about the clod of earth, is also the most tangible and certain affirmation of the potency of language, for the clod functions both as a metaphor and a metonymy. As the "seed of wide-dancing Libya" (42f.), the clod has a metaphorical association with the processes of fecundity, birth, and growth. As a piece of earth that contains in its part the whole of the future Cyrenaic land-mass, it has a metonymic contiguity with the earth that Arcesilaus is to rule. In Pindar's world the relation between signifier (clod) and signified (land of Cyrene) rests on a god-given (or, as Pindar might say, god-planted) coherence. It is a world of living, efficacious symbols. The further back one goes, the closer one is to the primordial creative power of first origins. The poet taps and continues the energies of first beginnings and first discoveries: the "seed" of Libya, the birth of Jason, Orpheus as "father of songs," the first creation of the iynx.

That moment of origins has been lost. The clod of earth, pressed from the hand of god to the hand of a mortal (37),

[48] See above, chap. 2, sec. II.

POETRY AND IDEOLOGY

is washed away into the sea (34-40). But even the loss is reported in the context of future recuperation. It is the task of the poet, as of the hero, to recover this lost point of contact with the divine. That moment of "receiving" from hand to hand (21-23, 34-37), like the touch between God the Creator and Adam in Michelangelo's Sistine fresco, remains alive throughout the poem as the model of mortal men touching the "imperishable" substance of the gods and of creation (*aphthiton . . . sperma*, 42f.). It is also a mythical model for the efficacy of poetic speech as the verbal mediation between humanity and divinity.

With our final movement back to the clod of earth in the remotest origins of Cyrene we are in a realm of signifiers which, for all their arbitrariness and fragility, remain potent with meaning. Medea's tale of the clod washed overboard as the dusk gathers around the solitary ship in its unknown ocean (38-40) conveys the precariousness of this contact with divinity. This loss of the god's gift is a failed version of a scene that has a more successful outcome in the stories of Pelops and Iamus in *Olympians* 1 and 6.[49] But the clod is not, ultimately, lost; the attainment of what it both contains and signifies is only postponed. In the clod metonymy and metaphor, the axis of contiguity and the axis of selection, are superimposed.[50] The structure of the ode is fulfilled (metonymically) and anticipated (metaphorically) in the overlapping of the clod's journey *to* Cyrene and the clod's identification *with* Cyrene.

The journey of the clod/seed from Lake Tritonis to Cyrene both makes manifest and mediates the distance be-

---

[49] *Ol.* 1.71ff.; *Ol.* 6. 57ff.

[50] I am utilizing here the terminology of Roman Jakobson, e.g., the celebrated formulation, "The poetic function projects the principle of equivalence from the axis of selection into the axis of combination" ("Linguistic and Poetics," 1960, in R. and F. DeGeorge, *The Structuralists* [Garden City, N.Y. 1972], 95).

CHAPTER 7

tween man and god. This spatial dimension of this passage has its temporal equivalent in the many generations between Euphamos, who lost the clod, and Battus who founded Cyrene. For the founding heroes time is measured by generations, by the mortal succession of fathers who beget sons who beget other sons. The poem, however, spans the gap of generations by its selective focus on prophecy. It thus transforms the emptiness of loss into the expectation of fulfilment, separation into mediation. Yet even as it does so, the ode marks the continuing distance from the past and from origins that is the condition of mortal life.

Time in the ode exists to be filled, to become part of a pattern of meaningful events. This is time in the eyes of the gods.[51] Its long vision takes in continuity, whereas mortals see only failure or delay. In the eyes of men, time remains the journey outward, the leaving of home, the loss of moments never to be recovered, the slipping away of a precious object into distant seas. Pindar's concern is to reveal mortal events in the perspective of the time of the gods; but the vision of immortal things takes place, necessarily, from the mortal perspective of painful effort, changeful passage, and loss.

[51] For this notion of time in Pindar, see Vivante, "On Time in Pindar," and Segal, "Time and the Hero"; also below, chap. 10.

8. Pindar's Post-Oral Poetics: Between Inspiration and Textuality

I. *PNEUMA* AND *GRAMMATA*

IN Medea's prophecy, as in all prophecy in Pindar, the power of language both indicates and fills the gap between origin and loss. It is, therefore, fundamentally ambiguous. It reveals what the divine will holds in store for mortals; but it also calls attention to the obscurity that veils those purposes as men try to understand them.

Medea's speech begins as a "pneumatological" voice, conveying the full force of divine presence and divine will. It then re-emerges as "grammatological" in the "ranks" of her utterances, which, while not explicitly meaning "verses," can imply the linear form of written words.[1] As such, these words are no longer the pure vehicle of divine wisdom, but bear the mark of their human instrumentality and poetic textuality, "dense craft" (58).

The pneumatological voice comes from the god, Muse or Apollo, who "breathes into" the mortal the supernatural power and knowledge that mark poetry as a privileged mode of access to the divine and the eternal.[2] The origins of this poetry are hidden in mystery, as Hesiod's Muses are veiled in mist (*Theogony* 9f.).[3] The "grammatological"

---

[1] For *pneumatological* and *grammatological*, see Jacques Derrida, *Of Grammatology*, trans. G. C. Spivak (Baltimore 1976), 11ff., especially 17.

[2] For the god's "breathing" the power of poetry into the singer, see Homer, *Odyssey* 22.347f.; Hesiod, *Theogony* 31. For a useful (if uncritical) survey of the divinity of poetry in early Greece, see Alice Sperduti, "The Divine Nature of Poetry in Antiquity," *TAPA* 81 (1950) 209-40, especially 224-33 on Homer and Hesiod and 233-37 on Pindar.

[3] As the origin of the divine gift of poetry is mysterious, so too its disappearance is mysterious: cf. the Muses' making Thamyris forget the divine song (*aoidē thespesiē*) in *Iliad* 2.594-600. For the reversibility of such divine gifts, cf. Aphrodite's threat to Helen in *Iliad* 3.414-17.

CHAPTER 8

voice, however, has a visible origin: it is defined by the human artifact by which it is recorded and preserved, as a text. Such poetry is a product, a creation of human device (*mētis*). The moment of its beginnings is known and perceptible. Viewed as a man's design or plan rather than a god's gift, such a work is less dependent for its realization on the poet's inspired presence. As a text, it can speak for itself (although, as Plato objects in a famous passage of the *Phaedrus*, it cannot answer back in self-defence); and it can dispense with the authority of the scepter-bearing bard whose god-sent inspiration is necessary to bring it to life in the oral performance. It can be fully effective as a text, a material thing that can be shipped overseas like any other piece of merchandise (*Pyth.* 2.67f.).[4] Pindar's vacillation between poet as craftsman and poet as inspired, untaught prophet reflects this transitional moment of his historical position. This issue, I suggest, is also reflected in his treatment of Medea's prophecy in *Pythian* 4.

Initially a hieratic voice, "breathed out of an immortal mouth," Medea's prophecy later appears as part of a graphic (or proto-graphic) space, the "ranks of speech" (*epeōn stiches*). The metaphor gives Medea's speech the spatial extension of a solid, visible object, even more concrete than the arrow-like "winged words" of Homer. Hence these ranks of words "speak forth" in the epic formula that regularly marks the end of a person's vocal utterance in direct discourse (ἥ ῥα Μηδείας ἐπέων στίχες, "So spoke the ranks of Medea's words," 57).[5]

---

[4] For an elaboration of some of these points, see my "Greek Tragedy: Truth, Writing, . . . Self," 44ff.

[5] This passage has been much discussed: most commentators believe that the *stiches* imply an oracle in hexameters: see Wilamowitz, p. 387, note 2; Farnell, ad loc. (2.153); Sandgren, 21; Schroeder, *Pindars Pythien*, 35; Duchemin, *Pythiques*, ad 57. The implication of "verses," however, here also carries with it the graphic space of their linear form. See also Cook, 128, for implications of fluid movement balanced by fixity in the

INSPIRATION AND TEXTUALITY

Medea's oracular voice at this point is the bearer of the divisions in the poetic voice generally, between Muse and mortal, message and vehicle, the unity of its truth and the daedalic multiplicity of its possible deceptions.[6] Her *logos* ultimately brings divine presence to mortals, but only through a long wandering and the detour of many generations. The divinely ordained implantation of the "immortal seed" of Libya risks dispersive dissemination in the chance landfall among dangerous women (cf. 50 and 254). Style and content work closely together to create a correspondence between the obscurity and discontinuity of Medea's oracular narrative and the postponements and discontinuities that attend the founding of Cyrene. At every point mortal action and mortal language are strung between revealing and obscuring the presence of the divine will or Being. On the level of language, the (grammatological) duplicity of *mētis* is the medium for the unitary, immortal, pneumatological voice of the gods.

The unusual distances that the text and/or poet (like his Argonaut hero) have to traverse and the unusual length of the ode may have led Pindar to a deeper than usual consideration of his work's double status, as embodied in Me-

---

form. Later in the ode *stiches* refer to the hostile forces of wild nature, "the ranks of heavy-roaring winds" around the Symplegades (210). Perhaps with this usage of the word in mind Bowra, 216, suggests that the phrase "can only mean something like 'Medea's words filed past.' " Although archaic poets could write their poetry without separation into verses, the disposition into the "ranks" of separate lines is common usage by the sixth century, as the funeral and other commemorative epigrams show. As early as the Ischia cup at the end of the eighth century verses are written as separate "lines": see Lillian Jeffery, *The Local Scripts of Archaic Greece* (Oxford 1961), plate 47. Although verse-by-verse division is rare for early archaic poetry (Jeffery, 236), it becomes common around 500 B.C.: cf. plate 4, numbers 32, 37, 43.

[6] Cf. *Ol.* 1.29ff. and on *poikilia* there, with its notions of shifting movement, multiplicity, reversibility, and tricky adaptability that it contains, as opposed to unity, simplicity, and stability, see Vernant and Detienne, *Cunning Intelligence*, passim, especially 18-23.

CHAPTER 8

dea / *mētis*, and therefore of its textuality. The ode, like the prophecy that organizes its dynamic movement between past and present, is quasi-oracular, inspired phonic utterance; but it is also "verses" that occupy the graphic space of ordered lines (*epeōn stiches*, 57), written down and sent overseas as a tangible product of "dense craft."⁷

In this awareness of his ode's textuality, Pindar is no longer a purely oral poet whose work takes place and is exhausted in the moment of the performance. Instead he views himself as the composer of a text which will make the passage overseas and will be recited (probably by others) at the court of a far-off monarch. The emphasis on inspiration, the Muse, direct utterance, and his presence "today" is a myth which overlays the self-conscious human artifice that crafts a tangible object that can be transported from one place to another and then re-created (from the presumably written text) as choral performance in the new locale.⁸

This conception of poetry as the crafting of an intricate art-work or tangible object emerges into greater prominence with increasing literacy. As poets make greater use of writing, if only to record and fix an orally composed work, they become more conscious of the textuality of what they have produced, the solidity and tangibility of something that can be seen as well as heard, an *ergon*, *agalma*, *daidalma*, like a statue (cf. *Nem.* 5.1ff.). The proc-

⁷ With the "ranks of words" in our ode contrast the "breeze of words" in *Nem.* 6.28b, (οὖρον ἐπέων), where, however, the poets are also "plowmen for the Pierian (Muses)" (32b) as well as sailors (32).

⁸ For the awareness of textuality in Pindar and other late archaic poets, see Jesper Svenbro, *La parole et le marbre* (Lund 1976), 186ff.; also Segal, "Greek Tragedy: Truth, Writing, ... Self," passim. It is not certain whether Pindar was actually present at his ode's performance in Cyrene, as has been argued by Chamoux, 175-79 and 185f., followed by Méautis, 216. For a more sceptical view, see Burton, 135, 145f.; Farnell, 1.367 and 2.168; Puech, ad *Pyth.* 5.87 (p. 96, note 1).

ess of recording orally composed texts in writing had been going on in Greece for at least two centuries before Pindar, but its implications for the conception of poetry begin to make themselves felt more forcefully around this time.[9] In the next generation Hecataeus, Thucydides, and Gorgias will refer to themselves explicitly as writers, *sungrapheis* or *grapheis*.[10]

Instead of the immediacy of presence in the oral performance, where the poet's living voice is a guarantor of truth and a token of authority, the poet of a written text is forced to confront the secondary set of symbols that he is utilizing. His artifice of language is raised to a second degree by the art and artifice of writing.[11] To a far greater degree than the oral poet, the text-poet who claims that his discourse is the pure phonic utterance of the Muse or the gods is conscious of the artfulness behind his claim and of the play of differences and deferrals that this artfulness contains. That distance from the unity of Being or from the divine presence is marked by the graphic space in which the voice now does its ambiguous speaking. The professional craftsman knows about the letters of a written text behind the apparently spontaneous phonic utterances, be they of Muse or of Pythian priestess. The poet is no longer the mouthpiece of the gods in any simple way; he is the producer of a text, with all the craft and multiplicity (*mētis, poikilia*) implied in that activity.

Medea's *mētis* on the open sea, however, is neutralized by the direct phonic utterances of the Pythia, of the Muse, and of the poet. All of these stand in direct or symbolical

[9] See the remarks on Theagenes of Rhegium on Homer in Detienne, *L'invention de la mythologie*, 129ff.; my remarks on *Ol.* 10 in *Poétique* 50.141f.

[10] Thuc. 1.1; Gorgias, *Helen* 21; Hecataeus frag. 4F1a Jacoby. See Detienne, *L'invention de la mythologie*, 134ff.

[11] See my remarks in *Poétique* 50. 131-54, especially 140ff.

CHAPTER 8

contact with the sacred Delphic earth and with the quasi-sacred place of the victory celebration (cf. 1-6). The directness of utterance that flows from Muse or divine inspiration is part of the myth of presence that Pindar uses (cf. the "spontaneous shout," *automatos kelados*, of the Pythia in 60b).

This phonic presence is no longer a given condition of the performance, as it is for the oral poet, but is something to be evoked and created as a mythical construct in both the frame and the narrative itself. This mythical construction is not just a fiction, an individual, ad hoc invention, as in a modern novel or poem. It rests, rather, on a long tradition of conceiving the contact between human and divine realms through the personal mediating presence of Muses and prophets. Pindar, however, self-consciously reconstitutes his text as both the oral, phonic truth of poetry and inspired, spontaneous utterance. He thereby exhibits the first, tentative stage of a grammatological mentality. The opening address to the Muse makes this evocation of voice a pre-condition of the ode. But the phonic presence is also created within the ode as the poet's equivalent to the goal of the heroic quest.

Pindar tentatively opens the gap between the invisible but immortal breath of Medea's inspired voice in 11 and the "marshalled lines" of dense craft in 57-58. This gap arises from the potential contradiction between Medea as spokesman of the gods, equivalent in function to the Pythian priestess, and Medea as the center of ambiguous behavior involving seduction, drugs, and craft.[12] Pindar opens that gap only to close it again in the assurances of

---

[12] This gap might be described in the Derridean terms of the "differance/deferral" between language and the presence that it seeks to re-create, the distance between the word and its re-presented object or as the (disguised) play of differences between the signifier and the signified that constitutes the "proto-writing" of language.

INSPIRATION AND TEXTUALITY

divine presence given in the account of the Pythia's welcome of Battus at Delphi. This movement of closure assumes a number of parallel or analogous forms in the ode: a movement from sea to land, from seduction to fertile marriage, from crafty to ambrosial verses (57f. and 299), from poetry as drug to poetry as healing medicine.

This proto-grammatological attitude arises at the end of the oral tradition, in which it still claims a place; but it can no longer ignore the medium of writing which makes possible its distinctive artistry and its heightened sense of its own complexity. Pindar's truth remains, ultimately, phonic and pneumatological; but it no longer exists in the innocence of *grammata*, letters.[13] Pindar may look back with nostalgia to the relative clarity of truth in the epic tradition, the "guileless art" or the "simple roads of life" that he so eagerly claims (*Ol*. 7.53; *Nem*. 8.35ff.). But he knows that his poetry is set apart from that of others and needs interpreters (*Ol*. 2. 85f.) for its "denser" weave. He knows too that the quasi-sacred solemnity (*semnon*) of Homer's bardic authority and his "winged device" may countenance lies (*Nem*. 7.21-25). Yet his own words' direct, "winged" flight to their recipient also depends on just such device or resource (*ema machana, Pyth*. 8.32-34). In his post-pneumatological consciousness, he also knows that *mythoi* are not just univocal vehicles to what the gods really are, but multiple, variegated, artful "tales" in which truth must be carefully and painfully separated from falsehood.[14] Pindar recognizes this human, gramma-

[13] See the beginning of *Ol*. 10, discussed in *Poétique* 50.141f., supra. On writing in *Pyth*. 4, but with an emphasis different from mine, see Farenga, 22ff.

[14] *Ol*. 1.29ff. For the criticism of variant versions of myth as a mark of the more critical mentality that accompanies writing, see J. Goody and I. Watt, "The Consequences of Literacy," in J. Goody, ed., *Literacy in Traditional Societies* (Cambridge 1968), 27-68, especially 44ff.; also Detienne, *L'invention*, 106ff., 134ff.

CHAPTER 8

tological dimension of artifice, craft, and guile, but can still insist on its proximity to the divine. His (and Medea's) craft of song can still give access to a divine grace or favor (*charis*), through which it overcomes the divisions, multiplicities, and distancings of its mortal origins.

For the poet's overcoming of craft by truth there are two major narrative analogues in the ode. First, the clod is a perishable seed delayed by mortal forgetfulness, *lēthē*, a term that also implies the darkness of oblivion that the immortalizing memory of poetry struggles to vanquish.[15] United with its destined Libyan earth, the seed will ripen to fruition and become part of a divine gift to the Battiads, a gift which includes the glory that the poet keeps alive in song (cf. 67-69 and 259f.). Parallel to the clod/seed and its eventual union with the Libyan earth is the Cyrenean exile, Damophilus, also separated from his Libyan soil and also, if the poem is efficacious, to be reunited with his lost homeland. The two temporal planes, remote myth of origins and contemporary circumstance, coexist in the larger myth of presence shaped by the ode, its regeneration of time as it harks back to primordial beginnings where all creative energies coexist.[16]

Near the end of the ode Pindar enjoins Damophilus' return by an obscure riddle introduced by the "finding out" of an "upright craft" at Cyrene (ὀρθόβουλον μῆτιν ἐφευρομένοις, 262); yet at his surrogate, temporary abode, in Thebes, he has "found a spring of ambrosial verses" (299). The pure stream of divine words invites us back beyond the textual distancings inherent in Medea's craft and lines of verses to something which is once more in touch with things immortal (cf. 11). Through these ambrosial words (*ambrosia epea*) Pindar would overcome the dangers of

---

[15] See Detienne, *Maîtres de vérité*, 21ff.; Pucci, *Hesiod*, 22ff., à propos of *Theogony*, 54f.; Komornicka (1972) 239ff.

[16] See above, chap. 5, sec. I.

INSPIRATION AND TEXTUALITY

craftiness, seduction, and multiplicity inherent in the *mētis* and *sophia* of his art.

The return of the clod from its formless state of wandering in the vast reaches of the sea parallels the movement of language from malformed stutter to clear oracle that "sets upright" and "reveals" (60, 62; cf. 262). In recuperating the divine potency of lost origins at the end of the myth (251ff.), Pindar shows himself the master of a *logos* that may wander between truth and guile, dangerous drug and healing, rooted earth and dispersive sea, but nevertheless always returns to its sources in the eternal and sacred vitality of creation (cf. 299). Like Odysseus, his tale traverses the marine realms of persuasion/seduction, erotic desire, craft, and drugs, but it also finds its way home to fulfil there the truth with which it set out in the divinely authorized messages of the opening strophes. Hence when Pindar praises Homer for saying that "the noble messenger wins the greatest honor in everything" (277f.), he is referring not only to himself as the mediator between Arcesilaus and Damophilus, but to the healing power of his poetry in general. The discourse of the ode will accomplish the healing that is the other side of its "drug."[17]

II. MEDEA, JASON, AND PINDAR (WOMAN, HERO, AND POET)

Pindar's poetry contains both Medea and Jason and has characteristics of both: craft and divine inspiration on the one hand; energy, authority, and the legitimacy of success with honor on the other. In its reflection on its own discourse this poetry partakes of the ambiguity of what mediates between opposing conditions. Jason's erotic cleverness (*sophia*) and persuasion (*peithō*), in all their

---

[17] On the motif of "healing," see Robbins, 211ff., and above, chap. 1, note 11.

ambiguity, parallel those of the poet who narrates his deeds (*sophia*, 248). Like Medea's prophecy, the poet shifts between a privileged male-centered transparency to action and the dangerous female ambiguities of seduction, mobility, and magic.[18] This is also a shift between the pneumatological and the grammatological forms of conveying truth. As inspired truth, the poet's words express a clear, linear direction that comes from the gods and proceeds straight to its goal of achieved communication. As verbal art, it is more fully immersed in the materiality of the medium, in the craft of expression, and hence takes delight in the manipulation of language for its own sake, in the digressions and excursions as much as in the end of the journey, whether geographical or poetic (the "road of song" in 247).

The overt commitment of the ode is obviously to direction given by god-sent messages. Hence at the end of the myth the byway of sexual adventure on an island inhabited by women proves the means for realizing the goal of implanting the seed/clod where it will take root (cf. 251f.). But by lingering over episodes and details that have little or nothing to do with the declared goal of the journey or the commissioned purpose of the ode, the poem introduces crosscurrents and eddies that carry us off course and redefine the nature of the poetic journey.

Jason runs the risk of submerging ends in means, just as the poet risks the loss of content in technique, epic tradition in lyric artistry. But these dangers also reflect the "grammatological" self-consciousness of a poet who stands between the oral tradition and a literate reflectiveness on his tradition and its media. Such a poet no longer

[18] On the ambiguity of the *pharmakon* when possessed by women and the masculine attempts to control it, see Ann Bergren, "Helen's Good Drug," in S. Kresic, ed., *Contemporary Literary Hermeneutics and Interpretation of Classical Texts* (Ottawa 1981), 200-14, especially 204.

INSPIRATION AND TEXTUALITY

can identify with his heroes in an uncomplicated way. He is sensitive to the discrepancies of using the unheroic and erotically colored thievery to accomplish the heroic violence of killing a male enemy (250); and he shares the fifth century's chronological and spiritual distance from the archaic myths that are the substance of its poetry. His song is no longer a medium transparent to the glorious deeds it tells. His identification with his material shifts between points of view which he crystallizes into the metaphors and narrative motifs of force and guile, simplicity and craft, direct attack and seductive persuasion. At the level of poetics, I would suggest, these tensions also appear in the double identification of his song with the deeds of heroes and the prophecies of wise women.

Both Jason and Medea are, at some level, projections of the poet's new and complex relation to his material. The poet shares the ambiguous role of Medea who narrates the whole action in the oracular synopsis of her dense craft (13-58) and is also a participant in that action. Like Medea too, his discourse spans the temporal distance between past and present and overcomes the spatial separation between Thebes and Cyrene, as previously between Thera and Libya. As the trustworthy vehicle of the Muse's voice, the poet is closely identified with the deeds of which he sings, for they are also a mythical paradigm of his own road of song. But as a practitioner of craft (*mētis*) and a manipulator of his special skill or *sophia* (248),[19] he also stands apart from those deeds and deliberately calls attention to that distance through the recessive frame that his opening strophe creates.

Were one to extend the grammatological implications of Medea's speech, the conscious "writing" of Gorgianic

---

[19] Cf. also the appearance of Orpheus, exemplar of poetry's power of enchantment, in 176f.

CHAPTER 8

rhetoric suggested by Farenga would be the logical conclusion. This is the self-consciousness of a text produced in full recognition of the opacity of language and as a deliberate act of "play," writing, and artifice.[20] But it would be anachronistic to project back upon Pindar's still protogrammatological awareness the full force of Gorgias' "pharmacological" rhetoric.[21] Whereas a Sophist like Gorgias eagerly espouses this textual production as his proper activity, Pindar keeps the seductive power of language within his myth (136-38), insists on its healing power (271), and views himself, like his hero, as a speaker of what is true and "straight." It is essential to his conception of his art that his *logos* traces its descent not from Medea's craft but from Apollo's upright prophecy and ultimately from Zeus, himself the father of Truth (*Ol.* 10.3f.). The operation is, as Farenga rightly points out, ideological, insofar as it enables Pindar to legitimize Arcesilaus' reign.[22] But, unlike Gorgias, Pindar is still far from viewing his work as a merely human instrument for praising powerful men for pay. His belief in his own myth of presence and in the divine authority of his song is still far more than a convenient fiction or a cynical mask. It was an attitude, possibly a self-deluding one, that could not endure much longer amid the rationalistic undercutting of myth from the mid-fifth century on. Only a generation older than Euripides, Pindar was already on the way to becoming an anachronism in his own day. But in 462 Euripides was still a youth; the Sophists had only barely, if at all, begun their work; and *mythos*, not *logos*, still held men's minds.

[20] In the last section of his *Encomium of Helen* (21) Gorgias speaks of having "written" the work as a "plaything," *paignion*. See my "Greek Tragedy: Writing, Truth, . . . Self," 51f.
[21] See Farenga, 19ff.
[22] Farenga, 21.

9. Sexual Conflict and Ideology

I. CONQUEST OF THE FEMALE

To Pindar, as to other Greek poets from Homer to Euripides, female sexuality appears as a mode of treacherous craft (*mētis*), deceptive ornamentation, beguiling persuasion, and quasi-magical drugs, unguents, or enchantments.[1] *Pythian* 4 combines traditional "wonder" at deeds of strength (cf. 238; also 80, 95, 163) with an undercurrent of dependence on feminine intelligence. The all-male band of heroes, like the male line of Aeolid and Cyrenean kings, needs the women they acquire on their travels. The unnamed Lemnian Women are the link, alien but indispensable, to the heroes' future and their realization of their divinely appointed destiny. Apollo makes use of a female voice, as Jason makes use of female *mētis*; but their goal is never deflected thereby. Although king, hero, and poet in *Pythian* 4 require the assistance of mysteriously powerful females, their efforts are overseen by Father Zeus and have as their goal the establishment of continuity and succession among males: the line of the Libyan royal house and its immediate epinician analogue, the glory of the male victors that lives on from generation to generation in the family, thanks to poetic memory.[2]

Medea's power and the magical silence that it commands controls the first section of the ode. She finishes

[1] See Pucci's remarks on Hesiod's Pandora in his *Hesiod and the Language of Poetry*, 92ff., 99ff.; cf. Pindar's implicit criticism of Hippolyta in *Nem.* 5.26ff. and of Clytaemnestra in *Pyth.* 11.17ff.

[2] Farenga is also concerned with uncovering the patriarchal ideology behind the ode, but he takes an approach quite different from mine, stressing Pindar's legitimation of Arcesilaus' authority on behalf of Damophilus, "the exiled, disenfranchised son of Cyrene," whose spokesman is "the poet and intimate of the father-tyrant" (p. 29).

CHAPTER 9

her prophecy, and the Argonauts "crouch subdued, motionless in silence" (ἔπταξαν δ' ἀκίνητοι σιωπᾷ, 57). The ominous overtones and the hints of danger are counterbalanced by the possibilities of success.[3] The verb *ptēssein* of the crouching of the Argonauts in motionless silence as they listen to Medea (57) occurs only here in Pindar; its associations in Homer and the tragedians are generally with fear. The phrasing is ambiguous, however, and can equally suggest the hero's amazement, in a good sense, at the wide future opened by their achievements.

Aphrodite's love-charm, the iynx, works in Jason's behalf to overcome Medea and to impel her to use her magic, in turn, in Jason's behalf. That aid then extends to the neutralization of another feminine danger, the "man-slaughtering Lemnian Women" (252) in Euphamus' union, from which the founders of Cyrene will spring. Initially, these last were described as only "a select race of foreign women," as Medea introduced them in her prophecy (50). At the end, however, after Jason's own victory of eros and seduction over Medea, they are called (in the poet's narrative voice) "a race of man-killing women," with a sharp juxtaposition of *gynai-* and *andro-* (γυναικῶν ἀνδροφόνων, 252). For both Jason and Euphamus victory takes the form, at the end, of a sexual conquest of a woman in a remote marine setting. Their triumph has an Odyssean rather than an Achillean cast.

Aphrodite's sharpest missiles (213) effect the triumphant return or *nostos* of a hero in control of a dangerous barbarian woman. Sexual desire (*pothos*), both for him and for Greece (218), work in the hero's favor.[4] The pattern is the reverse of that of tragedy. Aeschylus' Clytaemnestra and Sophocles' Deianeira destroy their husbands' *nostos*

[3] For the sinister implications of 57, see Farenga, 14f.

[4] For the dangers and ambiguities surrounding the *nostos* of the hero, of which Medea's eros is one, see Crotty, 106ff.

through an outburst of female sexual energy and contrivance. The Euripidean Helen in the *Trojan Women* can so bewitch Menelaus by her beauty that he takes her back on board his ship as a re-found bride instead of killing her (*Tro.* 891ff.). In Euripides, characteristically, the sexual conquest belongs to the woman, and the *nostos* too is hers; it is the triumph of her seductive power over the heroic endurance of her husband.[5] Pindar keeps feminine sexual power subordinate to the masculine heroic values of the *karteros anēr* and the admiration it inspires in his peers (239-41) and even in his enemy (237f.). He distributes his narrative accordingly: there is one strophe for Jason's love-episode but three for his encounter with Aeetes, bulls, and dragon (216-23 and 224-46 respectively).

The missiles of Pindar's love-goddess, however, have a sinister counterpart in the godless missiles with which Ino, the typical evil stepmother, drove her two stepchildren, Helle and Phrixus, from Greece to barbarian Colchis. Pindar alludes only briefly to this part of the myth when he tells how the ram of the Golden Fleece once saved Phrixus "from the sea and from his stepmother's godless missiles" (161b-62): τῷ ποτ' ἐκ πόντου σαώθη / ἔκ τε ματρυιᾶς ἀθέων βελέων. Even here the stepmother's evil appears only in its neutralized form, a bane of the remote past from which the persecuted son (Pindar is not interested in Helle) has been saved.

The movement of the ode from the shifting, metamorphic realm of the sea to the stability of land parallels the male hero's sexual victory. With the female magic of Aphrodite on his side, Jason wins Medea and the Golden

[5] For Euripides' undercutting of male heroic values by either attaching them to a woman (Medea) or feminizing the male protagonist (Pentheus), cf. B.M.W. Knox, "The *Medea* of Euripides," YCS 25 (1977) 193-225, especially 197ff., and my *Dionysiac Poetics*, chap. 6, especially 193-99; cf. also Sophocles, *Trach.* 1046-63, 1070-75.

CHAPTER 9

Fleece; Euphamus' success with the Lemnian Women follows immediately. Euphamus' victory, with its triple component of Argonautic voyage, winning a bride, and agricultural imagery also recapitulates Jason's, whose sexual conquest of Medea enables him to plow a foreign soil with the dangerous, fire-breathing bulls of Aeetes.

II. MASCULINE *MĒTIS*: *PYTHIAN* 9

In another Cyrenean ode, *Pythian* 9, Apollo again presides over a founding act wherein male initiative incorporates potentially dangerous female power through an act of sexual union. Chiron, who is also Jason's teacher in *Pythian* 4, gives the timely advice that averts possible rape. His *mētis* deflects Apollo's hand in 36—a glorious but nonetheless potentially heavy hand—to gentler ways (*Pyth.* 9.36ff.). The Nymph Cyrene is no passive victim of the god's intentions. A spurner of domestic arts, she hunts lions in the wild (17-22). Her descent from the elemental divinities Okeanos and Gaia (14-17) marks her as a powerful figure who might enlist strong forces in her defense. Her grandfather is the river-god Peneus, who intervened against Apollo in a more famous and less successful erotic pursuit, the god's attempt to win Daphne. Yet this potentially harsh aspect of Cyrene is softened and turned toward eventual union with the god, for her "killing of wild beasts" in the hunt has a civilizing function, "bringing serene peace in abundance to her father's cattle" (21-23). It thus looks ahead to her son by Apollo, Aristaeus, who is a divinity both of the wild countryside and of the protection of cattle (Agreus and Nomios, 64f.).

In the founding myths of Cyrene in both *Pythian* 9 and *Pythian* 4 the young, questing god or hero finds as his bride a potentially dangerous female in a foreign and hostile land. In *Pythian* 4, as we have noted, this motif has a doublet in the union of Euphamus with one of the "man-slaughtering" Lemnian Women. Both odes use variants of an underlying mythic pattern, of which the most famous version is Odysseus' conquest of Circe. In *Pythian* 4, however, the preventive medicine is not the moly-plant of the young god of *Odyssey* 10 or the advice of the wise teacher who instructs adolescent heroes in *Pythian* 9, but the seductive magic of Aphrodite. The neutralization of female sexual power by the representative of male Olympian initiative, therefore, is overdetermined: it operates both in the instrument (Aphrodite's iynx) and in the result (overpowering the enchantress and subduing her in marriage).[6]

In *Pythian* 9 Apollo acts directly upon the girl. The advice of the father-surrogate, Chiron, about Aphrodite's "hidden keys of clever Persuasion" transforms possible rape into seduction (38ff.). As this advice is explicitly called Chiron's *mētis* ("Chiron replied, with *mētis* in his answer," 39), guile serves the Olympian and patriarchal power in order to replace force (the "glorious hand" that Apollo would "bring upon" her in 36). In *Pythian* 4, Apollo acts only by his proxy, the Pythia, converting Medea's *mētis* to its hero-helping, Olympian aim. Here Aphrodite herself, instead of Chiron's advice *about* Aphrodite, bestows her seductive magic on the youthful hero (*Pyth.* 4. 214ff.).

Mētis, particularly in the sexual realm, is generally the sinister property of the woman: for example, Deianeira's "weaving of *mētis*" in Bacchylides 16 or Clytaemnestra's *mētis* in the *Agamemnon*.[7] In his account of Clytaemnestra in *Pythian* 11 ("pitiless woman," line 22), Pindar disapprovingly associates female sexuality with guile, trickery, and seduction (*Pyth.* 11.19-28).[8] In his Potiphar's wife

[6] On the male appropriation of the female power of *mētis* in the realm of language and poetry, see Arthur (1982) passim and (1983) 110f.; also Bergren (1983) 70f., 75.

[7] Bacchyl. 16.24f. and 30; Aesch., *Ag.* 1100 and 1426 and cf. 1636.

[8] On the negative values associated with Clytaemnestra in *Pyth.* 11, see Young, *Three Odes*, 19f.

CHAPTER 9

tale of *Nem.* 5.26-32 the woman gets the full share of the blame. In *Pythian* 11 too, female guile is matched and partially neutralized by another kind of feminine *dolos*, that of the old Nurse, here called Arsinoa. She is a kind of female counterpart to Chiron. She preserves the patriarchal line and the future instrument of patriarchal vengeance: she "takes (Orestes) forth from the grievous trickery (*ek dolou duspentheos*) when his father is killed beneath Clytaemnestra's strong hands" (*Pyth.* 11.17f.). In such a figure, as also in gratuitous narrative details like Chiron's daughters rearing Jason (*Pyth.* 4.103), we can see how Pindar softens the sharp sexual antinomies portrayed in the contemporary tragedies. His world-order utilizes a more harmonious cooperation between the sexes; but the firm patriarchal authority is always the implicit condition of that harmony.[9]

Both *Pythian* 4 and 9 place the erotic motifs of persuasion, seduction, and cunning intelligence on the side of male action. In *Pythian* 9 this *mētis* is bestowed on a sexually aggressive young male by a paternal figure associated with the Olympian order, the Centaur Chiron, and inhibits violence against a potential female victim. Both odes deliberately replace the mythical pattern of male violence

[9] Here too the ode has affinities with the *Odyssey*, which is probably the most elaborate model of such cooperation in the interest of the patriarchal order. See, for example, Norman Austin, *Archery at the Dark of the Moon* (Berkeley and Los Angeles 1975), chap. 4, especially 200ff. On the other hand, Pindar's condensed choral mode of telling the myth deepens the patriarchal sympathies of the Nurse by combining her rescue of Orestes with the description of Clytaemnestra's murder of Agamemnon and Cassandra: *Pyth.* 11.17-22. Aeschylus, by contrast, stresses the Nurse's love for Orestes and dislike of Clytaemnestra, but gives no particular emphasis to her allegiance to Agamemnon (unless something analogous to the Pindaric passage occurred in the lacuna posited by Hermann after *Choephoroe* 749-51). By giving a more pronounced role to the Nurse, however, Pindar also somewhat attenuates the gender division that is so sharp in Aeschylus.

SEXUAL CONFLICT

to ancient female divinities (ultimately, Zeus swallowing Metis) with a pattern of persuasive cooperation. What Chiron's *mētis* does for Apollo in *Pythian* 9, Aphrodite's iynx accomplishes for Jason in *Pythian* 4.[10] In both cases this narrative strategy seeks a balance between masculine heroism and female help. It thereby gives a gentler look and a broader legitimation to the subordination of female arts to patriarchal order.

III. THE MYTH OF PATRIARCHY

Unlike Aeschylus' place of prophecy, which once belonged to earth, darkness, and ancient female powers (*Eumenides* 1-19),[11] Pindar's oracular power is entirely under the domination of Apollo. Delphi is defined by the architectural clarity and wealth of the god's temple. His priestess is not the occupant of an underground hollow, but one "seated beside Zeus' golden eagles" (4). These are the pedimental statues that outline the roof of the temple against the sky. In the second reference to the Pythia's prophecy the mention of the oracular chamber is likewise suppressed in favor of the male-oriented agonistic space of the hippodrome, the place where both "Apollo and the Pythia gave honor" to Arcesilaus (65-67). Pindar will "now" (64) extend this gift of divine glory to the Cyrenean royal family by giving Arcesilaus' ancestor, Battus, to the Muses (67) at an occasion whose origins lie at Delphi (66-68). Even Medea's oracle is given as part of the Pythia's, and hence it is included in the voice that comes ultimately from Apollo.

For Pindar, as for Hesiod and the Aeschylean Apollo of

[10] For some aspects of this motif in *Pyth.* 9, with a rather different point of view, see Finley, 108-10. See also Nancy F. Rubin, "Narrative Structure in Pindar's Ninth Pythian," *CW* 71 (1977/78) 353-67, especially 358f.; Woodbury (1972) 567ff. See also chap. 1, note 33.

[11] See Zeitlin (1978) 162ff.

CHAPTER 9

the *Eumenides*, the essential female quality is to be medium and vessel, means rather than end, adornment rather than accomplishment.¹² As a prophetess Medea has a privileged role in and above the action. But the women of whom she speaks in her prophecy are limited to bearing the sons who will rule over the kingdoms that are in the process of being founded on these remote and dangerous travels. The daughter of Epaphus will "plant (*phuteusesthai*) the root of cities" in Libya (14f.). Euphamus, "whom Europa, Tityus' daughter bore by the banks of the Cephisus," will found the race of Libyan kings (45-48). He will find "a distinguished race of foreign women" for marriage (ἐν λέχεσιν, 51) with the sole purpose of begetting (τέκωνται, 52) the future "lord of the dark-clouded plains" (50-53). Jason, to be sure, calls Pelias by his matronymic, "descendant of Tyro of the desirable hair" (136), possibly to point up the contrast with Pelias' insulting reference to Jason's nameless mother in his opening address (98f.). But a few lines later Jason himself addresses Pelias as "son of Poseidon" and calls the unnamed mother of their common male ancestors, Cretheus and Salmoneus, a "cow" (μία βοῦς Κρηθεῖ τε μάτηρ / καὶ θρασυμήδεϊ Σαλμονεῖ, "One cow was mother to Cretheus and to Salmoneus of the daring counsels," 142f.). This startling image suggests that the woman is viewed as important only for her function of joining by blood the two male descendants here in conflict with one another.¹³

¹² The clearest mythical model is Hesiod's Pandora, on which see J.-P. Vernant, *Mythe et pensée chez les Grecs* (Paris 1974), 1.51ff.; *Mythe et société en Grèce ancienne* (Paris 1974), 187ff., 192ff., of which some portions are translated in R. L. Gordon, ed., *Myth, Religion, and Society* (Cambridge 1981), 51-56; also Pucci, *Hesiod*, 82ff.; Nicole Loraux, "Sur la race des femmes et quelques-unes de ses tribus," *Arethusa* 11 (1978) 43-88, especially 47ff., 55ff.; Arthur (1982) 111f.

¹³ For the abruptness of this image, cf. the "Boeotian sow" of *Ol.* 6.90, another animal comparison with a most unflattering ring. On the mat-

SEXUAL CONFLICT

The prophecy of Medea, as we have seen, is carefully paired with that of the Pythia, whose power emanates from the Olympian males, Zeus and Apollo (4f., 66). The aid of Hera, with its erotic-sounding elements of *peithō, pothos,* and *pharmakon* (184-87), is balanced by the powerful omens of Zeus: the sky god puts on a display of beneficent violence in the heavens to encourage his sons (193-202).[14] Jason's victory of seduction over Medea, thanks to Aphrodite's love-charm, is balanced by Euphamus' apparently unaided success with the Lemnian ladies. In both cases a potentially dangerous and possibly casual encounter leads to marriage and/or offspring. The epinician form of choral lyric tends to reconcile tensions that in tragedy burst out to rend the social fabric. Yet the resolution of the sexual tensions is not total. In both *Pythian* 9 and *Pythian* 4 the violence between the sexes is not fully masked by the myths of reconciliation. In *Pythian* 9 the possibility of rape is close to the surface (36f.); in *Pythian* 4 the Lemnian Women are still "killers of men."

Adventures at sea, both at the beginning and end of the ode, frame the land-based tale of a more traditional heroic encounter between males, Jason's meeting with Pelias in Iolcus. This episode is governed by the familiar epic values of straight speaking and strong doing, and it takes place in a virtually all-male world. We hear of Jason's birth, but not of his mother (111). Other references to the maternal parent are not flattering (98f., 142; cf. 162). The hero's first trial is a conflict with an older male who has displaced his own father and now holds the seat of power. It is a struggle

---

ronymics and the genealogy of Pelias and Jason here, see now Oddone Longo, "Su alcuni termini di parentela in Pindaro: classificatorio e descrittivo," in *Lirica greca da Archiloco ad Elitis: Studi in onore di Filippo Maria Pontani,* (Padua 1984), 167.

[14] Zeus' epithets, "with the spear of the thunderbolt" and "father of heavenly ones" in this context (194) also suggest a phallic component in this display of solidarity with the young heroes.

CHAPTER 9

to regain the inheritance and prerogatives that a father hands down to his son. Among these are belonging to his own land as a citizen (cf. 117) rather than being a stranger in another's land (cf.78, 118), his right to the house of his father (106, 117), with all the property and wealth (150) of the household (*oikos*, 148b-151), the honor or *timē* that goes with such a position (cf. 108, 147b), and the regal power, with its visible emblems of scepter and throne (cf.152 and 165f.).

Pelias' very terms of address deny Jason his right to these perquisites of his patrimony. They deny his place in the land by calling him "stranger" (97); and they deny his right to due inheritance from his father by labelling his origins as birth from his mother's *gastēr* or "belly," with its associations of corporeality, dependence on the female, and subjection to the biological immanence of man's mortal condition.[15] Pelias withholds the patronymic (98f.), in contrast to "fatherland," *patris*, in the previous clause. And he denies Jason's honor by suggesting that he might befoul or besmirch his race with lies (καταμιάναις γένναν, 100). Jason's calm reply establishes all these rights, as much by the manner as by the matter of his speech (101-19).[16] Pelias concludes his promise to restore the kingship with an oath to Zeus Genethlios (167b), the highest god of authority in the patriarchal family. As if in answer, three sons of Zeus are the first to respond to Jason's call for volunteers (Κρονίδαο Ζηνὸς υἱοὶ τρεῖς, 171).[17] The theme of reaching the home of one's fathers finds echoes in the personal history of Damophilus at the end of the poem.

[15] On the associations of the *gastēr* with man's subjection to mortality and consequent dependence on the female procreative power in Hesiod, see Arthur (1982) 74ff. and (1983) 111f.

[16] See above, chap. 2, sec. I.

[17] For the implication of the patronymic Κρονίδας in the ode, see above, chap. 2, note 36, and chap. 3, note 7.

SEXUAL CONFLICT

Like Atlas, he has been far from the earth of his fathers and his possessions (πατρῴας ἀπὸ γᾶς ἀπό τε κτεάνων, 290); and after being a *xenos* at Thebes (299) he hopes to "see his house." The metaphorical "bilging out of troubles" (διαντλήσαις ποτὲ οἶκον ἰδεῖν, 294) may also imply a trial by sea-journey.

Even in this patriarchal world, however, feminine guile has a role to play. As in the other parts of the ode, it is a role subordinate to but supportive of male heroism. The participles describing the act of spiriting away the newly born heir are all masculine, implying perhaps the men of the clan. They make use, however, of "the wailing of women" (113), which contributes to the secrecy that their plan requires ("in secret," *krubda*, 114). Presumably Jason's mother (who, incidentally, is never mentioned) has a role in saving her infant son; but Pindar refers to the agents of the flight only as parents (masculine plural) and frames the event in political rather than domestic terms. Thus Pelias' motives are to deprive the royal house of its legitimate honor (109) or prerogative (*tima*); and the point is continued, implicitly in the epithet *archedikai*, "legitimate rulers," applied to the parents (ἀρχεδικᾶν τοκέων, 110). Although an infant is involved, this is a conflict between males over honor, leadership, rule, and justice—all forms of power that emanate ultimately from Zeus, father of the gods (107).[18]

In *Pythian* 4, as in the *Odyssey*, the marine world suppresses or inverts traditional heroic norms. But in *Pythian* 4 Pindar has so arranged the events that Jason's encounter with Pelias at Iolcus—a tale only indirectly related to the main story of the founding of Cyrene—holds the center of the poem and stabilizes it in the traditional values of ac-

[18] So λαγέτας, "ruler of the people," 107; τιμάν, "honor," 109; ἀρχεδικᾶν, "ruling legitimately," 110b; ἀγεμών, "leader," 112.

tive masculine heroism and man-to-man conflict. Aphrodite helps Jason against Medea; but in the preceding section of the poem the divine helpers are Zeus and Hera, the paradigms of marital union, not of seductive eros. The explicitly sexual magic of Aphrodite is balanced by Hera's gift of longing for the *Argo* and by the martial drug of valor associated with it (184-87). The function of this latter is to send young heroes away from women to a society defined by the male-bonding of peers ("with other companions of the same age," ἄλιξιν σὺν ἄλλοις, 187). They are not to be "left behind and remain coddling a life without danger beside mother" (186f.).[19]

Like other Greek poets of the archaic and classical periods, Pindar presents this absorption of craft (*mētis*) into truth as an inevitable and "natural" evolutionary process whereby ambiguous female powers of seduction and procreation are brought under masculine control.[20] In tragedy the darker side of this myth surfaces, and the latent power of feminine cunning and sexuality and the female's resistance to the imposition of patriarchal authority hold the foreground.[21] In Pindar that myth of primordial sexual conflict is muted; and the surface myth is one of harmony after legitimate conquest, authorized by benign Olympian father-figures. Thus, as Nancy Rubin notes, Pindar omits Zeus' trickery and the primitive oral act of swallowing

---

[19] With this "not being left behind" cf. the story of Battus at the beginning of the ode, who must leave behind his homeland of Thera to found Cyrene (7).

[20] For this process in Hesiod, see Vernant and Detienne, *Cunning Intelligence*, 58ff., 108ff.; also Arthur (1982) 63-82, especially 77f. For its operation in the realm of poetic language, see Bergren (1983) 69-96, especially 82ff.

[21] Zeitlin (1978) 149, for example, defines the major issue of the *Oresteia* as "the establishment in the face of female resistance of the binding nature of patriarchal marriage where wife's subordination and patrilineal succession are reaffirmed."

SEXUAL CONFLICT

Metis from his account of the birth of Athena in *Olympian* 7.[22] Instead, he emphasizes the authority of Zeus as great king of the gods and as the father (34, 36) who guides the arts of Hephaestus. Father Zeus possesses the fertilizing power of procreation in the radiant, metallic form of the golden snowstorm (βρέχε ... χρυσέαις νιφάδεσσι, 34), an image as far removed as possible from the biological details of female parturition. Later in the ode Helios has the epithet *genethlios patēr* (70), a frequent epithet of Zeus as the source of procreative energy and the guardian of the patriarchal family.[23] Here this generative father figure firmly takes control of the processes of birth. He discerns the seed of Rhodes growing in the quasi-womb of the ocean (62), gives orders to Lachesis (also one of the Moirai), and after "mingling" seems to give birth to his three sons, the eponymous heroes of the three Rhodian cities (μειχθεὶς τέκεν, 71b; ἔτεκεν, 74). This use of τεκεῖν, in the active, for the father is rare; and these may be the only two places in Pindar where the verb is so used.[24]

The Muse whom Pindar invokes at the beginning of *Pythian* 4 is a pallid cousin to the figure of Athena in *Olympian* 7. She is the emblem of the feminine power in its transformed, harmonized state, subordinated to the Olympian patriarchy and allied to the masculine ends of glorifying a form of the Father. The voice of Apollo's desexualized priestess enframes the potentially disruptive *mētis* of the seductive and seduced Medea. The authority of Father Zeus, one might say, overshadows the danger of

[22] *Ol.* 7.34ff. See Rubin, "Epinician Symbols," 71-73.
[23] For Zeus *genethlios*, see Farnell, ad *Ol.* 8.15.
[24] The only other possible instance is *Pyth.* 9.33, where, however, the subject, τις ἀνθρώπων, may be the mother, particularly as Apollo is here speaking of someone's daughter (Cyrene). The collocation of "mingling" (in the aorist participle) with *tiktein* (active) is regularly used of the mother (e.g., *Ol.* 6.29, *Pyth.* 9.84), so that the combination used of Helios in *Ol.* 7.71b is particularly striking.

CHAPTER 9

Aeetes' potent daughter (10f.). Language as poison, associated especially with female passion, is offset by language as healing drug, associated especially with the male healers, Apollo, Chiron, and Asclepius (cf. 136f. and 270f.). Yet a trace of Medea's threatening power remains in the ambiguous epithet *zamenēs* (10) and in her dense craft beside the inspired pneumatological utterance of Apolline prophecy or of Olympian poetry.

The Pythia, whose power of potent speech comes from Apollo and who herself "sits beside the golden eagles of Zeus" (4), is exactly symmetrical with the Muse, daughter of Zeus and supporter (here and elsewhere) of his Olympian kingdom.[25] The Pythia's incorporation into Olympian patriarchy becomes even clearer later in the parallelism established by the contiguity of her prophecy and Medea's (53-58, 59-67). At this juncture too, the Pythia, Apollo, and the Muse all recur together, exactly as in the proem (66-68; cf. 3-6).

The Muse's patriarchal allegiance is a commonplace in early Greek poetry and needed no explicit statement.[26] Yet the residuum of guile in Medea's female *mētis* points, in its turn, to another concealed and ambiguous craft, the artful *sophia* of the hired professional behind the declaration of friendship (1) and the personal address (298). It is appropriate that the greatest ambiguities—those between inspiration and craft, truth and possible deception, oral utterance and the graphic space of writing, marriage and seduction—focus on the *mētis* of the quintessentially dangerous enchantress. Medea is an object of sexual desire who is both powerful and pliant, both threateningly

[25] In *Ol.* 14.9-12 the Charites, as "stewards of all deeds in the heavens place their thrones beside *Pythian* Apollo" and "revere the ever-flowing honor of the Olympian *father*." Cf. also the Golden Lyre of *Pyth.* 1.1ff., "joint possession of Apollo and the Muses" on Olympus.

[26] Cf. Hesiod, *Theog.* 25; Pindar, *Ol.* 10.3f. and 96, *Paean* 6.54-56.

"other" and able to be appropriated and possessed through her subjection to sexuality.

Pindar is aware of the fragmented, daedalic, crafty voices that later crystallize into the *technai* of the rhetorical schools.[27] On occasion he can even allow such voices into his poetry (*Pyth.* 2.81-85). But he always keeps the voice of deception subordinate to what he regards as the voice of truth, a poetry of praise rather than blame, of simplicity (*Nem.* 8.35f.) rather than multiplicity. Nothing would have surprised him more than to be regarded as a sort of proto-Gorgias; and yet such a description is not entirely wide of the mark, for this very emphasis on truth and simplicity is part of an implicitly ideological operation: his self-presentation as a practitioner of the older, more innocent, less crafty oral poetics. He sees himself as a prophet of the Muses; and yet he is a prophet who begins to know that he speaks through the written as well as the spoken word, through female artfulness as well as through Apolline prophecy or the Olympian inspiration of the Muse, through texts as well as through performance. He defines his poetic task as the conscious selection and support of myths of the "right" kind (*Ol.* 1.28ff.).[28] Yet it is probably inherent in the nature of enabling myths that in speaking about the sources of his own inspiration Pindar does not bring to conscious expression its underlying myth of Olympian patriarchy appropriating feminine *mētis*.[29]

[27] See Farenga, 18ff.

[28] On *mythos* in Pindar, see Detienne, *L'invention*, 96ff.

[29] Cf. the more direct suppression of this aspect of the myth in the account of the birth of Athena from the head of Zeus in *Ol.* 7.34ff: see above, note 22.

10. Conclusion. *Chronos*: Time and Structure

Pythian 4's interweaving of heroic myth with a historical founding legend grounds the remote past in the present, and vice versa. In the midst of distant voyages and fabulous geography there remain clarity, direction, and stability. Even the "real" geography that leads to the historical establishment of the city of Cyrene has a mythical aspect: "The Okeanos is not our Ocean, the Red Sea is not our Red Sea, the Lake Tritonis that we know is inland, and Pindar is poetry."[1] But the fabulous is firmly delimited by the definiteness of time and place given by the occasion of the ode. The present day is the ode's first word (σάμερον). The poet's first act is to station his Muse beside the king at the festive celebration now taking place in Cyrene (note the present participle, κωμάζοντι, 2b). Thus he grasps the passing moment of the festive happiness and sets it into contact with the goddess of eternizing commemoration, the Muse who brings present time into relation with past and future (cf. *Iliad* 2.485f.). Pindar closes the poem in his own native city of Thebes and in contact with the immortalizing power of his song (298f.).

More pervasive than Thebes and second only to Cyrene for the spatial stability of the ode is Delphi. It is both a real and a mythical place. "The mid-navel of the well-treed mother earth" (74), it is the seat of Apolline prophecy from which emanates the energy that governs all the movements in the ode. Delphi anchors the poem in a center. It is the point of the circle from which all motion radiates.[2]

---

[1] Gildersleeve, ad *Pyth.* 4.20.
[2] For aspects of the circular structure of the ode, see Cook, 120.

CONCLUSION

In its function as the place from which the divine will is communicated to men by oracles that foretell the future in the present, it also spans the distance between the remote and the tangibly real, between myth and history.

This spatial centering of the ode through Apollo has a temporal analogue in the role of *chronos*, the time that holds the fulfilment of the gods' design.³ The techniques of flashback, embedded narrative, and ring-composition in the ode's first section (1-69) create that circularity of form that governs the poem as a whole. Thus the end of the Argonaut myth harks back to Battus' departure (259-61 and 5f.) and to Medea's prophecy (254f. and 50f.). The themes of Thebes, divine song, and *xenia* at the very end also return us to the ode's opening words (cf. 298f. and 1-3; also *ouros* in 3b and 292).⁴

Jason's story, on the other hand, has a strong linear direction. There is a sharply demarcated "beginning" (*archa*, 70), and a clear progression toward a well defined and tangible goal, winning the Golden Fleece (159ff., 230ff.), which is the condition of winning back his kingdom. Pindar completes this impression of ongoing, continuous movement by filling in the period between Jason's secret exit from Iolcus as an infant and his return as a resplendent and mature twenty-year-old.

Just as centrifugal and centripetal movements in space have their center in Delphi, so the circularity and linearity of time have their stable center in *chronos*, the perspective of the gods that stands above the fragmented, limited time

---

³ On the meaning of *chronos*, see Hermann Fränkel, "Die Zeitauffassung in der frühgriechischen Literatur," *Wege und Formen frühgriechischen Denkens* (Munich 1960), 1-22, especially 10-12; Vivante, "On Time in Pindar," 107-31; and my "Time and the Hero," 29-39. See also Komornicka (1976) 9ff., who calls attention to the connection of time and cosmic Dike in Anaximander (12A9 DK; cf. Pindar frag. 145 Bo. = 159 Sn.).

⁴ For the ring-composition of the ode, see above, chap. 4, note 10.

CHAPTER 10

of mortal life and encompasses in a meaningful plan its temporal shifts and changes. Here are fit together all the separate pieces of time that men experience in their brief lives. The command of this unifying *chronos* enables the poet to present the events of the ode outside of their chronological sequence without losing the underlying pattern or meaning.

This encompassing divine plan fulfilled over time is established at the outset. The first strophe interweaves the poet's presence beside the king of "Cyrene excellent in horses" with the Muse who tells of a prophecy about founding a "city excellent in chariots" (εὐίππου βασιλῆϊ Κυράνας, 2; κτίσσειεν εὐάρματον πόλιν, 7f.). The two epithets of Cyrene, "excellent in horses" and "excellent in chariots," belong respectively to King Arcesilaus at his present celebration (the *kōmos*) and to the intended foundation of a remote ancestor. They draw the present chariot victory into the mythical event, the founding of a "city excellent in the chariots"; and they help blend together the poet's present journey (real or imagined) from Thebes to Cyrene, the Muse's metaphorical journey of song that stands outside of time, and the journey of the founding hero in the remote past as he left his sacred isle of Thera for a divinely appointed goal (6-9). Upon the Thera of Battus ("sacred isle," 6f.) is then superimposed the Thera of the Argonauts in the still remoter time of myth, when Medea uttered the "Therean word" of her prophecy that Battus, now at Delphi, is about to recover (9f.).

The overlay of the different temporal strata upon the moment of the present Cyrenean *kōmos* creates a dense complex of recessive panels of space and time that unfolds gradually as the narrative expands. Within the first ten lines Battus' departure from Thera (6f.) opens upon the scene, long before, of Medea's prophecy at Thera (9f.). The presence of the Muses beside Pindar at Cyrene (1-3) is the

CONCLUSION

contemporary analogue to the Pythia's oracular presence, with Zeus and Apollo, to Battus' at Delphi (4f.). Arcesilaus, ensconced as king in "Cyrene of the goodly horses" and subject of the present revel (2), leads us back to the remote king of "Cyrene of goodly chariots" as he leaves behind his land for the still uncertain quest (8). We can present these panels diagrammatically as follows:

Battus leaving Thera (6f.)	"Therean word" of Medea and Argonauts (9f.)
Pythia's prophecy to Battus at Delphi (4-6)	Muse's presence to Pindar at Cyrene (1-3)
"Chariot" as epithet of Battus' foundation (7)	"Chariot" of Arcesilaus' victory (2)

This dense oracular structure is the underlying shape of the history of Cyrene; and we reach this also through two prophecies and as an act of "recovery" in time ("to recover Medea's utterance at Thera *with* the seventeenth generation," 9f.). The motif of recovery, as we have seen, extends to the story of Jason (cf. 105, 159), and here too oracles make the events part of a divinely authorized design. Within the Cyrenean story the time of the divine plan operates also as the power of memory that spans centuries. The mortal heroes lose the clod because their "minds forgot" Medea's instructions (*elathonto phrenes*, 41b).[5] But seventeen generations later, Apollo himself at Delphi will remind (*amnasei*) Battus of his destined rule over the African land (54). Here it is significantly Apollo himself, not the Pythia, who "in accordance with his lawful enactments (*themissin*)" directly recalls this ancient promise (*Phoibos amnasei themissin*, 54).

As in *Olympian 7*, mortal forgetfulness is made good by

[5] On the motif of forgetting, see above, chap. 6, p. 111. See also Komornicka (1972) 239f.

CHAPTER 10

the remembering of the gods.[6] This memory spans past and future in the oracular structure of time in the ode. The mortals forget what was foretold them in the past, but the god reveals to a later descendant the fulfilment still to come. This fulfilment may be postponed because of the weakness of mortal *phrenes*, but in the steady flow of the divine *chronos* it is not cancelled.[7] The founding of Libya is completed as a collaboration of human energy and divine foresight. The mortal mind is subject to momentary aberrations or memory lapses, but the gods retain an unclouded perception of what will be. Indeed here, as in the corresponding passage of *Olympian* 7, Pindar does not even have to mention the specific intervention of the gods who correct mortal forgetfulness. After the "forgetting," Medea simply continues, "*And now* the immortal seed of Libya of the wide-dancing places has been poured forth on this island [Thera] before its season" (*Pyth.* 4.42f.: καί νυν ἐν τᾷδ' ἄφθιτον νάσῳ κέχυται Λιβύας / εὐρυχόρου σπέρμα πρὶν ὥρας). By suppressing the intermediate step of the god's remembering, Pindar indicates that the divine intention not only rectifies but even silently absorbs and cancels human error, so that for both Libya and Rhodes the destined events, in both cases a foundation, take their intended course.[8]

---

[6] Cf. *Ol.* 7.45ff., on which see most recently Shirley Darcus Sullivan, "A Strand of Thought in Pindar, *Olympians* 7," *TAPA* 112 (1982) 220-22, with the bibliography there cited.

[7] For the interplay of mortal and divine in the motif of forgetting, though with a different emphasis, see René Schaerer, "L'univers spirituel de Pindare," *Mélanges de philosophie grecque offerts à Mgr. Diès* (Paris 1956), 221-32, especially 226f. and 231. He notes the relation between 41 and 54 ("désir suivi par l'oubli," followed by "faveur divine") and remarks, "La conquête de la Libye était donc subordonée à la reconnaissance, par l'homme, de l'Intermédiaire divin: personne ne pouvait posséder ce pays sans passer par le dieu" (227). See also Méautis, 228.

[8] *Pyth.* 4.41ff.; *Ol.* 7.45ff. Note too the motif of "founding" here in *Ol.* 7.42 (κτίσαιεν βωμὸν ἐναργέα).

CONCLUSION

In the sacral time of the gods process and permanence are reconciled. This is the time of primordial beginnings, the *archai* to which the poet traces back the origins of men and of cities (cf. 70f., 144f.).⁹ It is the task of the poet to reveal behind the changeful, shifting rhythms of the irreversible time of mortal life this all-embracing, a-temporal duration of events in the time of the gods, *sub specie aeternitatis*. He participates in the abolition of profane time, to use Mircea Eliade's terminology, by taking us back to *illud tempus*, the moment at the commencement of time where all things share in the energies of creation. Or in the words of Wallace Stevens, "He hears the earliest poems of the world." He establishes contact between the mortal world and the reservoir of creative energies that move events from potentiality to actuality, pushing them across the barrier that separates being from non-being. In the human, anthropomorphic succession of moments what is a supra-temporal phenomenon, outside of time, becomes visible and comprehensible as event only in, and as, time.¹⁰

The creative energies that become visible in contemplating the mythical origins of lands and dynasties are also related to the moral forces that operate in the life of the individual and of the family. Jason speaks of his own origins

---

⁹ Note the recurrence of the first discovery or inventions of things in Pindar: the dithryramb (*Ol.* 13.17-19; frag. 61 Bo. = 70b Sn.); the horse's bridle (*Ol.* 13.85f.); the flute (*Pyth.* 12.20f.); the games at Olympia (*Ol.* 10.24ff. and cf. the continuing force of this πρωτόγονος τελετά and ἀρχαὶ πρότεραι in 51b and 78 respectively); the establishment of divinities of music and song (frag. 12 Bo. = 31 Sn.), and so on.

¹⁰ See M. Eliade, *Cosmos and History*, passim; Van Groningen, 96-102; also Pépin, 55-68, especially 57: "Le mythe s'étale, selon la succession du discours, des réalités simultanées; il prête un commencement à l'univers éternel, il parle à l'imparfait quand la vérité demanderait l'aoriste; il permet d'apprendre et d'enseigner parce qu'il décompose les difficultés, mais sous réserve de restituer l'unicité complexe du réel." Much of this formulation is applicable to Pindar's notion of *chronos*.

CHAPTER 10

in terms that connect human birth to the sources of life in the universe, "beholding the golden strength of the sun" (144). In the next lines, as he expounds to Pelias the respect or reverence (*aidōs*) that should govern righteous action among kinsmen, he invokes as its guardians the Moirai, the goddesses who are present at each mortal's birth (cf. *Ol.* 2.42f., 10.52f., *Nem.* 7.1).[11] The Moirai are the sign of connection between the individual life and the god-permeated order of nature and law. Their presence is also implied behind the *moiridion amar* ("destined day") in which golden-throned Cyrene's divine city is finally "planted" (255-61).

For the individual victor (or hero) the achievement in athletics (or martial deeds) is not narrowed down to the specialized, secular discipline of physical training and practice. It also partakes of reverence for sacred things and of the vital force, beauty, and creative thrust of sexuality and birth. Hence Pindar's erotic images in odes like *Pythian* 9 and *Nemean* 8 or the motifs of childbirth and marriage in *Nemean* 7 and *Olympian* 7 do not refer merely to the specific biographical circumstances of the athlete, but form part of the poet's mythic vision of unified life-energies in his world.[12] Among the exploits of the most physi-

[11] For the Moirai, see above, chap. 5, sec. II. Contrast the tale of Coronis in *Pyth.* 3, where the birth of a quasi-divine child is marred by a mortal's impatient desire and infidelity, so that the birth lacks the "fulfilment" brought by Eleithyia (9f.). This birth is attended not by the life-giving waters or the radiance of sunlight but by the destructive flash of Apollo's fire (35-44; cf. *Ol.* 6.43, *Pyth.* 4.144, *Nem.* 1.35).

[12] For *Nem.* 7 see my "Nemean 7," 456ff.; on *Pyth.* 9 Woodbury (1982) 245 opts, rather hesitantly, for the biographical view: "So insistent is the recurrence of this theme [sexuality, marriage, and procreation] that it becomes desirable to conjecture, if one assumes that literary forms and structures have their origins in people and society, that Telesicrates himself is, not only young, but also eligible to marry, if not promised in marriage. On that hypothesis, at least, it is possible to understand the relevance of love and marriage to the victor's praise." But literary forms and structures also have origins in symbol-making, analogy, imaginative association—that is to say, in poetry as well as in biographical factuality.

CONCLUSION

cally aggressive of his heroes, Heracles, Pindar includes the planting of trees at Olympia to shelter the valley from "the sun's sharp rays" (*Ol.* 3.23f. and 33f.) and marriage with "blooming Youth" (*Nem.* 1.71).[13] At the end of our ode the brief "epinician" allusion to the Argonauts' athletic victories in "contests of their limbs" includes, almost in the same breath, their procreative union with the Lemnian Women:

ἔνθα καὶ γυίων ἀέθλοις ἐπεδεί-
ξαντο ἵν' ἐσθᾶτος ἀμφίς,
καὶ συνεύνασθεν. (253f.)

Then in contests too did they display the strength of their limbs, for the prize of raiment, and were joined in union.[14]

The "planting" of the Libyan dynasty, with its imagery of agriculture and fertility, follows at once (254ff.).

The closing section of the myth of Pelops in *Olympian* 1 has a similar pattern:

ἕλεν δ' Οἰνομάου βίαν παρθένον τε σύνευνον·
ἃ τέκε λαγέτας ἓξ ἀρεταῖσι μεμαότας υἱούς. (88f.)

(Pelops) took Oenomaus' force and took also the girl as the consort of his bed, and she bore six sons, leaders of the people, eager for deeds of excellence.

Here, as in *Pythian 9*, the deed of masculine force (*bia*, 88) is closely associated with the hero's procreative power. The bride won by force will eventually produce the sons who continue the *aretē* inherited from their father, the

---

[13] On these passages, see, respectively, my essay, "God and Man in Pindar's First and Third Olympian Odes," *HSCP* 68 (1964) 228ff., especially 234-36, and Rose, "First Nemean," 167f.

[14] The reading in 253 is uncertain: the MSS. κρίσιν, retained by many editors, is metrically difficult but not impossible. In that case, the sense will be, "demonstrated a contest, decision, of their limbs. . . ." ἵν(α) is Kayser's emendation.

CHAPTER 10

founding hero of the place. In the footrace of *Pythian* 9.105-25 there is no mention of offspring resulting from the winner's marriage with the girl who is the prize of the contest; but by analogy with the myth of Apollo and Cyrene they are probably to be expected (cf. 59-66, and note the maidens' wish for Telesicrates as husband or *son* in 97-100).[15]

The large sweep of Pindar's *chronos* is closely related to his conception of his poetry as the vehicle of enduring Truth, *Alatheia*.[16] In the proem to the Sixth *Paean* he calls on Delphi, in company with Olympian Zeus, the Graces, and Aphrodite, to "receive (him) in hallowed time (ἐν ζαθέῳ με δέξαι χρόνῳ) as the songful prophet of the Muses" (*Pae.* 6.1-6). The poet's contact with the brilliant realm of the gods, whose beauty is here symbolized by the presence of the Charites and Aphrodite, takes place in "holy time." This is the timeless moment when the changeful time of mortal existence is intersected and irradiated by immortality.

This divine *chronos* is the dimension of time that the poet's *Alatheia*, the immortalizing Truth of his poetry, unveils to men.[17] In the brief but lovely Fourth *Olympian* the poet has been impelled by the Seasons (*Hōrai*), daughters of Zeus, to be witness to the victory and to place it in the divine *chronos*. Thus he invokes Zeus and the Graces

---

[15] For the interweaving of the two races, see Crotty, 95; also Jaume Pòrtulas, *Lectura de Píndar* (Barcelona 1977), 96f.

[16] In *Ol.* 10.50-55 Pindar closely associates truth and time: see Komornicka (1972) 241f. and (1976) 7f.; also Gretchen Kromer, "The Value of Time in Pindar's Olympian 10," *Hermes* 104 (1976) 420-36, especially 425ff. and 432ff.

[17] See Gianotti, 63ff., who cites a lemma of Hesychius, ἀλαθεῖς· οἱ μηδὲν ἐπιλανθανόμενοι ὡς Πίνδαρος (frag. 331 Sn.; cf. frag. 10.6 Bo. = 30.6 Sn.). See also Komornicka (1972) 239ff.; Kromer, "The Value of Time," 425f.; L. Woodbury, "Truth and the Song: Bacchyl. 3.96-98," *Phoenix* 23 (1969) 331-35, with bibliography, p. 333, note 10; Segal, "Messages," 200f.

CONCLUSION

to receive the *kōmos*, the festival celebrated by his song, which he calls "the radiance of strongest excellences that most endures in time" (χρονιώτατον φάος εὐρυσθενέων ἀρετᾶν, *Ol.* 4.12). In *Nemean* 4.6-8 the presence of the Graces likewise confers on the poet's words a more than mortal durability in *chronos*:

ῥῆμα δ' ἐργμάτων χρονιώτερον βιοτεύει,
ὅ τι κε σὺν Χαρίτων τύχᾳ
γλῶσσα φρενὸς ἐξέλοι βαθείας.

Longer life in time than deeds has the word that the tongue takes forth from deep thought, with the attending favor of the Graces.

The poet's capacity to make the momentary, fragmentary, durative time of men—the *kairos*, *hōra*, or *aiōn*—transparent to the timeless creative energies of the gods has as its other side Pindar's view of the poetic art as a self-conscious craft or skill (*mētis* or *sophia*) that must be kept apart from the falsehood, profit, or trickery to which it is also liable.[18] His poetics are also related to his conceptions of time. On the one hand the poet manipulates the *kairos* as a mortal who participates in discontinuous time, time as the succession of passing moments, of which the "right one" must be grasped in the "narrow measure" that it allows (ὁ γὰρ καιρὸς πρὸς ἀνθρώπων βραχὺ μέτρον ἔχει, *Pyth.* 4.286).[19] On the other hand he conveys to his fellow men the continuity of all time (*sumpas chronos*), that is the privileged perspective of the gods.[20] If he succeeds, his poetry of Truth not only escapes the deceitful side of craft

---

[18] E.g., *Ol.* 1.28ff.; *Pyth.* 2.73ff.; *Nem.* 7. 20ff. (with the remarks of Köhnken 49ff.); *Isth.* 2.5ff.

[19] On *kairos*, see Gundert, 63, 73; Vivante (1972) 116 ("the fleeting chance" or "happy coincidence which makes for effective action").

[20] For *sumpas chronos*, see *Ol.* 6.58, *Pyth.* 1.46, *Nem.* 1.69; also *Ol.* 10.53 and *Nem.* 4.42f.

CHAPTER 10

but is also the poetry of what time most sanctions and of what most reveals the ways and laws inherent in the time of the gods.

As a poet of Alatheia, daughter of Zeus (*Ol.* 10.3f.) and "foundation of great excellence" (frag. 194 Bo. = 205 Sn.),[21] Pindar attempts to assert the oral poet's privileged access to the divine and the imperishable. As the recipient and the vessel of the divine voices (*Pae.* 6.1-6), he possesses his knowledge as a god-given privilege rather than as a product of human effort. Such poetry, like the prophecy that Medea "breathes forth from immortal mouth" (*Pyth.* 4.10f.), is a magical power of mysterious origin rather than an intricate artifact devised by the wit and cunning skill of mortals.

This poetry partakes of the invisible and quasi-magical, incantatory power of the oral utterance, the "winged word."[22] It possesses the full potency and authority of the voice spoken by a commanding figure in the present. There is no mediation of its origins by writing, no material implement—tablet, roll, or parchment—to betray the traces of a human creation, the specific moment when the words become visible and tangible as objects fashioned by men. Although the result of poetry is often a monument of stone or bronze,[23] the operative metaphors for the process of poetic creation are of breath, air, and wind or of fluid substances like dew, wine, honey, springs of water.[24] Like oracles, such poetry has its origins in the realm of an un-

[21] On this fragment, see B. Gentili, *ICS* 6 (1981) 215-20.

[22] See my "Eros and Incantation: Sappho and Oral Poetry," *Arethusa* 8 (1974) 139-60.

[23] Cf. the temples of song in *Ol.* 6.1ff., *Pyth.* 6.7ff and 7.3; also my remarks on *Nem.* 5.1ff.: "Arrest and Movement: Pindar's Fifth Nemean," *Hermes* 102 (1974) 397-411, especially 409-11.

[24] In this perspective the more tangible "ranks of words" of *Pyth.* 4.57 perhaps stand out as especially significant, particularly if we contrast the "breeze of words" (οὖρον ἐπέων) of *Nem.* 6.28b.

CONCLUSION

seen, numinous power. In both cases the speaker does not merely re-present truth but unveils it: he makes it visible to men by becoming the spokesman or mouthpiece (*prophētēs*) of the gods.[25]

Pindar is also heir to the other tradition, and this goes back to Hesiod and Solon and is vigorously championed in his own day by Simonides and the early Sophists.[26] Here poetry is a crafted art-object wrought by men's craft and device (*mētis, technē, mēchanē, sophia*), with their concomitant proclivity for deviousness, lies, and deceptive appearances.

Standing at a point of transition between an oral and a written poetics, Pindar reflects an incipient conflict—perhaps at times even a conflict within himself—between a poetics of textuality and a poetics of presence, truth, and divine inspiration. We have labelled these two facets of his poetics a "grammatological" and a "pneumatological" consciousness of his art. For the grammatological or "textual" poet the human origins of the work—the intellectual effort, planning, shaping, and execution—are at or near the surface of the poem. For the pneumatological or inspirational poet the sources of the work are surrounded by divinity and therefore always partially concealed from the conscious, rational mind.

These conflicting views of poetry take many forms in Pindar: nature versus learning in the famous formulation of *Olympian* 2.86ff.; simplicity versus the variegation of artful elaboration; the straight road versus the crooked; poetry as truth versus poetry as fabrication.[27] Sometimes

[25] See J.-P. Vernant, "Le sujet tragique: historicité et transhistoricité," *Belfagor* 34 (1979) 639, on the notion of the potency of language for the oral poet: "Sa parole ne réprésente pas, elle rend l'être présent."

[26] For Simonides, see Detienne, *Maîtres de Vérité* 105ff.; Gentili, "Lirica greca arcaica e tardo arcaica," 77-79.

[27] E.g., *Ol.* 1.28ff., *Nem.* 7.20ff., *Nem.* 8.32ff. So too *epea* may be "marshalled ranks" or a sea-breeze: see above, note 24.

CHAPTER 10

Pindar seems to intimate a compromise position, suggesting that the devices and artfulness of *sophia* or *mēchanai* are themselves god-given.[28] But for the most part he asserts—one wonders with what occasional anxiety, need, or courage of affirmation in this post-Simonidean time— the divinity of his song and his belief that his poetry is an extension of the great Truth that comes from Zeus (*Ol.* 10.3f.) and shares in the gods' timeless energy of primordial creation. This is the birthing power that brings to completion the ever-fresh wonder of new life (to paraphrase the untranslatable *prōtogonos teleta* of *Ol.* 10.51). From this reservoir of creative energy flow also the new excellences and new foundations of men. Over these moments of creation preside the Moirai (*Ol.* 10.51f.), as they do also over the birth of heroes when they "first behold the Sun's golden strength" (*Pyth.* 4.144f.; cf. *Nem.* 7.1-8).

Of the great classical poets Pindar seems to us perhaps the most distant and the most foreign. Yet these issues in his poetry, though framed in his language of myth and divinity, may be closer than we sometimes allow, for they reflect fundamental attitudes in the response to and conceptualization of poetry that tend to recur, albeit differently formulated, whenever we think seriously about how men create art and how we receive the great art of remote times. A distinguished contemporary critic reflects as follows on the relation between poetry, mortal finitude, and death:

Finite men and women struggle in and against time, and with one another . . . Language does not become poetry for us until we know that language is telling us lies, because the truth is ambivalence and so also already death. Poetry has to be loved before we can know

[28] E.g., *Ol.* 9.26ff.; *Ol.* 14.5ff.; *Pyth.* 1.41ff.

CONCLUSION

it as poetry, and must inspire ambivalence in us at the center of that love.[29]

Pindar too has glimpses of this dark truth, most explicitly in *Olympian* 1.28ff. But his situation is far less desperate than ours; the worm at the center has not yet devoured the whole fruit. Against the "textual" poetry of device, cunning, and artifice, he can still assert the ancient oral tradition of divinely inspired song. Beside the utterances of *mētis* is heard the voice of Apollo. The poet may sometimes "tread in crooked paths" (*Pyth.* 2.85) or use deceptive "tales crafted with cunningly variegated falsehoods" (*Ol.* 1.29); but his words still flow ambrosial from the Theban spring (*Pyth.* 4.299).

[29] Harold Bloom, *Agon. Towards a Theory of Revisionism* (Oxford and New York 1982), 30.

Select Bibliography

Arthur, Marylin B., "Cultural Strategies in Hesiod's *Theogony*: Law, Family, Society," *Arethusa* 15 (1982) 63-82.

———, "The Dream of a World Without Women: Poetics and the Circles of Order in the *Theogony* Prooemium," *Arethusa* 16 (1983) 97-116.

Bergren, Ann L. T., "Language and the Female in Early Greek Thought," *Arethusa* 16 (1983) 69-96.

Bernadini, Paola Angeli, *Mito e attualità nelle odi di Pindaro* (Rome 1983).

Beye, Charles Rowan, *Epic and Romance in the Argonautica of Apollonius* (Carbondale, Ill. 1982).

Boedeker, Deborah, *Descent from Heaven: Images of Dew in Greek Poetry and Religion*, American Classical Studies 13 (Chico, California 1984).

Bowra, C. M., *Pindar* (Oxford 1964).

———, *Pindari Carmina* (Oxford 1947) (Oxford Classical Texts).

Bresson, A., *Mythe et contradiction. Analyse de la VIIe Olympique de Pindare* (Paris 1979).

Bundy, E. L., *Studia Pindarica*, University of California Publications in Classical Philology 18.1-2 (1962).

Burton, R.W.B., *Pindar's Pythian Odes* (Oxford 1962).

Calder, William M., III, and Jacob Stern, eds., *Pindaros und Bakchylides*, Wege der Forschung 134 (Darmstadt 1970).

Carey, Christopher C., "The Epilogue of Pindar's Fourth Pythian," *Maia* 32 (1980) 143-52.

Chamoux, François, *Cyrène sous la monarchie des Battiades*, Bibl. des Ecoles Françaises d'Athènes et de Rome 117 (Paris 1953).

Christ, Wilhelm, *Pindari Carmina* (Leipzig 1896).

Cook, Albert, *Myth and Language* (Bloomington 1980).

Crotty, Kevin, *Song and Action: The Victory Odes of Pindar* (Baltimore 1982).

Darcus, Shirley, "An Echo of Homer in Pindar, *Pythian* 4," *TAPA* 107 (1977) 93-102.

Detienne, Marcel, *Dionysus Slain* (1977), Eng. trans. L. and M. Muellner (Baltimore 1979).

SELECT BIBLIOGRAPHY

Detienne, Marcel, *Les jardins d'Adonis* (Paris 1972).
———, *Les maîtres de vérité dans la Grèce archaïque* (Paris 1967).
———, and Jean-Pierre Vernant, *Cunning Intelligence in Greek Culture and Society* (1974), Eng. trans. J. Lloyd (Atlantic Highlands, N.J. 1978).
Donlan, Walter, *The Aristocratic Ideal in Ancient Greece* (Lawrence, Kansas 1980).
Drachmann, A. B., ed., *Scholia Vetera in Pindari Carmina* (Leipzig 1903-27) 3 volumes.
Duchemin, Jacqueline, *Pindare poète et prophète* (Paris 1955).
———, *Pindare, Pythiques* (Paris 1967).
Eliade, Mircea, *Cosmos and History: the Myth of the Eternal Return* (1949), Engl. trans. W. Trask (Princeton 1954).
Farenga, Vincent, "Pindaric Craft and the Writing of *Pythia* IV," *Helios* 5 (1977) 3-37.
Farnell, Lewis R., *The Works of Pindar* (London 1930-32) 3 volumes.
Finley, John H., *Pindar and Aeschylus*, Martin Classical Lectures 14 (Cambridge, Mass. 1955).
Fontenrose, Joseph, "The Hero as Athlete," *California Studies in Classical Antiquity* 1 (1968) 73-104.
———, *Orion: The Myth of the Hunter and the Huntress*, Univ. of California Publications in Classical Studies 23 (Berkeley and Los Angeles 1981).
———, *Python* (Berkeley and Los Angeles 1959).
Fränkel, Hermann, *Dichtung und Philosophie des frühen Griechentums*, ed. 2 (Munich 1962).
Gentili, Bruno, "L'interpretazione dei lirici greci arcaici nella dimensione del nostro tempo," *QUCC* 8 (1969) 7-21.
———, "Lirica greca arcaica e tardo arcaica," in *Introduzione allo studio della cultura classica* (Milan 1972) 57-105.
Giannini, Pietro, "A proposito di Pindaro, *Pyth.* 4, 25-27," *QUCC* 22 (1976) 77-81.
———, "Interpretazione della *Pitica* 4 di Pindaro," *QUCC* 31 (n.s. 2) (1979) 35-63.
———, "Metis e Themis nella *Pitica* 4 di Pindaro," *Annali dell' Università di Lecce, Facoltà di Lettere e Filosofia*, 8-10 (1977-80) 133-44.
Gianotti, Gian Franco, *Per una poetica pindarica* (Torino 1975).
Gigante, G.E.V., "Per Pindaro narratore: in margine alla IV Pi-

tica," *Annali della Facoltà di Lettere, Naples* 17 (1974/75) 27-41.
Gildersleeve, Basil L., *Pindar: The Olympian and Pythian Odes* (New York 1885).
Greengard, Carola, *The Structure of Pindar's Epinician Odes* (Amsterdam 1980).
Gundert, Hermann, *Pindar und sein Dichterberuf* (Frankfurt 1935).
Hurst, André, "Temps du récit chez Pindare (Pyth. 4) et Bacchylide (11)," *Museum Helveticum* 40 (1983) 154-68.
Illig, Leonhard, *Zur Form der Pindarischen Erzählung. Interpretationen und Untersuchungen* (Berlin 1932).
Kirkwood, Gordon, *Selections from Pindar*, American Philological Association Textbook Series 7 (Chico, Calif. 1982).
Köhnken, Adolf, *Die Funktion des Mythos bei Pindar* (Berlin and New York 1971).
Komornicka, Anna M., "La notion du temps chez Pindare," *Eos* 64 (1976) 5-15.
———, "Quelques remarques sur la notion d' *Alatheia* et *Pseudos* chez Pindare," *Eos* 60 (1972) 235-53.
Lattimore, Richmond, "Pindar's Fourth Pythian Ode," *CW* 42 (1948/49) 19-25.
Lefkowitz, Mary R., *The Victory Ode* (Park Ridge, N.J. 1976).
Maehler, Herwig, *Die Auffassung des Dichterberufs im frühen Griechentum bis zur Zeit Pindars*, Hypomnemata 3 (Göttingen 1963).
Méautis, Georges, *Pindare le Dorien* (Neuchâtel 1962).
Mezger, Friedrich, *Pindars Siegeslieder* (Leipzig 1880).
Mullen, William, *Choreia: Pindar and the Dance* (Princeton 1982).
Nagy, Gregory, *The Best of the Achaeans* (Baltimore 1979).
Norwood, Gilbert, *Pindar* (Berkeley and Los Angeles 1945).
Pépin, Jean, "Le temps et le mythe," *Les Etudes Philosophiques*, n.s. 17 (1962) 55-68.
Péron, Jacques, *Les images maritimes de Pindare* (Paris 1974).
Puech, Aimé, *Pindare, II, Pythiques* (Paris 1922).
Pucci, Pietro, *Hesiod and the Language of Poetry* (Baltimore 1977).
Robbins, Emmet, "Jason and Chiron: The Myth of Pindar's Fourth Pythian," *Phoenix* 29 (1975) 205-13.
Robert, Carl, *Die griechische Heldensage*, ed. 4 (= Ludwig

SELECT BIBLIOGRAPHY

Preller and Carl Robert, *Griechische Mythologie*, II.3.1) (Berlin 1921) 757-875.
Rohde, Erwin, *Psyche*, ed. 8, Eng. trans. W. B. Hillis (London 1925).
Rose, Peter, "The Myth of Pindar's First Nemean: Sportsmen, Poetry, and Paideia," *HSCP* 78 (1974) 145-75.
———, "Towards a Dialectical Hermeneutic of Pindar's Pythian X," *Helios* 9 (1982) 49-73.
Rubin, Nancy, "Pindar's Creation of Epinician Symbols: *Olympians* 7 and 6," *CW* 74 (1980/81) 67-87.
Ruck, Carl, and William Matheson, *Pindar: Selected Odes* (Ann Arbor 1968).
Sandgren, Folke, "Funktion der Reden in Pindars Pythia IV," *Eranos* 70 (1972) 12-22.
Schadewaldt, Wolfgang, "Der Aufbau des Pindarischen Epinikion," *Schriften der Königsberger Gelehrten Gesellschaft* vol. 5, Heft 3 (Halle 1928).
Schroeder, Otto, *Pindars Pythien* (Leipzig and Berlin 1922).
Segal, Charles, *Dionysiac Poetics and Euripides' Bacchae* (Princeton 1982).
———, "Greek Tragedy: Truth, Writing, and the Representation of the Self," *Mnemai: Classical Studies in Memory of Karl K. Hulley*, ed. Harold J. Evjen (Scholars Press, Chico, Calif. 1984) 41-67.
———, "Messages to the Underworld: An Aspect of Poetic Immortalization in Pindar," *AJP* 106 (1985) 199-212.
———, "The Myth of Bacchylides 17: Heroic Quest and Heroic Identity," *Eranos* 77 (1979) 23-37.
———, "Myth, Cult, and Memory in Pindar's Third and Fourth *Isthmian* Odes," *Ramus* 10 (1981) 69-86.
———, "Pindar's Seventh *Nemean*," *TAPA* 98 (1967) 431-80.
———, "Time and the Hero: The Myth of Pindar's First Nemean," *RhM* 117 (1974) 29-39.
———, "Tragédie, Oralité, Ecriture," *Poétique* 50 (1982) 131-54.
———, *Tragedy and Civilization: An Interpretation of Sophocles*, Martin Class. Lect. 26 (Cambridge, Mass. 1981).
Slater, William J., *Lexicon to Pindar* (Berlin 1969).
Snell, Bruno, and Herwig Maehler, *Pindari Carmina cum Fragmentis* (Leipzig 1971, 1975) 2 volumes.
Stern, Jacob, "The Myth of Pindar's *Olympian* 6," *AJP* 91 (1970) 332-40.

SELECT BIBLIOGRAPHY

Thummer, Erich, *Pindar. Die isthmischen Gedichte* (Heidelberg 1968, 1969), 2 volumes.
Van der Kolf, Maria Christina, *Quaeritur Quo Modo Pindarus Fabulas Tractaverit Quidque in eis Mutarit*, Diss. Leiden (Rotterdam 1923).
Van Groningen, B. A., *In the Grip of the Past. Essay on an Aspect of Greek Thought* (Leiden 1953).
Verdenius, W. J., "Gorgias' Theory of Deception," in G. F. Kerferd, ed., *The Sophists and Their Legacy*, Hermes Einzelschrift 44 (Wiesbaden 1981) 116-28.
Vidal-Naquet, Pierre, *Le chasseur noir* (Paris 1981).
Vivante, Paolo, "On Time in Pindar," *Arethusa* 5 (1972) 107-31.
Walsh, George, *The Varieties of Enchantment* (Chapel Hill 1983).
Wilamowitz-Moellendorff, Ulrich von, *Pindaros* (Berlin 1922).
Woodbury, Leonard, "Apollo's First Love: *Pyth.* 9.26ff.," *TAPA* 103 (1972) 561-73.
———, "Cyrene and the Τελευτά of Marriage in Pindar's Ninth Pythian Ode," *TAPA* 112 (1982). 245-58.
Young, David C., *Pindar Isthmian 7, Myth and Exemplar*, Mnemosyne Supplement 15 (Leiden 1971).
———, *Three Odes of Pindar*, Mnemosyne Supplement 9 (Leiden 1968).
Zeitlin, Froma I., "The Dynamics of Misogyny: Myth and Mythmaking in the *Oresteia*," *Arethusa* 11 (1978) 149-84.
———, *Under the Sign of the Shield: Semiotics and Aeschylus' Seven Against Thebes* (Rome 1982).

Index of Works and Passages

Aeschylus,
  Agamemnon, 169
  Eumenides 1-19, 171f.
  Seven against Thebes, 59
Apollonius Rhodius,
  Argonautica, 16n4, 53, 53n4
Bacchylides, *Ode 16*, 169
Euripides,
  Medea, 52n1, 53
  Trojan Women 891ff., 167
Herodotus
  4.154, 14
  4.155, 31
  4.162-67, 13
  4.200-204, 13
Hesiod, *Theogony*
  9f., 153
  617-745, 144
  881-85, 105
Homer,
  Iliad
    1.188ff., 16
    1.234-38, 107
    2, 46
    2.485f., 180
    3.17f., 58
    3.30ff., 58
    6, 42
    9, 109
    11.740f., 53n2
    14, 62
  Odyssey, 16, 52, 55f., 72, 175
    1.337-40, 141n37
    4.413-25, 90
    4.456-61, 90
    9.319-24, 7n7
    10, 169
    11, 90
Parmenides *B1.22*, 47
Pindar,
  Isthmian Odes
    3.19, 129n17
    4, 12
    6.37, 110
    6.51ff., 48
    7, 109
    7.44ff., 133
    8.15f., 26
  Nemean Odes
    1.71, 187
    4.6-8, 189
    4.8, 99
    5.1ff., 156
    5.26ff., 165n1
    5.26-32, 170
    6.28, 190n24
    7, 128
    7.1, 186
    7.1-8, 192
    7.20ff., 12
    7.21-25, 159
    7.77-79, 69
    7.78f., 99
    8, 12, 186
    8.25-35, 26
    8.35ff., 159, 179
    8.36, 26
    10.73ff., 118
  Olympian Odes
    1, 23, 151
    1.6, 147
    1.28ff., 179, 193
    1.61, 110
    1.88f., 187
    1.97, 147
    1.113ff., 147
    2.31-37, 117
    2.37-42, 116
    2.42f., 186
    2.53-56, 126
    2.71-74, 91f.
    2.72, 127
    2.75-77, 127
    2.85f., 159
    2.86ff. 191
    3.23f., 187
    3.33f., 187
    4, 188

INDEX

Pindar (cont.)
    4.12, 189
    6, 61, 102, 151
    6.37f., 102
    6.47-57, 102
    6.54, 95
    6.55, 96
    6.56f., 99
    6.58, 96
    7, 97, 111, 177, 183f.
    7.34-36, 177
    7.53, 26, 159
    7.53-76, 104
    7.54-57, 94f.
    7.62-71, 69
    7.62-74, 177
    7.68f., 110
    7.69-71, 95
    10, 97-99
    10.1-3, 10n12
    10.3f., 164, 190, 192
    10.24ff., 25n27
    10.45-49, 97
    10.50-55, 97-99
    10.51f., 192
    10.52f., 186
    10.73-78, 98
    13, 133
    13.49-54, 53n2
  Paean 6.1-6, 188, 190
  Pythian Odes
    1, 9, 111, 131, 147
    2.67f., 10n13, 154
    2.74-92, 26f.
    2.81-85, 179
    2.83-89, 129
    2.85, 193
    2.91f., 27
    3, 9, 28
    3.1ff., 19
    3.52-67, 26
    3.54, 26
    4.1f., 180
    4.1-3, 33, 85f.
    4.2, 9
    4.2-4, 137
    4.4, 178
    4.5-11, 48
    4.6f., 44
    4.6-9, 182f.
    4.9, 74f.
    4.10f., 190
    4.10-13, 139f.
    4.12f., 6
    4.21ff., 43f., 47
    4.21-29, 92
    4.23-25, 49f.
    4.25-27, 80, 92
    4.34f., 31
    4.38-40, 81
    4.41, 183
    4.41f., 113
    4.42f., 184
    4.50f., 80
    4.50-53, 172
    4.53-67, 178
    4.56-63, 42
    4.57f., 38, 41, 154, 158
    4.57-69, 141f., 146, 148f
    4.59f., 47
    4.67f., 112
    4.69-71, 86
    4.71, 87
    4.71-74, 45
    4.72, 23f.
    4.75, 146
    4.78f., 76
    4.79f., 57-60
    4.82-84, 57
    4.87f., 29
    4.92, 29
    4.95, 38
    4.97, 35
    4.97f., 21
    4.97-119, 174
    4.101-19, 34f.
    4.106-8, 75
    4.109ff., 22
    4.109-13, 175
    4.109-15, 55, 102f.
    4.112-15, 21
    4.117f., 174
    4.120-23, 7, 36, 114
    4.120-24, 33
    4.129-31, 117
    4.129-33, 7
    4.129-35, 36f.
    4.133-35, 32
    4.136f., 15
    4.136-38, 19, 24

INDEX

4.138, 36
4.139f., 18
4.142f., 172
4.144-46, 100, 102f.
4.145f., 19
4.147f., 16
4.156, 38
4.157f., 114f.
4.159, 139
4.159f., 90
4.159-61, 76
4.161, 39
4.161f., 167
4.163f., 45f.
4.165, 39
4.178f., 114
4.184f., 15
4.184-87, 54f., 62f.
4.190-92, 50
4.193-202, 173
4.197-99, 43f.
4.204-6, 25
4.204-10, 83f.
4.209, 87
4.210-12, 61
4.212, 78
4.212f., 64
4.213-19, 20
4.214ff., 6, 15
4.215, 87
4.217f., 23
4.217-19, 18
4.218f., 54f.
4.219, 87
4.221f., 62
4.223f., 20
4.224, 87
4.229f., 60
4.229-31, 39f.
4.230, 7
4.230f., 112
4.233, 15, 62
4.233ff., 6, 15
4.234, 87
4.234-38, 65
4.237-41, 40f.
4.241, 6f.
4.247f., 5, 7
4.248, 32
4.249, 18n9

4.249f., 21, 66
4.250, 18, 25
4.250-61, 71
4.251f., 64
4.252, 166
4.253f., 187
4.254-57, 69f.
4.254-62, 79f.
4.255, 117f.
4.255-61, 186
4.257-59, 64
4.258-61, 77
4.259-61, 44
4.259-63, 22
4.261, 93
4.262, 160
4.263-69, 106-10
4.267, 25
4.273, 25
4.278f., 32f.
4.284, 31
4.286, 189
4.287, 108
4.290, 175
4.291, 33, 77
4.292f., 88
4.292-99, 84f.
4.294-96, 33
4.294-99, 99f.
4.298f., 88, 91, 180f.
4.299, 36, 111f., 160
5, 25n27
5.26-34, 9
5.49-53, 9
7.3, 25
8.32-34, 159
9, 28f., 168-71, 173, 186
9.12f., 20
9.14-23, 168
9.36ff., 168f.
9.38ff., 28
9.44-51, 27f.
9.62, 110
9.64f., 168
9.102-5, 188
10.27-30, 133
11.17ff., 165n1, 170
11.19-28, 169
12, 61

INDEX

Pindar (*cont.*)
  Fragments
    12 Bowra = 31 Snell, 111
    137 Bo. = 150 Sn., 149
    184 Bo. = 194 Sn., 25
    188 Bo. = 198 Sn., 110
    194 Bo. = 205 Sn., 190
Plato, *Phaedrus*, 154
Sophocles,
  Colchian Women, 53n4
  Oedipus Tyrannus, 145f.

Index of Names and Subjects

Achilles, 107-9, 112, 166
Aeacus, 126
Aeetes, character of, 38f.
Aepytus, in *Olympian 6*, 102
Aeschylus, 167
Aetnaea, and *Pythian 1*, 9
Agreus, 168
agriculture, and associations with marriage and creation, 68-70, 80f., 87, 104f., 150f., 187
aidōs, 19f., 61, 187
aisa, 44
Ajax, in Sophocles, 133
Alcman, 10
alētheia, 30, 111, 188-93. *See also* truth
Aloades, 29, 67f., 131
ambrosia, 110f.
anankē, 87
Aphrodite, 6, 17, 28f., 41f., 48, 54, 56, 61f., 66, 167f., 169, 188
Apollo, 19, 22, 28f., 47, 51, 60, 66, 78, 102, 133, 138-43, 147, 165; in *Pythian 9*, 20, 168-71
Arcesilaus III, king of Cyrene, 12f.
Arcesilaus IV, celebrated in *Pythian 4*, 9; political fortunes of, 13f.
Ares, 29, 67
Argo, origin of, 100f.
Aristaeus, 168
Arsinoa, in *Pythian 11*, 170
Artemis, 67
Asclepius, 178
Athena, in *Olympian 7*, 177
Atlas, 33, 103f., 108, 175

Bacchylides, 131, 169
Battus IV, king of Cyrene, 13
Bellerophon, 133
bia, 16, 31, 64-66, 187
birth, myths of, 68-70, 107f., 186-88, 192. *See also* origins

blame, 134, 149
Bloom, H., 192f.
Bundy, E. L., 3f., 9

Cadmus, 126
Cambyses, 13
Castor, 118
characterization, in *Pythian 4*, 7f.
Chariclo, 55
charis, 110
Charites, 188
Charybdis, 61
Chiron, 19, 55f., 82; in *Pythian 9*, 168-71, 178
choral lyric, archaic, 4f., 10
chronos. See time
Circe, 15, 55, 169
clod, in legend of Cyrene, 74f., 81f., 150-52, 160f.
Clytaemnestra, in Aeschylus, 166, 169; in *Pythian 11*, 169f.
Cretheus, 172
Croesus, in *Pythian 1*, 147
Cyrene, Nymph of *Pythian 9*, 168-71

Danae, 5
Daphne, 168
deconstruction, 123f., 143
Deianeira, 167
Delphi, 15, 36, 45, 47, 142f., 145, 171, 180f.
Detienne, M., 24
dialectical hermeneutic, 127
Diomedes, 42
dolos, 12, 15-29, 129
dreams, as prophetic, 46
drosos, 110
drugs. *See pharmakon*

Eliade, M., 92, 185
ephēmeros, 117

205

INDEX

Ephialtes, 29
erōs, 15-29, 52-68
Euphamus, and Triton in founding of Cyrene, 48-50
Euripides, 66, 164f.

Farenga, V., 123, 143, 164
Farnell, L. R., 6
fire, in myths of origin, 95f.; in trials of Jason, 62
foundation of cities, heroes in, 25. *See also* origins
Fränkel, H., 128

Gaia, 168
Geryon, 5
Gilgamesh, 90
Glaucus, 42
gold, and immortality, 113f.
Golden Fleece, 78f., 80, 113, 135, 167, 181; epithets for, 39f.
Gorgias, 157, 163f., 179
Graces. *See* Charites
grammatological, 153-64, 178f., 191
guile, and poetry, 15-29. See also *mētis*

Hades, 90
hair, and adolescent status, 57
healing, 19, 22, 134, 159-61
Hecataeus, 157
Helen, in Euripides, 167
Helios, 104, 177
Helle, 167
Hera, 48, 53f., 62, 68, 176
Heracles, 47f., 55, 97-99, 133, 187
Hesiod, 10, 127, 144, 171, 191
Hieron, 9, 13, 124, 130
Hölderlin, 4
Homer, 128, 159, 161, 165f. *See also* citations of *Iliad* and *Odyssey*
Horace, 4
hunting, 67

Iamus, 60, 95f., 133, 151
initiation, to manhood, 58-68

Ino, 157
iynx, 20, 24, 28, 40-42, 62-64, 69, 87, 100, 150, 166, 169, 171

kairos, 5, 133, 189
kerdos, 17
kleos, 107
kōmos, 9, 86, 137, 180, 182, 189

language, as self-conscious concern of *Pythian 4*, 30-42; oracular, 142f., 150; poisonous or healing, 178
Lemnian Women, 63f., 71, 79, 84, 166-68, 173
lēthē, 160. See also *alētheia*, memory
Longinus, 4
love. See *erōs*

magic. *See* iynx, *pharmakon*
marriage, and myths of creation, 62-64, 67f., 70f., 178, 186-88
mēdea, 63, 93. See also *mētis*
Medea, myths of, 52f.; as prophet, 135, 137-43, 157-61, 173; and love magic, 6, 17-19, 52f.
Medusa, 61
Meleager, 108f.
Memnon, 108f.
memory, 113, 160, 183
Menelaus, 90f., 167
mēnis, 16
mētis, 12, 15-29, 30f., 68, 93, 108, 118, 129, 154-57, 163, 169-71, 176-79, 189, 191-93
Metis, birth of, 176f.
Michelangelo, 151
moira, 44, 104f., 117f., 186
Moirai, 19, 103, 177, 186, 192
Mopsus, 49f., 117
Muse(s), 33, 86, 99, 127, 136f., 149, 153, 157f., 177-79, 180, 182

Nekyia, of *Odyssey*, 90
Neoptolemus, 133

INDEX

Nomios, 168
Norwood, G., 96
nostos, 89-93, 166

Odysseus, 15-17, 24, 30, 55, 61, 90, 161, 166, 169
Oedipus, 25, 88, 105, 106-19, 126, 135, 145f.
Okeanos, 168. *See also* sea, water
Olympia, founding myth of, 97-99
omens, 48-51, 95, 113, 173. *See also* oracles
Omphale, 55
oracles, 42-51, 74-76, 135, 137-44, 147f., 150, 152, 183
oral poetry, 9f., 154-60, 162, 178f., 190, 193
Orestes, 55
origins, myths of, 94-105, 111, 151, 160, 185-87
Orpheus, 100, 150
Otus, 29

panther, erotic association of, 59
Paris, and Jason, 58
Parthenopaeus, 59
patriarchy, myth of, 171-79
peithō, 15-29, 63, 161, 169-71, 173
Pelias, mode of speaking and character of, 33-40
Pelops, 133, 151
Peneus, 168
Phaleris, 131, 147
pharmakon, and male heroic values, 12, 15-29, 41f., 53n2, 63, 65, 173; and ambiguity of poetry, 159-61
Philyra, 55
Phrixus, 45f., 75f., 80, 90, 139, 167
plowing. *See* agriculture
pneumatological, 153-64, 178f., 191
poikilos, 18n9
Polydeuces, 118
pothos, 53, 63, 166, 173. *See also erōs*
prophecy. *See* oracles
Pythia, 33, 36, 41f., 63, 137-44, 157-61, 171, 173, 178f.

Rhodes, mythical origins of, 94f., 177, 184
Rose, P., 127
Rubin, N., 176

Salmoneus, 172
Schadewaldt, W., 9
Scylla, 61
sea, 16, 80-88, 92f., 160, 167, 173, 175
seduction. *See peithō*
sexual conflict, 165-79
silence, 37f., 165. *See also* language
Simonides, 5, 10, 191f.
Solon, 11, 191
sophia, 12, 15-29, 68, 161-63, 189, 191f.
Sophists, 164, 191
Sophocles, 166
Sphinx, 59f., 61. *See also* Oedipus
Stesichorus, 4f., 10, 90n4
Stevens, W., 185
Symplegades, 48, 61, 83, 87

Telemachus, 55
textuality, 30, 153-61, 190f., 193
themis, 22, 103, 183
Theron, 117, 124
Thersander, 117
Thucydides, 157
Thummer, E., 9
Tilphussa, 110
time, 51, 76f., 104, 152, 160, 181-90
Titans, 33, 77, 103-5, 137, 144f.
Tityos, 67f.
tragedy, 11, 147
Triton, 31f., 42f., 46-50, 70, 73, 91-94, 95f.
truth, 129, 133, 143, 157-64, 176-79, 188-93. *See also alētheia*
Typhon, 111

unity, of Pindaric ode, 8

Valéry, P., 4
Vernant, J.-P., 24
Vidal-Naquet, P., 58

207

INDEX

water, and myths of birth and creation, 82, 91-93, 95f., 104, 110f.
Wilamowitz-Moellendorff, U. von, 5, 123
writing, 9-12, 154-64, 178f., 190f. *See also* textuality

xenia, 35-37, 84f., 111, 181

Zeitlin, F., 59
Zeus, 33, 49f., 56, 61, 77f., 103f., 111, 131, 137, 144, 165, 173-79, 192

LIBRARY OF CONGRESS CATALOGING-IN-PUBLICATION DATA

Segal, Charles, 1936-
Pindar's mythmaking.

Bibliography: p.
Includes index.
1. Pindar. Pythian odes. 4. 2. Mythology, Greek, in literature.
3. Apollo (Greek diety) in literature. 4. Medea (Greek mythology)
in literature. I. Pindar. Pythian odes. 4. English. II. Title.

PA4274.P5S44 1986   884'.01   85-43312
ISBN 0-691-05473-8 (alk. paper)

GPSR Authorized Representative: Easy Access System Europe - Mustamäe tee
50, 10621 Tallinn, Estonia, gpsr.requests@easproject.com

www.ingramcontent.com/pod-product-compliance
Lightning Source LLC
Chambersburg PA
CBHW050633300426
44112CB00012B/1776